READING NEOPLATONISM

Neoplatonism is the term that designates the form of Platonic philosophy that developed in the Roman Empire from the third to the sixth century A.D. and that invests Plato's dialogues with a complex metaphysical interpretation.

Sara Rappe's challenging and innovative study is the first book to analyze Neoplatonic texts by using contemporary philosophy of language. The book covers the whole tradition of Neoplatonic writing, from Plotinus through Proclus to Damascius. Addressing the strain of mysticism in these works from a fresh perspective, Rappe shows how these texts reflect actual meditational practices, methods of concentrating the mind, and the other mental disciplines that informed the tradition.

As the broadest available survey of Neoplatonic writing, this book will appeal to classicists and philosophers, as well as to students of religious studies.

Sara Rappe is Associate Professor in the Department of Classical Studies at the University of Michigan.

READING NEOPLATONISM

Non-discursive Thinking in the Texts of Plotinus, Proclus, and Damascius

SARA RAPPE

University of Michigan

CAMBRIDGE
UNIVERSITY PRESS

CAMBRIDGE UNIVERSITY PRESS
Cambridge, New York, Melbourne, Madrid, Cape Town, Singapore, São Paulo

Cambridge University Press
The Edinburgh Building, Cambridge CB2 8RU, UK

Published in the United States of America by Cambridge University Press, New York

www.cambridge.org
Information on this title: www.cambridge.org/9780521651585

First published 2000
This digitally printed version 2007

A catalogue record for this publication is available from the British Library

Library of Congress Cataloguing in Publication data
Rappe, Sara, 1960–
Reading neoplatonism : non-discursive thinking in the texts of
Plotinus, Proclus, and Damscius / Sara Rappe.
p. cm.
Includes bibliographical references and index.
ISBN 0-521-65158-1 (hb)
1. Neoplatonism. 2. Reasoning – History. 3. Methodology – History.
I. Title.
B517.R36 1999
186'.4 – dc21 99–11395
CIP

ISBN 978-0-521-65158-5 hardback
ISBN 978-0-521-03942-0 paperback

For John Raugust and Eleanor Rappe-Raugust,
with love

Contents

Preface: *Discursive Strategies and Neoplatonic Texts*   *page* ix

Acknowledgments   xix

List of Abbreviations   xxi

1   Introduction. Representing a Tradition: Exegesis,
    Symbol, and Self-reflection   1

PART I: LANGUAGE IN THE *ENNEADS*

2   Plotinus' Critique of Discursive Thinking   23

3   Non-discursive Thinking in the *Enneads*   45

4   Introspection in the Dialectic of the *Enneads*   67

5   The Symbolism of the *Enneads*   91

PART II: TEXT AND TRADITION IN NEOPLATONISM

6   History of an Enigma: Mathematical Symbolism in the
    Neoplatonic Tradition   117

7   Transmigrations of a Myth: Orphic Texts and Platonic
    Contexts   143

8   Language and Theurgy in Proclus' *Platonic Theology*   167

9   Damascius' Ineffable Discourse   197

10 Conclusion: Reading Neoplatonism   231

References   245

General Index   261

Index Locorum   264

Preface: Discursive Strategies and Neoplatonic Texts

In *Reading Neoplatonism* I discuss the history and nature of Neoplatonic textuality. Over many centuries, Neoplatonism, based now in Alexandria, now in Athens, associated itself with a fixed textual tradition – the corpus of Plato's dialogues and the exegetical tradition associated with it – despite or perhaps even because of this temporal and geographic breadth. And yet more than the adherants of any other ancient philosophical lineage the Neoplatonists insisted that wisdom could be located only outside all texts and outside all language.

Why were the Neoplatonists, who explored so intensively non-discursive or non-propositional thinking, and who subjected formal dialectic to such criticism, exegetical beyond all other schools of ancient philosophy? And how does their suspicion of discursive thinking manifest itself in their texts? Working with the texts of Plotinus, Proclus, Damascius, and others, I show how lack of confidence in discursive argument shaped the textual strategies available to these authors. These texts often appropriate elements from ritual, repeatedly investigate the limits of discursive thinking, and try to illustrate how non-discursive thinking is supposed to work. We find texts that are at odds with their own textuality, discourses that deny that anything has been asserted, and discursive strategies that set themselves against their very discursivity. What are the issues that shaped the very distinctive textual practices reflected in the Neoplatonic tradition?[1]

---

[1] On the concept of textuality, see Silverman, *Textualities*, chap. 8, "The Language of Textuality." See also Paul Ricoeur, "Qu'est-ce qu'un texte?" in *Hermeneutik und*

In the following passages, two representatives of the Platonic tradition discuss the origins of writing, framing written language as somehow exotic or extopic, as non-native to the realms of truth and memory that writing appropriates to itself. For Plato, Egypt teaches the naive and untutored Greece to engage in a process of externalization by creating an artificial memory.[2] For Plotinus, Greece is derivative and mimetic, inventing philosophy as a science of representations that coincides with the deployment of written language.[3]

Socrates: The story is that in the region of Naucratis in Egypt there dwelt one of the old gods of the country, the god to whom the bird called Ibis is sacred, his own name being Theuth. He it was that invented number and calculation, geometry and astronomy, not to speak of draughts and dice, and above all writing. Now the king of the whole country at that time was Thamus . . . To him came Theuth, and revealed his arts, saying that they ought to be passed on to the Egyptians in general . . . "Here, O king, is a branch of learning that will make the people of Egypt wiser and improve their memories . . ."

The king answered and said, "O man full of arts, . . . if men learn this, it will implant forgetfulness in their souls; they will cease to exercise memory because they rely on that which is written, calling things to remembrance no longer from within themselves, but by means of external marks."[4] (*Phaedrus* 274c–275a, with omissions)

Dialektik: Festschrift fur Hans-Georg Gadamer, II, 181–200. Finally, see Gasché, *The Tain of the Mirror*, chap. 12, "The Inscription of Universality," especially p. 280: "In whatever terms – empirical, idealist, or dialectical – *text* is defined, it always implies a closure upon itself with a clear inside and outside, whether it is the empirical closure of the unity of a corpus, the intelligible unity of a work, or the dialectical totality of its formal or thematic meanings." Here Gasché articulates a theory of textuality that I would claim does not actually apply in Neoplatonic texts. Because these texts are premised on the condition that non-discursive thinking can never be formulated discursively, their textuality can no longer be considered primarily referential; the text as a discursive formulation is incommensurate with the theory of meaning on which a referential notion of textuality would rely. Hence the defect of self-enclosure, seemingly detected in postmodern critiques of textuality, is not necessarily a feature of Neoplatonic texts.

[2] For the notion of artificial memory, see Yates, *The Art of Memory*, especially chap. 2, "The Art of Memory in Greece: Memory and the Soul." See also Havelock, *The Muse Learns to Write. Reflections on Orality and Literacy from Antiquity to the Present.*

[3] On the geographical representation of linguistic history, see Rousseau, *Essay on the Origins of Language*, pp. 11–12, quoted in Derrida, *Margins of Philosophy*, p. 269. Cf. also the note there referring to Condillac's *Essai sur l'origine des conaissances humaines*, II, 1, chap. 10, sec. 103.

[4] Hackforth's translation, in *Plato: Collected Dialogues.*

The wise men of Egypt, I think, also understood this, either by scientific or innate knowledge, and when they wished to signify something wisely, did not use the forms of letters which follow the order of words and propositions and imitate sounds and the enunciations of philosophical statements, but by drawing images and inscribing in their temples one particular image of one particular thing they manifested the non-discursiveness of the intelligible world, that is, that every image is a kind of knowledge and wisdom and is a subject of statements, all together in one, and not discourse or deliberation. But only afterwards (others) discovered starting from it in its concentrated unity, a representation in something else, already unfolded and speaking it discursively . . . (*Enneads* V.8.6)[5]

I have juxtaposed the two texts so as to invent a dialogue between these two philosophers on the genealogy of textuality. Both passages lament a fall from innocence occasioned by writing and acknowledge the priority of spoken over written signs (Plotinus says that letters "imitate sounds"). Yet Plotinus seems to be recalling a unitary sign that fully reflected the wholeness of its object, a grammar without syntax that communicated the unabridged nature of what it described, whereas Plato recalls a form of interior memory that was able to forgo any kind of semiotic mnemonics, a self-recollection that disdained any record of itself.

If Plato and Plotinus could have engaged in a dialogue about the limitations of writing, what would each have said to the other? In the passages just quoted, one complaint seems salient – writing fails to capture certain features of what we might now call the subject of discourse. According to Plato, writing externalizes memory with the undesirable result that consciousness appears to fail to include its own contents. According to Plotinus, writing temporalizes the space of consciousness and translates the simultaneously present contents of consciousness as an extension within time.

Finally, however, both texts reveal themselves as part of a history, a temporally extended record of ideas that now inexorably form part of a textual tradition. These passages show us a tradition that is fully alive to the paradoxes of its own occurrence. What exactly is a philosophical tradition? Is its purpose to transmit texts, to authorize certain dogmas, or to communicate some kind of wisdom? If traditions are here to transmit texts, then what constitutes a text?

[5] Armstrong's translation.

What kinds of practices are involved in the creation of a specifically Neoplatonic textuality? We find, for example, Proclus writing in his *Commentary on the Timaeus:*

> And this is what theurgy reveals after Plato by means of the letters, namely theurgy fills the soul with the magical sign of the chiasma and the semicircles. Thus names and magical signs were first transmitted by Plato to us. (*IT* II 255–256)

Proclus is discussing *Timaeus* 36c1, the creation of the world soul from two strips consisting of compounds mixed out of Being and Becoming. The X of the world soul is a form of writing practiced by the Demiurge, while human beings imitate this divine inscription by means of magic rituals.[6] Here writing arrogates to itself an authority that belonged to the realm of the divine, and the text is woven out of signs that supersede the system of writing. Proclus interprets this text by attempting to reconstruct the talismanic force of the signs that are somehow disguised by writing. Again, Proclus' historical spin on the origins of his own tradition is instructive:

> All of Greek theology is the child of Orphic mystagogy: Pythagoras was the first to receive initiation from Aglaophamos, Plato in turn received from the Pythagorean and Orphic doctrines perfect knowledge concerning the gods. (Proclus *PT* I.5, 25–26)

According to Proclus, then, what is authentic in the tradition of which he himself is a member is not the body of writings that falls under the authorship of Plato. In the one case, the *Timaeus* text is shaped around the letter *chi*, a symbol whose efficacy involves a supernatural force not normally accorded to human writing. In the second case, the doctrines of Plato originate from a supernatural source in the revelations of Apollo, so that authorship is really subsidiary to the whole question of tradition. These two texts are only examples of the complex pragmatics of Neoplatonic textuality. By appealing to the ritual force of language and by deferring the location of authorship, these particular passages raise questions about the very nature of language and meaning, questions that have to be addressed as a part of the process of reading Neoplatonic texts.

Hence the purpose of this book is to pose questions about how to

---

[6] On this passage and on Proclus' theory of Demiurgic inscription, see Gersh, *From Iamblichus to Eriugena*, pp. 297–9.

read the texts of the Neoplatonic tradition. Over the next several chapters, I will be looking closely at the Neoplatonic treatment of language, metaphor, image, and text. I will be looking at the relationship between text and tradition and especially at the dialectical elements found within Neoplatonic texts. In the first part of the book, "Language in the *Enneads*," I discuss the textual strategies of the *Enneads*. Here I explore the parameters of discourse in the *Enneads* by examining its systems of organizing language: method, metaphor, and dialectic. In the book's second part, "Text and Tradition in Neoplatonism," I explore the textual practices of different adherents of the tradition and attempt to chart a history of Neoplatonic textuality.

The paradoxes of claiming that Neoplatonists avail themselves of discursive strategies in their attempts to avert the limitations of the discursive should by now be apparent. One of the claims that I make throughout this book is that Neoplatonic texts exhibit a self-consciousness about the methodologies that they employ precisely because of the difficulties caused by Neoplatonic notions of truth, philosophy, and tradition. Beyond any formal criterion shaping the tradition, Neoplatonists shared the belief that wisdom could not be expressed or transmitted by rational thought or language. Yet despite this repudiation of the discursive, their texts also possess a complex doctrinal content that operates in conjunction with these reservations. In fact, for Neoplatonists, there is one central metaphysical fact that grounds this attention to the non-discursive.

The identity theory of truth, the doctrine that intellect is its objects, and the self-disclosing nature of intellectual activity are at the center of Neoplatonic philosophizing and dialectic.[7] This theory of truth is notoriously difficult to demonstrate, and even if the Neoplatonists at times attempt to do so, they leave the central premise of

---

[7] In using the expression "identity theory of truth," I do not intend to imply that the Neoplatonists formulated such a doctrine merely as a theory or hypothesis explaining the nature of truth in dialectical contexts. Admittedly, the phrase "identity theory of truth" is probably ambiguous: Aristotle holds a theory that could be called an identity theory, but the Aristotelian version of the identity thesis is considerably different. Some of these differences are discussed in later chapters. On this topic, see Emilsson 1996, pp. 238–9. Emilsson refers to what I have been calling the "identity theory" as the "Internality Thesis." That said, it must be acknowledged that Plotinus does deploy this doctrine against Stoic or Stoicizing epistemology in *Enneads* V.3 and V.5, where he explores the nature of Intellect's incorrigibility.

this theory, that is, the existence of a faculty that incorrigibly grasps eternal truths, unargued for.[8] Surely such a conception of truth – truth that by definition cannot be communicated to another because any representation would rupture the unity of subject and object entailed by it – leaves the enterprise of philosophy in a predicament that can be solved only by paradox, compromise, or self-contradiction.

Nous, the faculty of intellectual intuition, functions in the texts of the Neoplatonists in terms of self-presence and immediacy; it enjoys a proximity to the truth that crosses over into self-encapsulation because intellect makes its own contents known to itself alone.[9] But what kind of language can be used to convey the truth that this faculty grasps? If the answer is that the language of nous must be metaphorical, it must be remembered that both conceptual and metaphorical representations fall short of its intuitions. This result may only confirm postmodern suspicions of philosophy when it attempts to appropriate or to authorize metaphor for its own constructions.[10]

---

[8] See Gerson, *Plotinus*, pp. 42–3, on the history of nous in Greek philosophy as a faculty whose "contents are universal truths." Gerson argues that one of the sources for Plotinus' doctrine of intellect is a traditional faculty psychology "that is largely unopposed within Greek philosophy." Strictly speaking, Plotinus departs from the psychological tradition in asserting that intellect "does not belong to the soul, though we can say that it is 'our' intellect, since it is distinct from the faculty that thinks discursively because it transcends [discursive thinking], but nevertheless it is ours, even if we do not count it among the faculties of the soul" (V.3.23–27). Although Plotinus does not proscribe language that describes the intellect as belonging to the person, he makes it clear that it cannot be attributed to the individual. There is no condition of the individual mind as such that operates as a guarantor for the apprehension of universal truth.

[9] *Enneads* V.5.2.18–20: ὥστε καὶ ἡ ὄντως ἀλήθεια οὐ συμφωνοῦσα ἄλλῳ ἀλλ' ἑαυτῇ, καὶ οὐδὲν παρ' αὐτὴν ἄλλο λέγει, ⟨ἀλλ' ὃ λέγει⟩, καὶ ἔστι, καὶ ὅ ἐστι, τοῦτο καὶ λέγει. [Therefore truth in reality does not correspond to something else, but to itself, and it says nothing other than itself, and what it says, it is, and what it is, this also it says]. Cf. V.3.6.24: "If intellect should be what it says, it would know itself exactly like this." On this self-communicating aspect of Intellect, see Emilsson 1996, pp. 237–8.

[10] I have in mind something like the following objection to the language of metaphysics, an objection that I do not share or endorse, but believe might profitably be addressed: "Henceforth the entire teleology of meaning, which constructs the philosophical concept of metaphor, coordinates metaphor with the manifestation of truth, with the production of truth as presence without veil, with the reappropriation of a full language without syntax" (Derrida 1982, p. 270). Derrida suggests that the Platonic tradition produces, by means of metaphor

If language is premised on the notion of a self-enclosing truth, then meaning itself risks losing its force. All statements about truth become metaphors or tropes because literal meaning has been proscribed from the outset as not available. To this objection to or warning about the role of metaphor within philosophy as an attempt to evade the question of meaning, one can only reply that the Neoplatonists refused to grant that truth could ever be fully disclosed; truth is itself a veil for an origin that falls outside of all representation. The chapters that follow detail and chronicle the texts and tradition that embody this paradox of meaning. The discursive strategies that inform Neoplatonic texts are a configuration of nondiscursive truth, just as the tradition as a whole is a record of its own appeal to what can only be called an unwritten tradition.

In Chapters 6 and 7 I document the significance of this appeal by showing how the Neoplatonists elaborate classical allusions to enigmatic traditions, to Orphics and Pythagoreans, to infamous lectures, and to obscure numerology. As we shall see, from the Neoplatonic perspective the superordinate position of Pythagoras over Plato in the historiography of Platonism is precisely informed by this notion of unwritten traditions. When seen in this light, the so-called oral-teachings hypothesis about Plato becomes part of a more elaborate yet ultimately consistent view of textuality within the Neoplatonic tradition.[11] Before turning to this tradition, I want to discuss more

the notion of a truth that is immediately present, a meaning not circumscribed by language, but one that has in reality no existence outside of metaphor. This challenge, how does language convey truth as self-presence, and how does the text create the illusion that this ambition is achievable, is a real concern and one that this book seeks to address. I do not see Neoplatonism as promulgating this notion of textually inscribed self-presence. Rather, my purpose in this book is to show that certain texts reflect or document the efforts of members of this tradition to achieve a kind of self-presence or self-knowledge that is precisely extra-linguistic, though it then becomes subject to linguistic description.

[11] In this book, I do not discuss the "esoteric doctrines" of Plato in terms of the historical validity of this concept. Readers interested in the "esoteric Plato" should consult the following works: Brisson 1995a; Findlay; Gaiser; Kraemer 1959; Kraemer 1990; Reale; and Schleiermacher.

One of the objections I have concerning the "esoteric interpretation" of Plato's dialogues, and *a fortiori*, of attempts to invoke Neoplatonic confirmation of this interpretation, concerns the notion of doctrine, teaching, or dogmatic formulation. If by imputing "unwritten doctrines" to Plato, the esotericist interpretation seeks to read Plato in the terms of an ontology that more closely resembles Neoplatonism because it includes such "unwritten principles" as the One (which would function

precisely the nature of Neoplatonic objections to discursive thinking or discursive arguments. The nature of this discussion is partially exclusive – we need to see the limitations of discursive thinking that the Neoplatonists worked so hard to overcome within those textual practices that came to be included in their works, many of which will strike the modern reader as bizarre, naive, even absurd. When Plotinus tells us that wisdom does not consist of propositions or statements or that truth is by nature non-representational, how big a leap is it from his remarks to a textuality that invokes theurgy, or to one that prefers Orphic cosmology to traditional metaphysics? I will try to demonstrate the intelligibility of the surprising forms that Neoplatonic textuality took, by insisting that we take the claims of the Neoplatonists to invoke non-discursive truth as foundational to their philosophical enterprise.

Finally, I must address what might be the most telling objection to the approach to Neoplatonic textuality that I am proposing to adopt in the following pages. Proclus wrote exegetical commentaries on many of the Platonic dialogues, as did the sixth-century scholarch Damascius. Moreover, it is clear that Plotinus adopts a scholastic approach in the majority of his treatises, arguing in detail against Stoic and Aristotelian category metaphysics, to take one prominent example. Why does this discursive form of philosophy preponderate in Neoplatonic texts if Neoplatonic textuality so readily accedes to the non-discursive? Here it must be said that the historical situation of Neoplatonism, a tradition that lasted for well over three centuries and that claimed to transmit the Platonic philosophy initiated a millennium before the appearance of its last exponent, Damascius, demanded a scrupulous adherence to the texts that informed it. In any event, rather than argue the merits of my approach from a perspective that surveys the sheer numbers of arguments and exegesis, it is perhaps just as useful to admit that the texts presented in this book could be exceptional. They presuppose a scholasticism without which their visionary flights, aporetic repetitions, or ritual

as a first cause), then this so-called Neoplatonic interpretation omits a crucial aspect of the Neoplatonists' own understanding of their tradition. In this book, I explain the Neoplatonic concept of unwritten teaching in terms of the philosophical *askesis* or practice of non-discursive modes of awareness. This *askesis* and its written counterpart, that is, the texts that constitute the record of Platonism, are never interchangeable.

formulae would remain opaque or uninteresting. This exploration of the hesitations experienced from within the tradition concerning the limits of discursive reason does not exhaust the limits of Neoplatonic textuality or seek to deny the inherent interest of Neoplatonic dialectic.

Acknowledgments

It is almost impossible to include the names of all those who helped in the writing of this book by reading various drafts and offering suggestions, inspiration, advice, encouragement, and friendship. My greatest debt is to Professor Lloyd Gerson of St. Michael's College, University of Toronto. I cannot express how much his own scholarship and activity in the field of Neoplatonism, as well as his generous encouragement of my work, have meant to me over the years. This book could never have been written without his help. Professors John Bussanich, University of New Mexico; Alessandro Linguiti, University of Milan; and Greg Shaw, Stonehill College, read and commented extensively on parts or all of the manuscript. Their criticisms and suggestions have been invaluable. I would also like to thank Professors Anthony A. Long and G. R. F. Ferrari of the University of California at Berkeley for their loyal support and intellectual mentoring throughout the long years of my graduate education and during my years as an assistant professor.

I offer my profound thanks to many of my colleagues in the International Society for Neoplatonic Studies, but especially to Jay Bregman and John Finamore. Other Neoplatonists and philosophers who have been extremely helpful are Professors John Dillon, Richard Sorabji, Steven Strange, and Harold Tarrant. Each of these scholars read through portions of the manuscript and offered sage advice; Professor Eyjolfur Emilsson also made important suggestions. Sally Haslanger, professor of philosophy and linguistics at the Massachussets Institute of Technology, read parts of the manuscript in detail. Her intelligent remarks saved me from many mistakes. I am grateful for the support of many, many classics colleagues, including the directors of the Center for Hellenic Studies, Deborah Boedeker and Kurt Raaflaub; Professors Ludwig Koenen and James Porter of the Department of Classical Studies at the University of Michigan; and Professor Sharon Herbert, the chair of the department. As this manuscript goes to press, I note with great sadness the unfortunate loss of my colleague, Professor Glenn Knudsvig; the memory of his warmth and kindness will be treasured by all who knew him. I also must thank Terence Moore, senior humanities editor at Cambridge University Press, and his editorial assistant, Gwen Seznec. Sincere thanks to copy editor Susan Greenberg and production editor Holly Johnson of Cambridge University Press. They greatly improved the manuscript. All of the already mentioned individuals contributed in one way or another to this work; however, they cannot be held responsible for the views or any errors in what follows.

My thanks to my sister, Audrey Rappe, and to Joshu for their support. Finally, my thanks to my mother, Eleanor Rappe-Raugust, and to John Raugust for all the years of unfailing love and encouragement.

The author gratefully acknowledges permission to reprint from "Metaphor in Plotinus," *Ancient Philosophy* 15, no. 1 (fall 1995), as the basis for Chapter 5, "The Symbolism of the *Enneads*"; "Self-Perception in Plotinus and the Later Neoplatonists," *American Catholic Philosophical Quarterly* 71, no. 3 (summer 1997), used in Chapter 3, "Non-discursive Thinking," in the *Enneads* "Skepticism in the Sixth Century? Damascius' *Doubts and Solutions Concerning First Principles*," *Journal of the History of Philosophy* 36; no. 3 (July 1998), as the basis for part of Chapter 9, "Damascius' Ineffable Discourse" and for small portions of the Introduction; and "Damascius' Skeptical Affiliations," *The Ancient World* 29, no.2 (1998), in the opening remarks of Chapter 9.

Abbreviations

Alc.	Proclus. *Commentary on the First Alcibiades of Plato.* Edited by L. G. Westerink. Amsterdam, 1954. English translation by W. O'Neill. The Hague, 1971.
CH	*Corpus Hermeticum.* Tome 1. Traités I–XII. Edited by A. D. Nock. French translation by A.-J. Festugière. 1946. Reprint, Paris, 1991.
CO	Julianus. *The Chaldean Oracles.* Edited and translated by R. Majercik. Leiden, 1989.
C-W	Damascius. *Doubts and Solutions Concerning First Principles.* 3 Volumes. Edited by J. Combès and L. G. Westerink. Paris, 1986–91.
DM	Iamblichus. *On the Mysteries of the Egyptians.* Edited and translated by E. des Places. Paris, 1989.
Hermetica	*Hermetica: The Ancient Greek and Latin Writings which Contain Religious or Philosophic Teachings Ascribed to Hermes Trismegistus.* Edited and translated by Walter Scott. Vol. I, *Texts and Translation.* Reprint, London, 1968. New English translation in B. Copenhaver, *Hermetica.* Cambridge, 1992.
In Crat.	*Proclus' Commentary on Plato's Cratylus.* Edited by G. Pasquali. Teubner, 1908.
IE	Proclus. *A Commentary on the First Book of Euclid's Elements.* Translated by G. Morrow. Princeton, 1970. Second edition, 1992.

IP *Proclus' Commentary on Plato's Parmenides. Procli Commentarium in Platonis Parmenidem,* In *Procli Opera Inedita.* Second ed. Edited by V. Cousin. Paris, 1864. Reprint, Hildesheim, 1961. English translation by J. Dillon and G. Morrow. Princeton, 1987.

In Rem. *Proclus' Commentary on Plato's Republic. Procli in Rem publicam commentarii.* 2 vols. Edited by G. Kroll. Leipzig, 1903–6. Reprint, 1965.

IT *Proclus' Commentary on the Timaeus. Procli in Platonis Timaeum commentaria.* 3 vols. Edited by E. Diehl. 1903–6. Reprint, 1965. French translation by A. J. Festugière. 5 vols. Paris, 1966–8.

Or. Chald. *Oracles chaldaïques.* Avec un choix de commentaires anciens. 3ᵉ rev. et corr. Texte établi et traduit par E. des Places, Paris, 1996.

Phil. Chal. Proclus. *Eclogae de Philosophia Chaldaica.* Edited by H. Jahn, Halis Saxonum, Preffer, 1891.

PT Proclus. *Platonic Theology. Theologie Platonicienne.* Edited by H. D. Saffrey and L. G. Westerink. 5 vols. Paris, 1968–87. *Procli in Platonis Theologiam.* Portus ed. Hamburg, 1618. Reprint, Frankfurt, 1960.

1

Introduction. Representing a Tradition: Exegesis, Symbol, and Self-reflection

Reading Neoplatonism touches on issues as diverse as Plotinus' critique of essentialism and Proclus' references to theurgy. What brings these strands of thought together, and how can a scholar justify tracing these disparate phenomena back to a single source? In this book, I claim that the wide variety of textual strategies we find in the Neoplatonic tradition arises largely as a means of circumventing the hesitations that the tradition as a whole has about discursive thinking. There is a diachronic movement to the book: I begin at the start of the Neoplatonic tradition and end with the last Platonic successor, Damascius.

What makes Neoplatonism a unified tradition, and what kinds of resources enabled Neoplatonists to maintain the continuity of this tradition? Formally, Neoplatonists remained allied over the acceptance of Plato's dialogues as constituting something like a foundational discourse. Yet obviously there is a great deal more to the tradition that brought about its cohesion, above all its metaphysical structures and its associations with pagan religiosity. In short, Neoplatonism was a textual tradition as well as a living school; its adherents practiced a minority religion that struggled to define and maintain itself against an increasingly intolerant mainstream ideology.

But if the Neoplatonists rely on the writings of Plato for their metaphysical enterprise, the central feature of this enterprise is nevertheless its insistence on the faculty of intuition, nous, for the truth of its deliverances. Therefore, the Neoplatonists faced issues very much like our own as they continued to identify themselves with their philosophical tradition. They had to account for the question of transmissability: how is intuitive wisdom communicated, especially within the context of a philosophy that repudiates language but continues to practice speculative metaphysics? Linguistic theory was just as significant for the Neoplatonists as it is for modern philosophers, as they worked with such issues as the origins of signification and designation and the problematics of translation.[1] Finally, the Neoplatonists were confronted as we are with an amazing history of competing philosophical schools, with an eclectic scholasticism formed and reformulated throughout the centuries of theorizing that preceded them.

Yet there are factors that show up in virtually any Neoplatonist text, factors that help us to gauge a text's distance from our own modern way of conducting philosophical discourse. I have attempted to identify as one such factor the Neoplatonic insistence on the limitations of discursive thinking and, therefore, on the textual conveyance of non-discursive methodologies. To be sure, due to current research in this area, no scholar would now dispute that there is a strong doctrinal component to Neoplatonist metaphysics and that Plotinus, above all, argues cogently and forcefully for what can rightfully be called his philosophical system. Such doctrines as the theory of emanation, the causal role of the One with respect to the two other primary hypostases, and the relationship between body and soul, as well as aspects of human psychology such as virtue and free will, all constitute a definite philosophical teaching that purports to describe, more or less accurately, what reality is like and what human beings are like.[2] Plotinus also attempts to sketch, hint at, and otherwise indicate a method that one might say oversteps speculative metaphysics as such. The *Enneads* and the texts that follow in its train represent a disciplined attempt to foster, to awaken, or at least to acknowledge what the Neoplatonists conceived to be a sometimes

---

[1] Cf. M. Hirschle, *Sprachphilosophie und Namenmagie im Neuplatonismus* (Meisenheim am Glan, 1979).

[2] On the doctrinal aspects of Plotinus' philosophical system and for his strength as an exponent of original philosophical doctrine, see the highly persuasive monograph of Gerson 1994.

Gerson views Plotinus as an innovative, systematic philosopher, who attempts to provide ontological solutions to "inadequacies in the accounts of Plato and Aristotle" (Gerson 1994, p. 67) concerning such issues as, for example, the role of the One as a causal principle, or the need for an explanatory principle that transcends the intellect.

dormant capacity in human beings, for *theoria* or vision, for insight and self-awakening.[3] These texts are written to convey to the reader a wisdom that must simultaneously be discovered either outside the text or beyond the text. But how is it that this tradition concerns itself with what could be called a non-discursive pedagogy, especially given that the tradition itself, as we shall see, places such tremendous weight on textual exegesis? The answer to this question ought to go beyond the merely empirical observation that Neoplatonic philosophical discourse can take several different forms: theurgic ritual, radical Skepticism, visionary journeys, or visual exercises. That much will be obvious to any reader of the tradition.

Decoding these texts involves seeing them as something like meditation manuals rather than mere texts. The non-discursive aspects of the text – the symbols, ritual formulae, myths, and images – are the locus of this pedagogy. Their purpose is to help the reader to learn how to contemplate, to awaken the eye of wisdom, to, in the words of the Chaldean Oracles. "Open the immortal depth of the soul: open all [your] eyes up in the heights."[4] In other words, these texts constitute a language of vision.

In the remaining pages of this introduction, I consider in more detail the very concept of the exegetical tradition as practiced by the Neoplatonists. The Neoplatonists answered for themselves such questions as how to invoke Platonic authority for their own metaphysical doctrines, how to evaluate the literal meaning of Plato's texts, and how to interpret Plato's figurative language, by means of a hermeneutics that first elaborated these seemingly transparent concepts. For example, the word "symbol" (*symbolon*) has certain ritual affiliations that informed the Neoplatonists' readings of texts as well as

---

[3] Plotinus, for example, thinks that there is an innate capacity in all human beings, by which they can enjoy "contact with god" (*Enneads* V.1.11.14), although this faculty is largely dormant. Cf. *Enneads* V.1.12.1: "But how is it that although we have such great possessions, we are not aware of them?"

For Plotinus, the task of the philosopher will not be to deliver a discursive exposition concerning the principles of reality, but rather to remind his reader to "turn the act of awareness inward, and insist that it hold attention there" (*Enneads* V.1.12.15).

[4] *Chaldean Oracles*, fragment 112.

the Neoplatonic texts themselves. Likewise, since the question of Plato's own teaching methods is under dispute for some of the Neoplatonists,[5] their notion of what constitutes Platonic doctrine can also be opaque. Even the concept of a text as a neutral medium for conveying doctrine receives scrutiny. Thus, there are esoteric texts, sacred texts, public texts and ritual texts, and all of these texts presuppose the appropriate context for their decipherment.

Platonic Exegesis before Plotinus and after Damascius

Even if we confine a study of Neoplatonic textuality to its exegetical nature, and see Neoplatonism as literally a series of footnotes on Plato, this textuality is still fraught with difficulties, as any student of Plato will observe. There is neither space nor necessity to rehearse here the familiar difficulties raised by Schleiermacher and advanced by the Tübingen school concerning the allusions to extratextual wisdom embedded within Plato's texts, the "things of more value than the things . . . composed" (*Phaedrus* 278d9).[6] Instead, I would like to frame Neoplatonism by looking at the history of ancient Platonic exegesis.

Ancient philosophers tended to see themselves as exegetes of previous texts or doctrines and the Neoplatonists were no exception.[7] Perhaps the most famous example of this traditional claim to orthodoxy is found in *Enneads* V.1.8, Plotinus' doxography concerning his doctrine of the three primary hypostases, the soul, the intel-

---

[5] For example, in the so-called *Anonymous Prolegomena to the Study of Plato's Doctrines*, the sixth-century Neoplatonist Olympiodorus suggests that Plato teaches by emphasizing the contrast between divine and human intelligence, or by means of maieutics or by helping the student cultivate self-knowledge. English translations by L. G. Westerink (Amsterdam, 1962).

[6] Cf. Krämer, *Plato and the Foundations of Metaphysics*, for a history of the notion of the Unwritten Doctrines. Kraemer and Reale suggest that Unwritten Doctrines are principles that form a foundation for the metaphysics adumbrated in the main corpus of the Platonic dialogues but that were, for various reasons, never explicitly espoused as foundational. I do not pursue this line of inquiry in this book for the simple reason that I am concerned here with non-discursive thinking. Since these principles were discursively formulated, according to Krämer and others who take this line of approach, it seems to me to make little difference as to whether they were orally transmitted or inscribed in the dialogues of Plato.

[7] On Plotinus as exegete of Plato, see Charrue 1978, Dörrie 1974, and most recently Gatti in Gerson 1996, pp. 10–38.

4

lect, and the One: "our present doctrines are an exegesis of those [ancient teachings], and so the writings of Plato himself provide evidence that our doctrines are of ancient origin. (V.1.8.11–15)."[8] Plotinus elaborates this programmatic statement regarding the exegetical nature of his teaching elsewhere in his works. In particular, Plotinus raises the question of how the methods of the Platonic exegete differ from the methods employed by members of other schools. Because intellectual knowledge resists discursive formulation, Platonic exegesis turns out to be, perhaps surprisingly, fundamentally extratextual. In the following passage, Plotinus is expounding the difficulties surrounding an inquiry into the nature of intellectual knowledge: "We have failed to arrive at understanding because we think that this knowledge consists in theorems, or in drawing conclusions from premises; but that kind of thing has nothing to do with knowledge here. Now if someone wishes to argue about these matters, he is permitted to do so for the time being. As for the knowledge [in intellect] which Plato has in sight when he says, 'It is not one thing, distinct from that in which it exists . . . ' " (V.8.4.48–53).

Plotinus suggests that one can interpret Plato only by relying on an intuition that fully assimilates the doctrine in question; one must, according to Plotinus, become the exegesis. If Plotinus' Platonic exegesis implies a paradoxical devaluation of the text, it is because the status of the text is always in question throughout the long history of the Platonic tradition. Throughout this history, the one question repeatedly asked is, what were the doctrines of Plato and how does one recognize Platonic teaching? By looking at this question of what constitutes Platonic dogmatism in the history of exegesis, we gain a vantage point from which to view the texts of Neoplatonism.

We know that the Middle Platonists practiced an unusual form of textual exegesis, in which so-called items of doctrine found within the text were marked with an obelisk to signify their doctrinality, and then imported wholesale and without any dialogic contextualization, into a series of dogmata, or teachings, that were thought to contain the most important aspects of Plato's philosophy. Any reader who has had the occasion to plod through the somewhat disengaged

---

[8] On this passage, see the commentary of Atkinson 1983, p. 192.

5

Didaskalikos of Alcinous or analog handbooks[9] recognizes at once the artificiality of excerpting what are purportedly Platonic tenets from the dramatic and disputational arena in which those same tenets were originally framed. The credibility of the *Handbook of Platonism* is further strained since it purports to be a literal summary of Plato's principal doctrines and yet attributes to Plato innovations in the areas of ethics and logic that were never even conceived by him.[10] At any rate, the point of this example is to remind the reader of one extreme version of textual literalism, in which philosophy is thought to consist of a list of tenets, even if in some cases that list is supplemented by anachronistic material culled from the current philosophical vocabulary.

What strikes me about such works as the *Didaskalikos* is the boldness by which they are produced, an audacity occasioned by the handbook approach that displays an insensitivity to the hesitations Plato himself expressed over the written method of conveying doctrines as well as to the literary form of the dialogues. If the Middle Platonists shared with the Neoplatonists that peculiar amalgam of Hellenistic and Peripatetic philosophy that formed the basis of their scholastic disputes, they most certainly did not share the Neoplatonists' heartfelt, passionate scrutiny concerning the true meaning of almost every word in Plato's texts. This overconfidence in the transparency of the text, a rashness signified by the exegete's dogmatizing obelisk, can be strikingly contrasted with the diffidence that one sees at the very end of the Neoplatonic era. Glancing at the Platonic commentaries and handbooks produced in the sixth century, in the school of Olympiodorus, one notices a veritable obsession with the issue of Plato's own hesitations as evinced in his texts.

Olympiodorus devotes chapter 10 of his *Prolegomena to the Study of Platonic Philosophy* to the refutation of an *ephectic*, or non-dogmatic, Plato:

---

[9] As, for example, Apuleius' *De Platone et eius dogmate.* See Dillon 1993 and Whittaker 1990 for the most recent and authoritative texts and translations of the *Didaskalikos.*

[10] For example, Alcinous attributes to Plato what amounts to the entire system of Peripatetic ethics. See *Didaskalikos* and Dillon's commentary on chapters 5 and 6. Perhaps "credibility" is the wrong word, since the purpose of the *Handbook* remains unknown. There seem to be Peripatetic sources in use throughout and a particularly close connection to the Peripatetic ethics of Arius Didymus.

Plato also superseded the philosophy of the New Academy since that school gave precedence to *akatalepsia*, while Plato demonstrated that there do exist cognitions grounded in genuine knowledge. Nevertheless, some assert, assimilating Plato to the *ephectics* and to the Academicians, that he too maintained the doctrine of *akatalepsia*.

These remarks are curious, for we have no indication that a Skeptical reading of Plato was current or even conceivable at this time. In fact, as the context makes clear, the Skeptics are represented in this passage as a prior philosophical school; chapters 7 through 10 present a concise history of philosophy that is remarkably free from any notions of philosophical currency attributable to the views that fall under its purview: "there has been no shortage of philosophical *haireseis* (schools) both before and after Plato, yet he surpassed all of them by his teaching, his thought, and in every possible way" (*Prolegomena* 7.1).

Olympiodorus performs the exegete's role throughout his refutation of a non-dogmatic Plato, turning first to the grammatical item, Plato's use of what Olympiodorus terms the "hesitating" adverbs, such as "probably" (εἴκος), "perhaps" (ἴσος), and "as I imagine" (τάχ᾽ ὡς οἶμαι). Nevertheless, Olympiodorus manages to sustain a superficially pedantic tone in the four pages he devotes to this end, eschewing any close reading of the dialogues, briefly glossing topoi such as recollection, and importing issues that have no foundation in Plato, as, for example, his refutation of the tabula rasa theory of the soul (10.27).

In short, Olympiodorus' schoolroom lesson has little interest as a document of sixth-century Skepticism: one wonders, for example, if Olympiodorus was familiar with any of the writings of Sextus Empiricus or was more likely using the brief paragraph in Diogenes' *Life of Plato* to inform his topic.[11] Nor indeed has it much value as an exegetical text, as we have seen. Its importance, if it can be said to have any, lies rather in the particular fascination that Plato's teach-

---

[11] The word *ephektikos*, used of Plato in *Prolegomena* 10, is found in Diogenes Laertius. At any rate, Sextus at *PH* I 221 does not in fact define Plato as a Skeptic. An alternative possibility is that the Neoplatonists were familiar, not with the works of Sextus Empiricus, but with those of Aenesidemus. We know that Aenesidemus' book survived until the time of Photius because of Photius' synopsis of the ten modes associated with Aenesidemus.

7

ing seems to have held for the school of Ammonius, the teacher of Olympiodorus and of Damascius.

We know from Olympiodorus' commentaries on the *Gorgias* and on the *Phaedo* that Ammonius had written a treatise devoted to *Phaedo* 69D4–6 in which he proved that this passage did not call into question or cast doubt upon the immortality of the soul.[12] For now, we note that Olympiodorus transmitted his obsession with the dogmatic Plato to his own student, the Christian Neoplatonist Elias, who again discusses the Ephectics as a distinct philosophical school in the preface to his *Commentary on the Categories*. In this charming rendition of Plato as a champion of truth against its arch detractors, the Ephectics, who deny that anything can be known, and the Protagoreans, who assert that everything is true, Elias too alludes to the immortality of the soul to illustrate his theme:

[The Ephectics] suppressed the refutation of a premise. And this school is also known as the Three-footed, since they answered with three alternatives: when asked the definition of soul, whether it was mortal or immortal, they answered, "it is either mortal or immortal or neither or both." The school is also known as "aporematic," because it maintains a state of aporia and does not permit solutions.

And they oppose the Protagoreans. The Protagoreans maintained that truth prevailed, saying that what each person believes is actually true. But Plato takes both schools to task in his own terms, refuting the Ephectics in the *Theaetetus* thus:

"Do you maintain that nothing can be known as a result of knowing [this fact] or as a result of not knowing it? For if you do so knowingly, then behold, there is knowledge. But if not knowingly, then we shall not accept what you say, since you don't know [what you are talking about] when you say that nothing is knowable." Plato refutes the Protagoreans in the *Protagoras*, as follows: "Are we right or wrong when we say that you are wrong, Protagoras? If we are right, then you are wrong, and therefore, there is falsehood. But if we are wrong while you are right, there again falsehood exists. Therefore, whether you are right or wrong, you are wrong." (Elias *In Cat.* Profemium 109.24–110.8)

These dialogues are used to invent a dilemma concerning the existence of propositional truth. In what follows, we see that Elias is

---

[12] We also know that the subject of Plato's dogmatism or Skepticism was frequently raised in the introductions of the Aristotelian Commentators, possibily due to the influence of Ammonius. See the introduction to *Prolegomena*, p. lxiii.

concerned once more to portray Plato as a dogmatic philosopher, and so to rescue him from what he sees as a pair of unattractive, sophistic alternatives. In the next passage there is an almost verbatim echo of the *Prolegomena's* interest in the grammar of doubt: "Some have thought that Plato too belonged to the [Ephectic] school, above all since he used adverbs that indicated doubt, as when he said, 'I think,' 'Perhaps,' 'Maybe,' and 'I guess.' " This quotation from Elias repeats many themes found in the *Prolegomena*; perhaps the prefaces to these works were stamped out of a single mold. Whether this material became some kind of scholastic siglum, a seal of orthodoxy, or had perhaps a propagandistic purpose, is a question worth exploring, but one that must be postponed for the present.[13] Meanwhile, it is enough to notice not only that Ammonius, Olympiodorus, and Elias all belonged to the Commentator tradition and therefore that their works could well be sets of lecture notes, school disputations, or textbook material, but also that their work on Plato was rather mediocre.[14] According to Damascius, these teachers were entrenched Aristotelians; posterity has disposed of their Platonic Commentaries, which had to compete with the more brilliant works of Proclus and Damascius. We should not expect to find great insights or staggering hermeneutics on the subject of Platonism in these prefaces or textbooks.[15]

Instead, we do find a consistently developed theme, which has to do with the dogmatic reading of Plato's dialogues. Although it is not clear how thoroughgoing these authors proved to be in their scrutiny of Plato's dialogic epistemology, one fact seems trenchant: they associated Plato with an ambivalent dogmatism. That is, their concern to defend the dogmatism of Plato arose out of their sensitivity to the qualified, possibly hesitant nature of his assertions, and no doubt to the negotiable character of truth that inevitably arises in the dia-

---

[13] On the contents of the Proemia to the Aristotelian Commentators on Plato, see the work of Phillipe Hoffman 1987a.

[14] Still useful on the subject of Olympiodorus is R. Vancourt, *Les derniers Commentateurs Alexandrins d'Aristote. L' École d' Olympiodore* (Lille, 1941).

[15] Damascius *Life of Isidore*, p. 110: "Ammonius was extremely diligent and proved to be of the utmost assistance to the various Commentators of his generation. But he was a rather entrenched Aristotelian" (my trans.). For a comparison between the *Prolegomena* and the *Didaskalikos* of Alcinous, see Segonds's *Introduction*, p. vii (*Prolégomènes à la philosophie de Platon*, texte établi par Westerink et traduit par Trouillord avec la collaboration de A. Segonds (Paris, 1990).

9

logue form and is marked by the adverbs of hesitation. Olympiodorus casually inserts the Neoplatonic interpretation of Socrates' denial
that he is a teacher: "again [Plato] says, 'I teach no one,' " in the
sense of "I do not impart [my own] teachings to anyone," and caps
this gloss with a paraphrase of the *Theaetetus* and the *Seventh Letter*.
In reply to these worries, Olympiodorus and Elias cull sentences
from the dialogues that reveal a bias toward what they might regard
as true teaching. For example, Olympiodorus ends his refutation of
Plato's Skepticism with a paraphrase from the *Gorgias:* "If you do not
listen when you yourself are making assertions, then you will not be
convinced if someone else is the speaker. How could we consider
[the author of this sentence] to be a Skeptic?" (*Prolegomena* 11.25).

To summarize this discussion, Ammonius and his school are at
least somewhat ambivalent in their assessment of Plato's dogmatism;
they clearly distinguish the style and teaching methods that he culti-
vates from ordinary dogmatism. At times, they hint that Plato's teachings involve an appeal to a kind of intuitive wisdom, based on introspection, on divine or innate knowledge.[16] Finally, this hermeneutics
of ambivalence is peculiarly associated with one particular exegete,
Ammonius, and his immediate students and philosophical descen-
dants. We have evidence that Olympiodorus and Elias were students
of Ammonius, and we have very strong verbal agreements within the
prefatory material to the Commentary works that these philosophers
authored.[17] With these conclusions in mind, let us turn to consider
Damascius, the last Platonic successor and the figure with whom I
end this study.

We know from the *Life of Isidore* that Damascius at some time had
studied with Ammonius (*V.I.* 111.10: "Damascius records that Ammonius had expounded Plato to him").[18] However remote his intel-

---

[16] *Prolegomena* 10.
[17] Cf. p. 61 of Segonds' commentary on the *Prolegomena*, and the references cited
there. See also the following passages. I am extremely indebted to Professor Harold
Tarrant of New Castle College for these references. See now Tarrant's translation
of Olympiodorus' *Commentary on the Gorgias* (Leiden, 1998). Indeed, it is Tarrant's
work on the exegetical works of the Alexandrian school that has made possible my
own very limited inquiry. Hermias, *In Phaedrum* 20.7; Proclus *In Alc.* 21.10–24.10
95.25–96.22; Olympiodorus *In Alc.* 24.11–20; 33.21–34.2; 212.14–18; Olymp. *In
Phae.* I 8.3; 6; 14; Olymp. *In Gorg.* 60.11–15; 188.15–17.
[18] Zintzen, *Damascii vitae Isidori Reliquiae,* 1976 fr. 128. From Suda IV 761, 3, s.v.
φρενοβλαβεῖς.

lectual affiliation with the Alexandrian school, Damascius makes a point of reporting on and recording the activities of this group in the *Life of Isidore*, so that we can safely assume his familiarity with its exegetical methods. This path of inquiry has at least enabled us to track the exegetical puzzle of a non-dogmatic Plato back into the Late Athenian Academy, via the shadowy figure of Ammonius. And it has confirmed the fact that Neoplatonism is partially informed by ancient difficulties surrounding the interpretation of Plato.

What I hope I have accomplished by framing the Neoplatonist tradition with this cursory look at Middle Platonism and the Commentators is to suggest that the issues of textual practice, of dogmatism and exegesis, were very much alive for the ancient students of Plato, just as they are for us today. Just as it has become fashionable for some modern students of Plato to refuse to attribute to Plato any of the interlocutors' statements as constituting a doctrinal position, so some strands within the Commentator tradition emphasized the difficulty of ascertaining the existence of any theses Plato might have held with conviction. An even earlier exegetical style evinced in Middle Platonism completely ignored the dialogic presentation of the doctrines that it literally ascribed to Plato, in a way that might remind one of the criticism practiced earlier in our own academic tradition. Although Neoplatonists practiced a distinctive method of exegesis, this is not to confine Neoplatonism to its role as an exegetical school. In fact, the Neoplatonists promulgated a number of doctrines deliberately designed to support the notion of a tradition outside the texts as well as a transmission of wisdom outside the literal teachings of Plato.

The Symbol

One question concerning the relative place of texts within the tradition of Neoplatonism and, particularly, the Neoplatonic valuation of texts is bound up with the dispute between theurgy and philosophy in the third and fourth centuries.[19] At the center of this dispute are the place and significance of the symbol, or *sunthema,* the ritual object by means of which theurgic elevation was thought to take

---

[19] On this dispute, see Sheppard, Shaw, and Smith.

place.[20] Thus what I am interested in is not so much a contemporary discussion of the place of the symbolic within exegesis, that is, a philosophy of hermeneutics in the abstract. Rather, what I propose to look at is the place of the *symbolon*, or *sunthema*, the ritual object in Neoplatonism, as a way of grounding a discussion of symbolism, and how to read it in the exegesis of Neoplatonic texts. Although chapter 5 applies contemporary linguistic theory to what I there call Plotinus' metaphors, I would like in this introduction to suggest that the role of metaphor in the *Enneads* of Plotinus is linked to the larger question of symbolism as construed by the Neoplatonists.

I define "symbol" as any structure of signification in which a direct, primary, literal meaning designates, in addition, another meaning which is indirect, secondary, and figurative and which can be apprehended only through the first. . . . Interpretation is the work of thought which consists in deciphering the hidden meaning in the apparent meaning, in unfolding the levels of meaning implied in the literal meaning.[21]

This quotation, from Ricoeur's *The Conflict of Interpretations* indicates a theory of exegesis that goes exactly *against* the spirit of Neoplatonic symbolism, or so I would argue. For the theurgists, a *symbolon* is not a meaning at all, nor is a *symbolon* subsidiary to, derivative of, or referential to a literal meaning. Instead, the *symbolon* is a divinely installed switch, so to speak, that operates within the context of ritual. Symbols function as crossroads, as junctures that allow the soul to trace its path back to its origins. For Neoplatonists, the process of interpreting symbols involves a complex mixture of traditional lore and radical self-reflection.

What does it mean to interpret the symbolic expressions of Neoplatonism, and how should we proceed when we encounter a symbol or, as we would say, a metaphor, within the text? By looking at the tradition as a whole in the light of these questions, we gain a foothold by which to perform an exegesis that may coincide more exactly with the terms of Neoplatonic theory. Moreover, this approach reveals, somewhat unexpectedly, a certain unity in a tradition that is normally thought to have been ruptured by the split between theurgy and philosophy in the third and fourth centuries.

To take one example, we know that Iamblichus composed a work

---

[20] See Coulter for a history of the word *symbolon*.
[21] Ricoeur, *The Conflict of Interpretations*, p. 12.

entitled "A Compendium of Pythagorean Teachings,"[22] of which one book comprised the *Protrepticus*, or "Exhortation to Philosophy." This work, still extant, is a kind of exegesis of the Platonic tradition, as well as a discourse on how to read the texts of philosophy in general, and how to read Pythagorean symbolism in particular. Thus in chapter 21 of the *Protrepticus*, we find a catalogue of the so-called Pythagorean *symbola* as well as a method of decoding them according to Neoplatonic principles of exegesis. In this text also we find Iamblichus remarking that the entire philosophical tradition in which he finds himself participating (the Pythagorean, which was for Iamblichus the pristine form of Platonism)[23] employs symbols as its primary method of teaching: "the whole of Pythagorean teaching is unique in that it is symbolic" (*Prot.* 34, p. 247).[24] What characterizes this tradition, according to Iamblichus, is its reliance on symbolic modes of discourse. Iamblichus' *Protrepticus* culminates in his gradual revelations concerning the meaning of Pythagorean symbolism, as if to suggest that they constitute in themselves an initiation into the contemplative life.[25]

> The final method for exhortation is the one [that makes use of different kinds of] symbols: the kind unique to this sect and not revealed to other schools; the public kind shared with the other schools. . . . Accordingly we will introduce in our discourse certain exoteric explanations, those shared with all philosophy . . . and then gradually mix in the more authentic teachings of the Pythagoreans . . . and this method will lead us imperceptibly from exoteric conceptions . . . into the heights, elevating the thoughts of everyone who approaches with genuine effort. (*Prot.* 29, p. 132, with omissions)

Iamblichus goes on to discuss the importance of the distinction between esoteric and exoteric doctrines, pointing to the Pythagorean separation of mere auditors from the actual followers of Pythagoras, as well as to the Pythagorean rule of silence and nondisclosure to the uninitiated. What follows is an utterly fascinating interpretation of 39 Pythagorean *akousmata*, or sayings that are available to the general public but whose meanings are divulged only

---

[22] Cf. Larsen 1972 Chapitre II, "Synagoge Pythagorica," and the Budé edition of the *De Mysteriis Aegyptorum*, Notice, pp. 5–7. Five books belonged to this collection.

[23] Cf. Larsen 1972, pp. 70–90; O'Meara 1989; and for a still briefer survey of the relevant material, chapter 6 below.

[24] Cited by Larsen 1972, p. 88 ft. 101.

[25] Larsen 1972, p. 103. Iamblichus *Prot.* 29, pp. 130–1.

according to Pythagorean teaching. The general tendency within this interpretation is to remind the student of the priority of developing an accurate conception of wisdom, and in this sense the text becomes quite self-referential, as in the following interpretation of the Pythagorean saying, "Avoid the highways and take the short-cuts" (*Prot.*, p. 137):

> I think this saying tends in the same direction. For it exhorts one to keep away from the vulgar and merely human life, and thinks it better to follow the detached, divine life, and it asserts that one ought to ignore *communis opinio* and value instead one's own thoughts, which are secret, etc. (*Prot.*, pp. 137–8)

So in this book, we can imagine Iamblichus providing the student with a kind of counter-*Didaskalikos*, an esoteric handbook that invokes symbols rather than tenets.[26] A thorough exhortation to philosophy, it includes a series of precautions, embodied in the *akousmata*, concerning the form, accessibility, and practice of genuine wisdom. Iamblichus here warns the would-be student that wisdom is not publicly available in the sense that the true purport of its deliverances can be discovered only when one is willing to venture beyond the texts that commonly circulate.[27] Although this example concerns itself once more with exegesis and reliance on the literal text, it also introduces the crucial concept of the symbol.

This concept is so crucial because it has come to signify a breach in the Neoplatonic tradition, manifested in the polemics between Plotinus' disciple Porphyry and the Syrian philosopher Iamblichus, concerning the place and function of ritual *askesis* in the philosophic life. We know about this dispute from Iamblichus' work *On the Mysteries of the Egyptians*, which is prefaced with the following words: "the teacher Abammon's reply to a letter of Porphyry and solutions to the difficulties [posed] in it" (*DM*, Scholion). The book opens with Iamblichus' adopting the persona of an Egyptian prophet who will

---

[26] Not that Iamblichus is writing in the tradition of the *Didaskalikos*, of course, since he is writing in the tradition of Aristotle's *Protrepticus*. See Larsen on the Protreptic tradition.

[27] On the initiatory uses of Pythagorean maxims, see I. Hadot 1978, who discusses the place of Simplicus' *Commentary on the Manual of Epictetus*. According to Hadot, the importance of the Pythagorean *Sentences* as well as the maxims of Epictetus' *Handbook* is due to the method of moral education in this epoch. On the question of precepts, moral rules, and the value of *Sententiae*, see Seneca, Epistle 94.

attempt to answer Porphyry's difficulties concerning the practice of theurgy. As is well known, behind Iamblichus' insistence, contra Porphyry, on the ritual efficacy of certain symbols for the purpose of uniting the individual soul with the gods, lies a psychological tenet. Iamblichus follows Aristotle in holding that the human soul is fully embodied; he denies Plotinus' doctrine that the highest part of the soul always remains undescended, permanently attached to the intellectual realm.

From this conception of the soul, Iamblichus argues that knowledge or intellection necessarily fails to allow the individual soul to free itself from its human limitations: "not even gnosis [grants] contact with the divine. For gnosis remains barred [from its object] because of a certain otherness" (*DM* 7, p. 42). Again Iamblichus maintains that "thinking does not connect theurgists with divine beings, for what would prevent those who philosophize theoretically from having theurgic union with the gods? Rather . . . it is the power of ineffable symbols comprehended by the gods alone, that establishes theurgical union"[28] (*DM* 96, 13). Lack of space prohibits more details here about the dispute between Porphyry and Iamblichus.[29] What is important is that this dispute has suggested to some scholars that the theurgic Neoplatonism of Iamblichus and its associated religiosity represent a foreign and divergent philosophy from that of Plotinus' school. Perhaps too this scholarly judgment has resulted in a way of reading Plotinus' *Enneads* that ultimately overlooks its ritual affiliations and its symbolism as subordinate to or superseded by discursively expressed doctrine.[30] In fact, recent studies of Iamblichus and Plotinus have suggested that both philosophers employ mathematical symbolism not just to represent features of the intelligible world but also as part of a contemplative language intended to convey a sense of the unitive knowing celebrated as the hallmark of the tradition.[31]

This brief excursus on the nature of Neoplatonic symbolism allows us once more to consider what a proper Neoplatonic herme-

---

[28] Translation of Gregory Shaw. Shaw 1995, p. 84.

[29] Readers should consult Shaw 1995, pp. 13–15; Wallis 1972, pp. 107–10; Dillon 1987, and especially Finamore 1985 on this topic.

[30] See chapter 5 below for this scholarly controversy and for an attempt to read the *Enneads* in light of theurgic practices.

[31] Bussanich 1997; Shaw 1995; Shaw 1993.

neutics would be like. On the one hand, Neoplatonic texts can be considered in terms of their own exegetical functions; they represent a pedagogical tradition that nevertheless repudiates, as we have seen, a literal interpretation of the text. On the other hand, these same texts are also the main vehicle of expression for a tradition that explicates its original insights in terms of a theory of non-discursive thinking. It is not simply the conventional contrast between primary and secondary meanings or the literary contrast between literal and metaphorical utterances that is at stake in a Neoplatonic hermeneutics. Rather, what this book attempts, in its chapters on metaphor, Orphic and Pythagorean symbolism, and Proclus' theurgic discourse, is an interpretation of Neoplatonic texts within the framework of the tradition's own pronouncements about the meaning of symbols. And this attempt lands us in an ancient hermeneutic circle. For many of these symbolisms invoke a context of tradition and suggest that to be appreciated, the symbols must be expounded by and for those who belong to the tradition. We saw this in the case of Iamblichus' *Protrepticus*. In this sense, perhaps Ricouer's way of describing the hermeneutic circle, "you must understand in order to believe but you must believe in order to understand,"[32] has some relevance for Neoplatonism.

As examples of this Neoplatonic promotion of tradition, one may cite the almost uniform invocation of Pythagoras' divine initiation and the consequent prestige of mathematical symbolism, or again, the frequent allusions to the Orphic theogony as anchoring Neoplatonic cosmological speculation in divine revelation. In fact, the very institution of *Diadoche*, the transmission of the Neoplatonic mantle within the revived academy, is once more part of this prestige accorded to tradition.[33] Celebration of the master's birthday, hagiographic bibliographies, and general veneration of the teacher as the most authoritative source of wisdom are all purposefully deployed by the Neoplatonists (witness Porphyry's hagiographic *Life of Plotinus* attached as preface to the *Enneads*) to remind the reader of the appropriate context for interpretation.

---

[32] Ricouer, *Conflict of Interpretations*, p. 298.
[33] See Lim 1995 and Fowden 1989 and the references that they cite.

Reflection

Still, we today do not belong to the Neoplatonic tradition; we cannot be initiated into the inner circle of Plotinus' listeners, and we have no one to instruct us in theurgic practice. If the context for Neoplatonic exegesis is the (at least partially fabricated) notion of tradition, in reality the symbols and doctrines encountered in these texts are presumably thought by their authors to be accessible. Their meaning is to be recovered, in Plotinus' words, by self-inquiry (Plotinus insists that "knowing something in the strict sense amounts to knowing oneself" [V.3.61]) or by "turning within oneself and seeing the vision as one [with the self] and as oneself" (V.8.10.40). Throughout this book, I am concerned to discuss not only Neoplatonic textuality but also Neoplatonic pedagogy by means of the doctrine of non-discursive thinking. This pedagogy was foremost and always conceived by the Neoplatonists as a search for self-knowledge, a contemplative *askesis* that demands from its practitioner not just a familiarity with the texts of the tradition but also the effort to assimilate those texts.

The questions that remain to be asked are how such assimilation is thought to take place and whether or not the texts themselves provide clues to this process. Part of the appeal for Iamblichus and Porphyry of the Pythagorean tradition is that it allows them to envision philosophical speculation within the environment of the Pythagorean modus vivendi. Other Neoplatonists rely on the doctrine of contemplative virtues, grades or stations of wisdom by which one traverses the path that theory sets out. For example, although in the *Sententiae ad Intelligibilia Ducentes* (Sentences Leading to the Intelligible World)[34] Porphyry distinguishes among four classes of *arete*, it is clear that each kind – civic, kathartic, noetic, and paradigmatic – is a mode of training the mind, of transforming one's consciousness so that this assimilation can take place. In this treatise, Porphyry offers an excursus on the practice of contemplation, affording the modern reader a rare glimpse of Neoplatonic pedagogy.

The first grade, civic virtue, allows the student to govern the

---

[34] This treatise is more or less a compendium containing extracts from the *Enneads*, with some additions by Porphyry, particularly in the area of Neoplatonic ethics. The modern critical text is by E. Lamberz (Leipzig, 1975).

emotions and to integrate the personality around the practice of contemplation.[35] Kathartic, or contemplative, virtue results in *apatheia*, in the complete detachment of the self from its embodied condition and the refusal to identify with the body as defining the self.[36] The third class comprises the noetic virtues, those that permit the soul a deeper form of self-discovery: "without that which is prior to soul [e.g., nous] the soul does not see what belongs to it" (*Sent.* 32, p. 37). These virtues are defined in terms of the soul's ability to direct its attention inwardly, to abide in a state of contemplation, and to become one with the object of contemplation. Attention, concentration, control of thoughts, and absorption in the object to which the mind is present are all governed by practice at this stage. Porphyry thus defines a very precise contemplative psychology as a gradual process of inner transformation, of identifying, purifying, and concentrating the faculty of awareness to cultivate wisdom, which is defined as the native work of this faculty (*Sent.* 32, p. 29).[37]

What this contemplative psychology, or *askesis*, shows us is that self-reflection is construed as a process of working with the mind and developing its powers of concentration. This training in concentration is part of the non-discursive methodology that complements the textual side of the tradition. Several chapters in this book address the psychology of contemplation and even suggest that the symbol, as it is found in Neoplatonic texts, often becomes a contemplative object, one whose meaning can be discovered only through an intense process of concentration, assimilation, and self-reflection. The process of interpreting the Neoplatonic symbol, and hence the Neoplatonic text, is entirely dependent on the act of self-reflection.

This hermeneutic conclusion should not come as a complete surprise. In modern hermeneutic theory, imagination and the phenomenology of experience are sometimes given priority over de-

---

[35] Porphyry *Sent.* 32, p. 23: "sophrosune is the agreement and harmony of the appetitive faculty with the rational faculty."

[36] Porphyry *Sent.* 32, p. 25: "Being established in theoretic [e.g., kathartic] virtue results in apatheia."

[37] Porphyry *Sent.* 32, p. 29: "The fourth class of virtues are the paradigmatic, which are seated in the intellect and are more potent than the psychic virtues and function as the causes of these."

scriptive metaphysics.[38] Certainly the great modern exponent of symbolic hermeneutics, Paul Ricouer, has emphasized the links between reflection and interpretation. As he puts it: "reflection is the effort to recomprehend the *ego* of the *ego cogito* in the mirror of its object, its works, and ultimately its acts."[39] And very few will fail to be aware that psychoanalytic models provide us with grounds for associating the act of interpretation with the practice of self-reflection.[40]

Conclusion: Non-discursive Methodology in the Tradition

Let me try now to reiterate some of the themes touched on this introduction by way of summarizing the main argument of the book. The Neoplatonists rely on and defer to nous, a faculty or perhaps principle of intuition that, the majority of Plotinus scholars would now agree,[41] is characterized by self-reflection.[42] Not only does this principle ground the metaphysical insights that go into making up a body of philosophical truths, but this faculty is also the source of self-knowledge.[43] These two kinds of knowledge, philosophical insight and self-knowledge, turn out to be one and the same thing for the

---

[38] Cf. Sellers, *Delimitations. Phenomenology and the Demise of Metaphysics*. Bloomington, 1997.

[39] Ricouer, "The Hermeneutics of Symbols," in *Conflict of Interpretations*.

[40] I am not here applying a psychoanalytic reading to Neoplatonic texts, even though, for the most part, this book is concerned with the third hypostasis, the level of soul. The reason for my concentration on this hypostasis is that the soul, according to Plotinus, is characterized by discursive thinking; the texts that become important in the following chapters are aimed primarily at directing the discursively operating mind to a different mode of thinking. Psychoanalytic interpretations of Neoplatonic doctrines would not be valid from within the perspective of Neoplatonism, since for the Neoplatonists, intellect is not, properly speaking, a faculty that belongs to the human psyche. Hence intellect cannot be understood primarily through studying the history of the individual mind or soul. See Blumenthal 1971 and Blumenthal 1996.

[41] See especially Gerson 1997 and 1994, p. 55: "For Plotinus, we might say that since Intellect is immaterial, it naturally follows that knowing is essentially self-knowing. Knowing implies infallibility and infallibility can only obtain when there is self-reflexivity."

[42] Emilsson 1996 speaks rather of intellect's "self-consciousness."

[43] In using the word "faculty," I do not mean to imply that the Neoplatonists conceived of intellect as a capacity purely or even substantially belonging to the individual human soul. Perhaps it is better to speak of the intellect as a principle rather than as a faculty.

Neoplatonists. However elaborate their metaphysics may sometimes appear, the structures reported and discovered by Neoplatonists are part and parcel with self-discovery.

What characterizes the faculty of insight is unitive knowing, non-separation of subject and object, or complete assimilation to and identification with the object of knowledge. And this form of unitive knowing is non-discursive. But what exactly is nous, and how does one gain access to it? Could it be that the Neoplatonists were uninterested in answering these questions and instead relied on the authoritative pronouncements of tradition to dispel or defer any anxiety about the existence of nous and the availability of intellectually grounded truth?

I doubt this. In addition to the metaphysical structures assumed and elaborated in the tradition, this tradition also transmitted a non-discursive methodology. We saw earlier that Iamblichus in his *Protrepticus* warns the student that wisdom is not publicly available, that it instead demands both initiation and *askesis* if it is to become available at all. To the questions, what is this *askesis*, and how did the Neoplatonists think one ought to practice it, we glimpsed possible answers in the contemplative virtues of Porphyry, who describes a gradual training that develops the mind's capacity for non-discursive, or unitive, thinking.

In the following chapters, I treat the non-discursive or non-doctrinal aspects of the texts – symbols, visualizations, and so on – as further elements of this tradition. That is, I show that the texts reveal an inclination to non-discursive methodologies and, further, that the symbol can and sometimes does function as the locus for inculcating this kind of method. In the first part of the book, in the chapters that center on Plotinus' thought exercises and metaphors, I try to reconstitute the kind of non-discursive methodology that I suspect is operating between the lines of the literal text. This methodology relies on self-reflection, on introspection, and on self-awareness, but of a highly specialized sort, one that I will now attempt to outline, but which I elaborate in more detail in chapters 3 through 7. Let me ask the reader's indulgence as I briefly list the features of this self-reflection and also suggest that the individual chapters provide greater clarification.

Non-discursive thinking does not involve thinking about anything either by way of propositions or by way of theorems, and so on (chapter 2). Instead, non-discursive thinking involves, perhaps para-doxically, a kind of objectless knowing, an activity that is self-directed but refrains from any definitions or objectification of the self (chapter 3). This form of self-directed activity is self-transparent, involving a turning of the attention toward the pure act of awareness as such, and a detachment from all other objects of awareness (chapter 4). Non-discursive thinking involves concentration, a setting aside of the entire panoply of objects, both perceptual and conceptual, and an identification with the object of contemplation (chapter 5). This object of contemplation, examples of which are given in chapters 3, 4, and 5, is a matter of intense theoretical and practical speculation within the tradition. The object of contemplation can be connected to the practice of theurgy and very often is selected from a set of traditionally revered symbols, such as mathematical objects (chapter 6), traditional myths or ritually oriented narratives (chapter 7), and divine names (chapter 8). Finally, whatever insights are gained from this practice of intellectual *askesis*, the results obtained are never equivalent to any discursive formulation or expression (chapter 9).

In this Introduction, I have attempted to tie together the apparently disparate themes of the chapters that follow. I have also no doubt deferred responsibility for the variety of textual practices treated in this book by claiming that we, as readers of these texts, have no choice but to confront and accept the multiplicity of these practices if we are to comprehend the tradition. Finally, however, I should admit that the reader will find in what follows a record of my own attempts to read the texts of Neoplatonism, alongside the efforts of a growing scholarly community that is engaged in this enterprise. It is my sincerest wish that readers of this book will find that these texts speak to them and become the occasion for their own strategies, both discursive and non-discursive.

PART ONE

Language in the *Enneads*

2

Plotinus' Critique of Discursive Thinking

In this chapter, I want to look more closely at the Neoplatonic critique of discursive thinking, as part of a more general discussion of philosophical method in the *Enneads*. One issue that demands immediate attention is how we ought to conceive of philosophical method in Neoplatonic texts. This chapter will explore dialectic in the *Enneads*, with particular emphasis on its contrasts with both Stoic and Aristotelian dialectic, as well as with more contemporary philosophical methodologies. This chapter is largely negative in its conclusions, showing more what the dialectic is not than what Neoplatonic dialectic includes. In this respect, it introduces the subsequent chapters that explore a variety of dialectical strategies that nevertheless presuppose this central critique of discursive thinking.

Let me start with the modern distinction between ontological commitments and epistemological commitments invoked, for example, to examine versions of philosophical realism. Realism has been described as the belief that reality exists independently of any [human] representation of it.[1] Expressed in this way, modern philosophical realism is not an epistemological theory and entails neither a theory of truth nor a privileged, unique description of the world.[2] In other words, if one holds some version of philosophical realism, it may turn out that truth (one's representation of the world) and reality coincide – that our representations accurately reflect the way things are – or it may not. It may further turn out to be the case that

[1] Searle 1995, pp. 151–3.
[2] Searle 1995 pp. 154–5, arguing against Putnam's definition of realism. See also Farrell, chapter 5.

a plurality (even an indefinite plurality) of descriptions can be used to represent reality. In this example, ontology and epistemology are conceived as separate philosophical realms, whose conclusions may operate quite independently of each other. Such was not true of ancient philosophical methodology.

In the history of ancient philosophy, realism has coincided with theories of truth that entail very specific ways of representing the world. Plato's Theory of Forms, for example, ties a type of ontological objectivism to a theory of language: language refers to and depends on the existence of real entities that directly inform linguistic usage. Similarly, Aristotle's notion of first philosophy also relies on a theory of truth:

> In every systematic inquiry where there are first principles, or causes, or elements, knowledge and science result from acquiring knowledge of these. (*Phys.* 184a10)

Aristotle's philosophical realism entails ontological objectivism – the existence of objective first principles in nature – as well as a correspondence theory of truth. For Aristotle, these first principles that exist in nature also determine the truth of our statements about them. Facts about reality bring about the truth of our representations, so that definitions adequately reflect the essences of primary substances.[3] One philosopher has even generalized this kind of theorizing in the history of Western philosophy, stating that:

> One of the oldest urges in Western philosophy is to think that somehow or other truth and reality should coincide, that somehow or other, if there really were such things as truth and reality, as we normally think of them, then truth would have to provide an exact mirror of reality. The nature of reality itself would have to provide the exact structure of true statements.[4]

What kind of emphasis a particular variety of realism gives to epistemological considerations varies, no doubt, with the intensity of epistemological debate that realism addresses. Scholars have remarked that, for example, Aristotelian epistemology is almost surprisingly unproblematic in certain ways: since Aristotle never doubts that knowledge of the world is available for human knowers, doubts as to whether or not private experience links up with a public reality

---

[3] On Aristotle's philosophical realism, see Irwin, pp. 4–6.
[4] Searle 1995, p. 175.

hardly arise for him.[5] Conversely, if Platonic epistemology is particularly concerned with distinguishing the faculty of intellect as capable of somehow conceiving infallible knowledge, it is also concerned to represent that knowledge as not subject to derailment by Sophistic persuasion. Plotinus inherits the "faculty" approach to intellect that characterizes the epistemologies of Plato and Aristotle, but shares in common with Plato a sensitivity to possible epistemological challenges, a sensitivity that exerts a definite influence on his theory of truth.

So far we have seen that although epistemology and ontology are intertwined in ancient thought, either the epistemological side or the ontological side of a given question will often prevail. Often dialectic operates out in the open in a Neoplatonic text, whereas its ontological or epistemological correlates have to be inferred from or even teased out of this operation. Neither a theory of truth that is isolable from ontological assumptions nor an ontology that operates independently of epistemology, Plotinus' dialectic plays upon the inadequacy of discursive thinking while simultaneously insisting that truth is unproblematically available to human knowers. Precisely because intellectual knowledge is infallible due to intellect's inherent self-reflexivity (intellect is its objects), for Plotinus, philosophical activity operates beyond the constraints of epistemology. Thus the doctrine of infallible intellectual knowledge is common to Platonic, Aristotelian, and Neoplatonic epistemologies. But unlike Plato, who subjected his own epistemological constructions (for example, the Theory of Forms, or the ontological basis of predication and negation) to a fairly rigid rational scrutiny, the Neoplatonists made no such attempt to do the same for their intellect. And despite the formal similarity to the Aristotelian doctrine that intellect is its objects, the Neoplatonic identity thesis had radically dissimilar consequences for Neoplatonic methodology.

In the case of Plotinus' theory that intellect is its objects, this means that knowing the truth is a state utterly unlike that of normal thinking. Precisely because intellectual knowledge is not intentional, in the sense that it is not directed at things outside of itself, the contents of intellect cannot be disclosed by means of linguistic representations. Nor can the metaphysical structures revealed by the

---

[5] Taylor 1990, pp. 116–17.

intellect be described by means of propositions without suffering a great deal in the process of translation. Hence the locus of the representational gap has migrated in the philosophy of Plotinus. He does not ask how it comes about that intellect adequately represents features of the world because he is more troubled by how the world that is known by intellect can be philosophically represented. The problem with such representation is not only the obvious one, that any representation is selectively aspectual, capturing certain features and omitting others of the object represented. Plotinus' problem is that he needs to convey a theory of truth that is precisely non-representational, without the unwanted result that reality collapses into mere representation.

If truth is inherently non-representational, not based on a representational relationship between subject and object, then how can it be revealed? What kind of truth can be communicated if truth just is, as Plotinus notoriously remarks, "what it says."[6] We need to distinguish Plotinus' methodology from subjectivism, from the epistemological stance that equates the world with one's representations of it. The doctrine that intellect is its objects does not imply a subjectivist theory of truth, according to which the immediacy of consciousness stands in for an otherwise elusive and mediated reality. The difficulty of locating truth on the subjective side of the representational gap is a topic to which I will return in chapter 3. For now, I turn to Plotinus' critique of discursive thinking.

Philosphical Methods

Epistemological idealism picks up where Cartesian confidence leaves off.[7] Because the Cartesian solution privileges the representational nature of the mental, it actually leaves the representational gap, the cognitive dissonance that arises from the private nature of subjectiv-

---

[6] Cf. *Enneads* V.3.5.25: "Truth ought not to be of something other [than itself], but what truth says, this too it ought to be." And again, *Enneads* V.3.10.35: "If [intellect] says 'I am this,' and the 'this' is different from that which speaks it, it will utter falsehood."

[7] Here I use the term "epistemological idealism" to refer to Nagel's definition of idealism as the view that "what there is is what we can think about or conceive of ... and that this is necessarily true because the idea of something that we could not think about or conceive of makes no sense" (Nagel 1986, p. 90).

ity, fully intact. One very broad response to this dilemma has been the anti-foundationalist epistemologies of Bernard Williams and Thomas Nagel. These philosophers search for objectivity as an approximate goal that is brought about by the reflexive critique of idiosyncratic representations. As Paul Redding puts it, "subjectivity is understood in a particular way: it is understood in terms of the idea of the particularity of the conditions under which the belief is formed, an idea expressed by the metaphor of the conditions under which one 'views' the world – one's 'perspective.' "[8] This search for objectivity in turn leads to a relatively less perspectival truth, an aperspectival truth or "view from Nowhere," which in some ways forms the modern equivalent of the absolute or of absolute truth. Williams discusses this notion of truth in his book *Descartes: The Project of Pure Inquiry:* "That surely must be identical with a conception which, if we are not idealists, we need: a conception of the world as it is independently of all observers."[9]

This way of construing objectivity seeks to remove the particularity of the subject as a partial or limited perspective on what might be thought of as an absolute conception of the truth. This modern debate about what constitutes philosophical truth, especially an absolute conception of truth, takes as its parameters the scientific model that Williams explicitly endorses as one extreme position. The other extreme presents the viewpoint of the subject as always already conditioning the reality that any absolute conception of truth would pretend to be about. But these two views would be seen as flawed, though perhaps in different degrees, from within the terms of Plotinus' own theorizing about the nature of truth. The identity theory of truth for the Neoplatonists does not seek to discover objective essences, if that search is thought to take place outside of the searcher. Certainly, scholars have rightly emphasized the metaphysical or ontological concomitants of Plotinus' theory of self-reflection. Much like Aristotle's God, the contents of that intellect are simply the forms. Hence self-reflection will turn out to be knowl-

---

[8] Redding, p. 6. Cf. also Nagel: "A view or form of thought is more objective than another if it relies less on the specifics of the individual's makeup and position in the world, or on the character of the particular type of creature he is" (Nagel 1986, p. 5).

[9] Bernard Williams, *The Project of Pure Enquiry* (Sussex, 1978), p. 241.

edge of reality. The idea here is that self-reflection functions like a principle of truth; knowing that one knows is the foundation for knowledge of truth. In this sense, there could be no knowledge of reality without self-reflection.[10]

Now this is an important dimension of Plotinus' epistemology, and Plotinus does explicitly suggest (in V.5) that self-knowledge is the principle of all truths. The problem is that thinking about an object does not, for Plotinus, equate with knowing it objectively, that is, knowing it as it is in itself. Plotinus is concerned to show that human beings cannot think their way out of a limited point of view, since discursive thinking itself constitutes one such limited perspective.

Again, like Williams and Nagel, Plotinus does insist upon the reflexive critique of thought as a condition for its correction, but he offers cautions about a metaphysical realism that too easily assumes that our accounts of the world correspond to features of the world as it is in itself.[11] In short, it may well be that intellect grounds its intuitions according to the ontologically prior nature of the forms. Nevertheless, this notion of objectivity is not a conceptual one; the objects known in this way cannot be the subjects of propositions nor can they be about individual particulars in the world. The reason for this caution is, once more, that conceptual activity, far from observing the nature of things as they are in themselves, actually obstructs our view. It prevents us from seeing things as they are in themselves. In the remainder of this chapter, I will be looking at Plotinus' own formulation of the problematics of perspective.

Philosophical Explanation in *Enneads* VI.7

Enneads VI.7, "How the Multitude of Forms Came into Being and On the Good," opens with a criticism of Plato's account of Demiurgic creation in the *Timaeus*. Under Plotinus' direct fire is language that describes the Craftsman as calculating, planning, or entertaining reasons for his act of production.[12] What is the philosophical

---

[10] See Gerson 1997 who best explicates this position.
[11] On ancient philosophy and metaphysical realism, see Irwin 1988, chapter 1, section 2.
[12] The first lines quote *Timaeus* 45b3, directly alluding to the younger gods' dispatch

context for this exegesis?[13] Our treatise's structure is guided by a series of six *aporiae*, each concerned with a Platonic text frequently adverted to within the tradition.[14] Yet the same denial of discursive thought to God is found in several other treatises, namely, "On Providence" and "On Problems Concerning the Soul" and in the Grossschrift, all of which are non-Platonic contexts.[15] Because of the very similar language employed in a parallel passage in II.9, "Against the Gnostics,"[16] most scholars agree that our passage alludes to the Gnostic interpretation of Plato's Demiurge as the planning mind,[17] or *"nous dianooumenos,"*[18] and to the Gnostic idea that Thought, unaccountably hypostasized, planned and carried out the work of creation, albeit faultily. More recent scholarship views the denial of discursive thought to the Demiurge as an attack upon the Stoic view of deity that identifies human reason and divine intelligence and holds that in this Plotinus was informed by earlier Academic criticisms of such anthropomorphism. Here III.2 is adduced.[19] To be sure, there continued a long-standing debate in the annals of Ancient Greek philosophy over whether God thinks the

---

of the souls into the world of space and time, but the general issue is the language of deliberation that Plato uses in the narrative. Cf. *Timaeus* 30b1, λογισάμενος; 29c1, πρόνοιαν; 34a9, λογισμός, etc.

[13] For general discussions of VI.7 1–15 in light of Plotinus' philosophical treatment of the idea of *Pronoia*, see Leroux 1990, pp. 31–2; Theiler 1966; Schubert 1968; P. Hadot 1988, pp. 31–6; Schroeder 1992, pp. 16–20.

[14] On the overall structure of VI.7, see Hadot 1987c; Hadot 1988.

[15] Schubert 1968, Leroux 1990, and Wallis 1987.

[16] II.9.8.20. In chapters 5 and 6, Plotinus censures the opponents' falsification of Plato's account of creation: "often they have soul as the maker instead of the planning mind and they think that this is the maker according to Plato, being a long way from knowing who the maker is. And in general they falsify Plato's account of the manner of the making" (II.9.6.23–26). For a discussion of whose views precisely are being criticized, see Peuch 1960, Roloff 1970, pp. 169–79, and Elsas 1975, in the appendix of Roloff's monograph. Both II.9 and VI.7 oppose a literal reading of the *Timaeus* creation account not only because of Gnostic renderings that hypostatize the planning mind but also because a literal rendering assumes that the world had a beginning in time.

[17] The conception of a Demiurge, or Creator God, who uses the forms as a blueprint for the world is of course central to most Middle Platonic discussions that try to explain how God interacts with the world. See Witt 1930, p. 199; Dillon 1977, pp. 46–9 and passim.

[18] II.9.6.21.

[19] See Wallis 1987, pp. 942–52.

way we think, and Aristotle's negative answer[20] was definitive for the later Platonists.[21] However in VI.7 itself, within the chapters that immediately follow the criticism of *Timaeus*, Plotinus refers neither to the Gnostics nor to the Stoics, but rather to Aristotelian teleological explanations of the kind adumbrated at *Physics* II 199b34 and *PA* 1641b25, as well as to the Aristotelian account of definition in *Metaphysics* Zeta 3.

In this section, I want to discuss the doctrine that is, the denial of discursive reasoning to God, in terms of Plotinus's own philosophical methodology,[22] since source criticism has yielded such a plethora of interpretations. Within our treatise, this denial is tied to a discussion of the limits of philosophical explanation: even though we may *describe* it by means of discursive thought, there is no such thing as a unique explanation for the structure of the world. A good statement of this position may be found in V.8, περὶ τοῦ νοητοῦ κάλλους, "On the Intelligible Beauty." The explanations by which we humans try to account for the world, using discursive thought as we must, are always underdetermined by the available evidence:

> You can explain the reason why the earth is in the middle and round, but it is not because you can do this that things are so There; they were not planned like this because it was *necessary* for them to be like this, but because all things There are disposed as they are, the things here are well disposed, as if the conclusion was there before the syllogism which showed the cause, and the conclusion did not follow from the premises. (*Enneads* V.8.7, Armstrong's translation)

The word that Armstrong translates as "reason" is *aitia.* In Aristotle's *Posterior Analytics* it bears the meaning of "explanation." Ac-

---

[20] *Metaphysics* Lamba chapter 9 and *De anima* II. For the Aristotelianized Platonism of the Imperial period, see Blumenthal 1987b.

[21] It could be said that Plotinus reversed the terms of the debate and asked whether the human soul could ever think like the divine mind. For his positive answer to this question in the form of the concept of the undescended soul and its heterodoxy within the Platonist tradition, see Blumenthal 1987b.

[22] Throughout the *Enneads* we find the insistence that the world is not an artifact whose genesis is owed to someone's intentions, associated with the "two acts' theory of causation, wherein every level of reality must of necessity produce an image of itself in the form of a "lower" existent. However, what follows is a methodological interpretation rather than a strictly metaphysical one. For caution against a purely source critical approach to Plotinus, see Schlette 1974 and more recently, Leroux 1990, pp. 23–6.

cording to Aristotle,[23] if we come to know the *aitia* we know both the reason for a given state of affairs and that, on account of the *aitia*, it is not possible for the state of affairs to be otherwise. Such knowledge is said to constitute knowledge in its most proper sense. But things could not be more different with Plotinus. For him, the condition sine qua non for knowledge is the unity of the knower and the object of knowledge, a condition that discursive thought of any kind necessarily precludes.[24] Our blueprints for the world do not correspond to the architect's because there simply is no discursive thought in intellect. Now, causal relations are a prime instance of a ready-made structure. And Plotinus declines to discuss the structure of nature in terms of standard causal explanations, including teleology, one-directional causal connection, essentialism, and metaphysical dualism, all of which are characterized in various ways by the limitations of discursive thought. In this treatise, Plotinus refuses to subscribe to such explanations because he denies that discursive thought can ever be absolute. This is not to say that Plotinus refuses ever to invoke essentialism or completely denies the ordinary structure of causal sequences. Here we see Plotinus operating at the limits of philosophical discourse, taking a critical turn to investigate the forms of philosophical explanation, ultimately to introduce a form of philosophy that is not explanatory in any of the usual senses.

We turn now to the critique of causal explanations offered in treatise VI.7. Plotinus' arguments seem to cut in two directions. Plotinus corrects Platonic teleology with a healthy dose of what is ostensibly Aristotelian essentialism. But this essentialism is in turn modified beyond anything recognizably Aristotelian when Plotinus insists upon the unity of *ousia* with the second hypostasis, *nous*. Aristotle's theory of explanation, according to which what a thing is, τὸ τί ἦν εἶναι, is identical to the reason for its existence, τὸ διὰ τί,[25] shows up in chapter 2 of VI.7 as a corrective to the idea that the

---

[23] *Post. An.* I.71a16.
  Ἐπιστάμεθα δὲ οἰόμεθ'ἕκαστον ἁπλῶς, ἀλλὰ μὴ τὸν σοφιστικὸν τρόπον τὸν κατὰ συμβεβηκός, ὅταν τὴν αἰτίαν οἰώμεθα γινώσκειν δι' ἣν τὸ πρᾶγμα ἐστιν, ὅτι ἐκείνου αἰτία ἐστί, καὶ μὴ ἐνδέχεσθαι τοῦτ'ἄλλως ἔχειν.
[24] See below chapter 3.
[25] *Physics* 197a32. Cf. *G.A.* II 742b23–36.

teleological disposition of the world is imposed from outside.[26] In fact, there really is no teleological disposition of the universe, although the world is well-disposed, not as the result of an accident, but because it subsists together with its intelligible cause.[27] Likewise, due to the doctrine of the unity of all Forms with the second hypostasis, we cannot explain the world by appealing to the discrete essences of hylomorphic compounds anymore than we can by appealing to the Demiurgic imitation of the Forms. Essences at the level of nous are not discrete. Instead of trying to explain the nature of the particular, we must go to the intelligible and see how the particular looks from that point of view.

Plotinus enhances these causal theories with the concept of coordinate arising. This doctrine presents a twofold analysis of the phenomenal world, both parts of which are intended to break up any belief in an independently real or self-subsistent external world. The first theme is a description of the world as an interdependent nexus of beings. Under this description, the familiar Stoic idea of *cosmic harmonia* receives a more profound philosophical interpretation as a system of relationships that can be described as mutually reflective points of view.[28] The second theme treats the multiplicity of individuals more on the analogy of thoughts arising in the mind, each expressing the nature of the thinker who has them.

The treatise begins with an attempt to understand why the individual has been endowed with the faculties of sensation. "God or a god sent souls into genesis, endowed with sense organs." But why was this provision made? Answer: for the sake of preservation, which is to be accomplished by the activities of pursuit and avoidance (of sense objects).

Plotinus follows a strictly teleological model of explanation to

---

[26] On Aristotle as a corrector of Platonic notions of teleology, see Balme 1987, p. 275.
[27] Cf. VI.7.3.9 and II.9.8, "Against the Gnostics," for Plotinus' denial of teleology "To ask why soul made the universe is like asking why there is a soul and why the Maker makes. First it is the question of people who assume a beginning of that which always is" (II.9.8). And later in the same chapter: "The image [i.e., the cosmos] had to exist, necessarily, not as the result of thought and contrivance" (II.9.8.22). Cf. also V.8.7.
[28] On Stoic cosmic harmonia, see Cicero *De Finibus* III, section 38 ff.; Edelstein-Kidd 1989–90, fragments 104 and 106. For Plotinus' familiarity with this Stoic tenet, and the probable influence of Posidonius, see Reinhardt 1924, Graeser 1972, Witt 1930 Theiler 1966.

what he considers an absurd conclusion: God endowed living beings with sense organs out of foreknowledge that this would tend toward their bodily preservation. Since perception is a function of the soul and not of the body, souls must possess some faculty for sense perception even before entering the world of genesis. Otherwise they would lack psychic faculties that constitute part of the definition of soul. Hence the conclusion must be that souls are endowed with sense capacities by nature. The purely noetic condition would therefore be unnatural for the soul. So the nature of the soul is to exist in a state wherein the sense faculties may be used, and so it must live in the sense world. The soul is designed by nature then to exist in a state of embodiment, multiplicity, and in general, evil. But if the same intelligence responsible for the creation of the soul could be responsible for its being endowed with the ability for self-preservation, we would have contradictory purposes in the very creation of the soul. "The exercise of providence would amount to no more than the purpose, that the soul be preserved in evil."

And yet the sensible exists; its cause can only be the intelligible. So the intelligible brings about the sensible in a way that does not involve the production of something outside of itself. The conclusion is that the sensible already exists within the intelligible. At this stage of the argument, Plotinus does not yet tell us how the sensible exists within the intelligible. He seems content to exploit the rhetorical reversal of roles and to leave the language of the sensible intact as a kind of metaphorical or extended usage.[29]

Thus after proscribing teleological views, Plotinus proceeds with his own account of the relation between the intelligible and the sensible. The immediate and glaring difference between the banned account and the kind of account found at the end of chapter 1 in the treatise VI.7 is the manner of reference to time. In the *Timaeus* narrative, events unfold temporally, and causation is a developmental sequence that ends in the individual realization (ἑκάστην ἐνέργειαν) of a form within matter.[30] But this type of analysis is false

---

[29] Thus we find him talking about "the perceptibles that exist there" (VI.7.6.2), "the eyes they have there" (V.8.4.26), εἶναι τὰς αἰσθήσεις ταύτας ἀμυδρὰς νοήσεις, τὰς δὲ ἐκεῖ νοήσεις ἐναργεῖς αἰσθήσεις. (VI.7.7.31), "Our sensations are dim intellections; intellections are clear sensations."

[30] Readers will no doubt be aware of the history of *Timaeus* interpretation as providing one of the great intellectual fora in antiquity for thinkers of all creeds. From Proclus

because of the view that it adopts, which looks at reality as if it were a succession of temporal segments that somehow have to be linked to each other through the explanations we give. Instead of trying to explain the world in this way, we should start with the realization that "no 'later' exists in the intellect" (VI.7.1.40). So when we try to understand reality, we should start with a perspective that sees different states of the world as present altogether, though without temporal existence.

Several recent studies have called our attention to the Neoplatonists' interest in theories of causation.[31] Of interest to moderns is the outright denial of horizontal or one-directional causal sequence among sensible particulars, or the denial that bodies are causally efficient.[32] Conversely, only incorporeal beings such as form, intellect, and soul are agents. The Neoplatonists regularly accounted for the emergence of substances as well as the processes of the natural world by appealing to the idea of immanent causation, the doctrine that effects are contained within their causes. Therefore the sensible particular, inasmuch as it is not incorporeal, cannot be designated or isolated as the cause of a given individual or event. In the following passage, we see the denial of something that could be likened to a modern notion of cause, in which an event A precedes another event B, such that B would not have come about without the presence of A.

Fire does not arise without a cause – What is its cause? Not friction, as one might assume, since fire already exists in the universe and friction takes place with the bodies undergoing friction [already] containing [fire]. (VI.7.10.40, Armstrong's translation modified, reading ἐχόντων as temporal not causal participle)

Here event A, the friction, is not the cause of event B, the conflagration. Rather, the cause of the conflagration is just the fact that

---

to Philoponus, pagans, Christians, and Jews debated how to read the *Timaeus* myth. For an interesting account of certain aspects of this interpretation, see Jarislov Pelikan 1997, the Jerome Lectures, *What has Athens to do with Jerusalem?* Ann Arbor, University of Michigan Press.

[31] Barnes 1983b; Sorabji 1987; Wagner 1982b.

[32] Barnes 1983b, p. 175, for example, concisely summarizes Proclus' presentation of this view (*ET* 80): (1) all bodies are passive; (2) everything incorporeal is active; (3) no body is active; (4) no incorporeal thing is passive. Barnes supplies the conclusion to the argument: only incorporeal things are active.

the element fire exists and, presumably, does so in dependence upon the form. This appears to be a denial of what is often called the counter-factual version of horizontal causation. That is, the conflagration might have occurred even without the friction. Yet in other places, Plotinus seems more concerned not to deny horizontal causal sequences but rather to illustrate the difficulties involved in trying to specify just how events are supposed to be related to each other if one is to say that they are causally related.[33] One very basic issue involves the difficulty of picking out just what a cause is, such that it is both necessary and sufficient for the bringing about of a given effect. The problem has to do with being able to distinguish such a unique cause from what might be called the total causal field, in being able to distinguish a background condition from a cause. Hillary Putnam, for instance, illustrates the problem in this way:[34]

Imagine that Venusians land on earth and observe a forest fire. One of them says, "I know what caused that – the atmosphere of the darned planet is saturated with oxygen" . . . What is and what is not a "cause" or "explanation" depends on background knowledge and our reason for asking the question.

The problem here arises from the ambivalent context in which the explanation is given, but we can generalize from this example. If for any given query we find that a complete answer will have to specify all of the relevant background conditions, then it seems that our answer will be reduced to something that does not look like an explanation for the event at all. Plotinus has this in mind when he asserts that the only real explanation for an event is to say that it belongs to a totality.[35] The theoretical background for this kind of problem is sketched at VI.7.2.35, in what I will refer to as Plotinus' doctrine of simultaneous arising:[36]

In fact just as in our universe, which subsists from a multiplicity of elements, all things are linked with each other, and the explanation for the individual consists in its being a member of the totality (that is, just as the part in the case of every individual is perceived in terms of its relation to the whole), it

---

[33] On the difficulties of specifying the nature of causal connection between events, see Davidson 1980.
[34] Putnam 1983, p. 214.
[35] Cf. VI.7.2.35, discussed in the next paragraph.
[36] My translation.

is not the case that first one thing arises, and then after that, this, but rather things subsist in relation to each other, both the cause and the effect.

The first part of the conclusion seems to sketch and then to deny a theory of causation that could easily be compared to the Humean account of cause as: "An object precedent and contiguous to another, and so united with it in the imagination, that the idea of the one determines the mind to form the idea of the other."[37] Obviously things do arise one after the next. What this phrase means is that although there may be sequences of events, these sequences are not causal sequences. The next part of the sentence presents an alternative causal theory: the cause and the effect come to be in reciprocal origination from each other.

This alternative, non-teleological method of explanation, in which the relationship between cause and effect is one of co-arising, shows up in the subsequent puzzles of VI.7.1–15. In VI.7.1 it appears to be the inspiration behind the constant refrain in which the logic of temporal sucession, τόδε μετὰ τόδε,[38] is denied. Rather, the sensible arises as an immediate and necessary expression of the intelligible. Chapter 3 of VI.7 applies this theory to an analysis of soul and concludes that soul must arise simultaneously with its sense faculties. Chapters 8 and 9 show that the objects of sense, and so the whole realm of sentient beings, must arise simultaneously from the intelligible world. In chapter 10 all sentient beings must arise simultaneously, as must the gross elements together with their inhabitants (chapter 12).

In chapter 3, Plotinus applies his theory of interdependent causation to the analysis of the human form: if we ask, why does man have eyes or eyebrows, the only answer can be, ἵνα πάντα, in order that all things might come to be. Why should this kind of answer constitute any kind of an explanation at all? Taking the example of eyes first, we can see that Aristotle would certainly find this answer unsatisfactory. Since it is a part of human nature to be a sighted being, we have eyes because they are components without which the human form would be incomplete. Aristotle describes this preferred type of explanation as follows (*PA* 1640a 33–b4):

---

[37] Hume, book I, part III, *A Treatise of Human Nature,* quoted by Mackie 1974, p. 3.
[38] Cf. VI.7.1.37: ὁ λογισμὸς τοῦτο ἀντὶ τοῦτο; VI.7.1.40: τοῦτο, ἵνα μὴ τοῦτο; VI.7.1.56: τόδε μετὰ τόδε.

This is why we should for preference say (a) that man has these parts because this is what it is for a man to be. For without these parts he cannot be. Failing that, the next nearest thing: that is either (a') that it is altogether impossible otherwise, or at any rate (b) that it is good this way.

At this point we can see a difficulty emerging in the view that is explored in chapter 2 of VI.7. There, we read that each being has its reason why within itself, and that on a secondary level (in the order of individuals) the form is the cause of each individual's coming to be. Such a concession would seem to be completely in agreement with what Aristotle says here about the preferred form of natural explanation. Yet in this treatise Plotinus asserts that the reason why human beings have eyes is in order that everything may come to be: διὰ τί οὖν ὀφθαλμοί· ἵνα πάντα.

In fact, Plotinus goes on to suggest in this treatise that not only is the essence/accident distinction invalid, but it is so because the very differentia that are said in Aristotelian parlance to constitute the definition of something, and so to constitute its essence, are in fact inessential, or strictly accidental for that substance. In this section, Plotinus pursues his attack upon essentialism by means of a favorite strategy. He attempts to prize apart the essence/accident distinction by showing that it has no explanatory power, and thus that the individual substance lacks essential properites.

Aristotle seems to have thought that the concept of hypothetical necessity could be applied to the parts of an organism,[39] such that there were "features of a kind that explain other features of that kind without themselves being explained by features of that kind."[40] If we say that it is part of the human essence to be a sighted being, then eyebrows will be necessitated given this essential structure. So in this case we should be able to designate the eyebrows as φυλακτικόν and so as something that contributes to the end but is in fact not the end. But then the reason for the eyebrows – the form of man – must exist before the safeguard, since it determines that there be a safeguard. Plotinus concludes that the safeguard is not after all contributory to the essence, but is a part of the essence.

Thus it is extremely difficult to come up with a functional analysis

---

[39] For a list of Aristotelian passages that apply a teleological analysis to the parts of an individual organism, see Gotthelf 1987, pp. 190–1.
[40] Gotthelf 1987, p. 189.

of the parts of an individual in such a way that one could specify which elements function for the sake of others: πάντα ὅσα ἔχει ἔχοις ἂν εἰπεῖν διότι ἕκαστον (VI.7.2.44). "One could say that all that belongs to an individual is its reason why." The undermining of the concept of definitional necessity is based upon the rejection of the distinction between the parts of an individual that are components of the essence and the parts of the individual that are contributory toward the essence. And again, Aristotelian essentialism is based on the ability to specify what belongs to a susbstance essentially. The erasure of the essence/accident distinction in this case seems to erode this essentialist construction.

This is not to say that the Neoplatonists rejected Aristotelian logic as incapable of yielding valid results for the reasoning process. Rather, the results obtained by this process will not yield necessary propositions about the reality that they describe.[41] In V.8.7.41 we read:

> as if the conclusion was there before the syllogism which showed the cause, and the conclusion did not follow from the premises; [the world order] is not the result of following out a train of logical consequences and purposive thought; it is before consequential and discursive thinking.

It seems that the Stoic philosopher Poseidonius attributed the intelligibility of the world's structure to the fact that the designing intelligence, God, and human intelligence shared the same thought processes, since human souls were *apospasmata* of God.[42] Therefore, the Stoics hold that a teleological description of the world is a factual description of a state of affairs that inheres within the cosmic structure.[43] Thus this very structure, the systematic cohesion of individuals

---

[41] A great deal of scholarly work has been devoted over the last several decades to the exposition of Plotinus' notorious critique of Aristotle's categories, presented in *Enneads* VI.1–VI.3. To name but a few of the major works: Lloyd 1955–6; Lloyd 1990; Wurm 1973; Strange 1981; Rist 1967, chapter 8, "The Sensible Object" Corrigan 1981, pp. 98–121.

[42] See Reinhardt, pp. 116–17.

[43] It is not that we find Plotinus denying Providence, but that we find Plotinus consistently denying what he considers to be an anthropomorphic conception of Providence. Plotinus' most explicit definitions of Providence not only do not rely on any notion of teleology, but in fact go out of their way to distinguish between teleology and Providence. Thus in Treatise III.2, "On Providence," we find what is perhaps

within their order of being, is understood by Plotinus as a reflection of the inherence of our world within its intelligible cause. And this latter, the *cosmos noetos*, is not systematic in the way that the physical cosmos is.

Dialectic in Treatise VI.7

The exploration of teleology and paradigmatism in chapters VI.7.1–11 ends on an entirely different note. At the beginning of this treatise, Plotinus tries to demonstrate some of the conceptual difficulties he has with traditional teleology, as well as to sketch an alternative causal analysis of individuals. But any such theory of causation is open to at least the following criticism: to say that the reason why something is the way it is is simply because it is the way it is, or because it belongs to the totality of things, is perhaps to eschew philosophical explanation altogether. This position seems philosophically weak and, if asserted in some dialectical contexts, leaves such issues as theodicy entirely unanswered.

Part of the problem with this explanation is that Plotinus seems uncomfortable with the question. As he says in the treatise "On Providence," "What reason could [Intellect] have for making, since it lacks absolutely nothing?" If Providence is a doctrine that attempts to explain why things are the way they are in the universe, or why the universe is as it is, then this is not a question that Plotinus is willing to address when formulated in this way.

I have been dwelling at length on Plotinus' arguments in treatise VI.7 because of their dialectical function. Indeed, I think that Plotinus' notion of interdependent causation is not asserted as a doctrine at all, but is largely a dialectical device, designed to impugn or arrest

Plotinus' clearest statement of his doctrine:
> If our doctrine maintained that the universe came to be, starting from a specific point of time, after previously being non-existent, then our doctrine would affirm that Providence was the same [for the universe] as it is for individual things, that is, a foreseeing and rational planning on the part of God, who [would calculate] how this universe could arise, and also how things would be as perfect as possible. But since we maintain that this universe is everlasting and has never not been, we could correctly say that Providence for the universe is its being in accord with intellect. (III.2.1.15)

confidence in the explanatory power of discursive thinking, and designed, in the words of one scholar, "to break the hold on the mind caused by physical realitites and spatio-temporal limitations."[44]

Here one sees the direct bearing of how Plotinus' reservations about the limitations of discursive thinking come to affect Plotinus' methods and language. In our treatise, discursive thinking takes the form of a variety of philosophical explanations, culled from the history of prior theorizing. Plotinus seems to think that the available models can never solve questions as profound as "why are things the way they are." This diffidence too may seem weak, evasive, and not entirely satisfactory. If philosophy has been so unsuccessful in grappling with such issues, why practice it? Furthermore, one might ask, if I can't use human rationality to think about things, what other rationality can I use? So it is of no small interest that Plotinus ends a discussion in which he proscribes rational explanations, with a non-discursive answer to the question of how this universe came to be the way it is. He closes this section with a visionary passage, the first of many to be considered in this book.

In this passage, Plotinus continues to ask a series of questions that seem to demand a philosophical explanation. He starts with the question, where does everything come from? But this question quickly leads to others, until finally one is left asking questions that simply cannot be answered by a philosophical explanation:

> If someone asks what is the source of sentient beings, one is also asking what is the source of heaven there. And asking this is asking where [the Form] of the sentient being comes from, and this is the same as asking what is the source of life, and of universal life, and of universal soul, and of universal intellect. (VI.7.12.15)

What counts as an adequate understanding of individuals? Plotinus provisionally seems to suggest that we can understand the universe as a kind of mutual coming-to-be, or interdependent causal nexus: sentient beings all arise together as manifestations of a world soul or universal form of life. But this answer is just provisional, and the point of the passage is to suggest that once philosophical explanations come to an end, we are still left with work to do. Plotinus concludes with a most surprising suggestion: the physical aspect of

---

[44] Bussanich 1997, p. 5307.

living beings, by means of which they express their individuality, can be seen as a unity – objectively, as constituting one world body, and subjectively, as constituting one phenomenal presentation. The qualities that are known to comprise, on the Neoplatonist's account, the sum reality of the individual[45] are no longer capable of doing the work of presenting attributes by which an individual might be discriminated from another individual. Instead, these qualities should be apprehended in the most general form as one unified field of sense presentations:

The emergence of [all things] is from a single source, so to speak, but the source is not like some one particular breath or like a single feeling of warmth. Rather, it is as if a single quality contained all qualities in itself, and actually preserved them, so that [the quality of] sweetness [would be preserved] together with the [quality of] fragrance, and this single quality were [to become] simultaneously the taste of wine, and all of the modes of taste, and sights of colors, and all the sensations of touch. The quality would bring about whatever sounds are heard, all songs and every rhythm.

This passage has been interpreted in connection with Plotinus' cosmic and intellectual mysticism.[46] One question that arises in reading this passage concerns the apparent phenomenalism implied by the *aisthetic* nature of this description. Are we here dealing with a form of idealism? Is Plotinus in effect suggesting that all things arise as ideas in the mind? Most scholars think not, but on the surface, this appears to be the case.[47] The progress of the passage is from the objective description of the quality, as sweetness or smell, to its fundamental nature as a kind of awareness on the part of the perceiver. This passage is a description of the external world dissolving into the soul; in it we watch the world of objective qualities transmuted into a world of flowing qualia.

The world appears before us in this visionary passage as bereft of individual essences, a world whose content is apparently appropriated by a subject. What is more, this subject appears to view the entire cosmic panorama as its own act of awareness. Perhaps the loss

---

[45] *Enneads* II.6.3. On the purely qualitative existence of the individual, see the extensive discussion of Wurm 1973.

[46] Bussanich 1997.

[47] Bussanich points out that mystical visions often use sensory imagery to convey the experience.

of an objective world is too high a price to pay for the rejection of an essentialism that could vouch for the existence of such a world.

To address this issue, I would like to turn to the work of a scholar who writes on the religious dimensions of Plotinus' thought. Commenting on the nature of Plotinus' cosmic religiosity, this scholar writes:

The place to begin is not actually on the noetic level itself, but very close to it, on the psychic level. The trajectory of the mystical ascent extends from the material world and the experiences the embodied lower soul has in it to union with the One. However, the first level of reality superior to the material world is not the intelligible world, but the soul, both individual souls and the World soul. But does it make sense to speak of a distinct psychic level of entities, experience, and awareness?[48]

I think that this is exactly what Plotinus is doing in our visionary passage. He wants to lead the mind out of its habit of looking at the world as essentially outside of the self, as composed of a number of objects with discrete essences that are known in all sorts of ways, but primarily through the senses and through thinking about essences.

Plotinus attempts to weaken the claims of philosophical explanation as a way of luring the reader into a distance from the ordinary worldview. Suddenly, Plotinus suggests that the world can be seen as from within the mind. This move, this claim about the world, is going to occupy Plotinus in many of the passages to be considered in the following chapters. But it represents not a final position or an absolute truth. It is a provisional step, designed to bring the reader closer to the world of nous, by revealing something about the nature of the soul. This entire treatise is ultimately an exercise in self-knowledge and represents a dialectical progression, starting from the physical world and ending in the self-revelation of the One.

[48] Bussanich 1997, p. 5306.

3

Non-discursive Thinking in the *Enneads*

In the last chapter, we looked at Plotinus' visionary approach to Plato's Demiurge and wondered if the unitary world of the soul threatened to elide and engulf the ordinary world of objective essences. The question before us is now, how does Plotinus' conception of the soul overcome, so to speak, the temptations of this unlimited enrichment and avoid falling into a solipsistic dream. In what follows, I will explore the limitations of the soul's world and the soul's vision, showing in particular that Plotinus' views on discursive thinking point to a form of knowledge that asks the individual soul to step outside of its own constructions and its own contents. As we will see in the following chapters, because non-discursive thinking ultimately circumvents the intentional structures of thought, the intentional stance cannot be reified in such a way as to substitute for an objective world order.

Plotinus' views on method and truth involve a rejection of essentialism and a generally cautionary attitude toward discursive thinking. Some features of his anti-essentialism might lead us to think that he does hold to a kind of subjectivism, but in what follows I would like to suggest that this is not accurate. To clarify the problems with characterizing Plotinus as a subjectivist, I turn to a modern critique of subjectivism. In his book, *Subjectivity, Realism, and Postmodernism*, Frank Farrell points out the hidden ironies of what amounts to a self-deception implicit within Cartesian epistemology. This self-deception appears when we contrast ancient and modern Skepticism:

Whereas the ancient skeptic recommends withholding judgment about any proposition, his modern counterpart is skeptical about the world in a way that he is not skeptical about the contents of inner life. Things in the world may be worthy of doubt in every respect, but at least my ideas give themselves to me as what they really are, and while natural entities can no longer have natures, the inner objects do have natures, in that it is clear to the thinker what counts as the same idea reappearing.

A certain disenchantment of the world, an emptying out or a loss of content within the world, is the result of the unlimited enrichment of the subject. It seems that this Demiurgic conception of the self, automatically knowing, possessing, and ascertaining the nature of its ideational creations, is the counterpart of a Promethean division according to which what formerly belonged to the world outside of the subject now is reappropriated by the subject.[1]

The visionary counterpart to Plotinus' antiessentialist views, glimpsed at the end of *Enneads* VI.7, "How the Forms Came into Being," might seem to augur just this unlimited expansion of the subject, with a corresponding collapse of the world: "the emergence of [all things] is from a single source, as if a single quality contained all qualities in itself" (chapter 12, lines 23–4). As Burnyeat has shown, this danger of the idealistic subject who usurps the content of the world seems foreign to Ancient Greek forms of idealism in general and to Plotinus' noetic cosmos in particular. In Plato's *Parmenides*, for example, when the young Socrates suggests (*Parmenides* 132 b4) that the Forms are thoughts and hence located in minds, Parmenides secures his agreement that such a thought must still be "of" an existing reality: "What then, said [Parmenides], each Form is a thought, but is the thought [the thought of] nothing?" "But that is impossible," said [Socrates]. "Then it is of something?" "Yes." "Of something that exists or something that does not exist?" "Of something that exists" (*Parmenides* 132 b11–c1).

Plotinus too excludes any purely subjectivist tendency from his account of intellect, by emphasizing the priority of Forms or Being to intellect and by denying that a Form is a Form only when or because intellect is aware of it:[2]

It is, then, incorrect to say that the Forms are thought if what is meant by this is that when Intellect thought this particular Form came into existence

---

[1] On the Demiurgic self, see Farrell, chapter 1.

[2] On this point see Gerson 1994, chapter 3 and ft. 53, where he quotes V.9.7.14 requoted from Gerson above.

or is this particular Form; for what is thought must be prior to this thinking [of a particular Form]. (V.9.7.14–17)

Consequently, there is no impoverishment of the world implied in Plotinus' conception of the subject, and it could even be said that his views of the subject instead entail a further enrichment and proliferation of Being. Plotinus holds both that intellect is identical with its object and that intellect as a whole is all the Forms (V.9.8.3–4).[3] As he says of the intellectual object, "apparently it is a part, but when [someone] looks into the appearance clearly, [it is] a whole, [that is, all the Forms]." This cognitive complexity is both intersubjective, as the intellect knows all the other intellects, as well as prolific, as each object is all other objects. In fact, there is no conceptual equivalent to this intersubjective realm of truth characterized by mutual entailment among the Forms.[4] Hence, the structure known by intellect is emphatically not an invention of the individual mind, but becomes available to the individual only when she has succeeded in putting aside her particular point of view, or more accurately, when she has succeeded in increasing her point of view. Finally, it must be said that Plotinus seems to think that human beings develop a viewpoint that transcends the subjective when those same human beings fully apprehend the nature of the subject.

Epistemology and Introspection

As Farrell has recently argued, the modern subject boasts an ancient lineage whose ancestry can be traced far beyond its incarnation in the Cartesian *res cogitans*.[5] Many if not most modern philosophers start their examinations of subjectivity and the dialectics of subjectivity with a critique of the Cartesian "invention" of the mental world and its counterpart, the mental substance.[6] Although recent work

---

[3] On the controversial translation of the second half of this clause, ἕκαστον δὲ εἶδος νοῦς ἕκαστος, see Gerson 1994, p. 55 and ff.

[4] Cf. Gerson 1994, pp. 48–58, on the topic of intersubjectivity in the intellectual order of reality.

[5] Farrell 1994. See also below chapter 3 for an extended discussion of Descartes' roots in the medieval tradition. See also now Stephen Menn's *Descartes and Augustine*, chapter 4, "Augustine," on the Augustinian background of Descartes' *Meditations*, and chapter 3, "Plotinus," on Augustine and Plotinus.

[6] Rorty 1979; Redding 1996; Gillespie 1995; Zizek 1993.

has successfully traced the path of Cartesian dualism back to a medieval or even an Augustinian conception of the divinized cognitive self, one that "borrows" the attributes of a creationist god and authors its own private world through a series of projections that effectively seal its epistemological limitations,[7] modern theorists still find that the *res cogitans* provides a most useful target. The Cartesian mental self (whose very formulation as the indubitable subject of its own doubts suggests its dialectical origins in an epistemological debate) has become a veritable *pharmakos* on whom is foisted every fallacy of the modern age and has been almost ritually exorcised from the pages of our texts.[8]

On the one hand, historians of philosophy have been perhaps overly anxious to seal off hermetically the Cartesian self and its privileging of one feature of the mind, namely, its self-transparency.[9] On the other hand, even if it wishes to deny that the modern notion of consciousness has recognizable analogues in ancient epistemology, this story of the invention of the mind leaves out a chapter on Descartes' pragmatic appeal to the subjective states, an appeal that Descartes shares with a far more ancient tradition involving therapy of the soul. For although the introspective stance features heavily in Cartesian epistemology, in fact the "retreat within" as a philosophi-

---

[7] On the theological origins of the Cartesian subject, see Gillespie and Farrell, and especially Hans Blumenberg, *The Legitimacy of the Modern Age* (Cambridge, 1983).

[8] Objections are legion. One could cite, for example, Freudian objections (the denial that consciousness is self-transparent), methodological objections that introspection is not an adequate way of getting at the nature of the mental, anachronistic invocations of the Aristotelian psyche that seems to lack self-consciousness or any trace of mentalism, postmodern attacks on the Cartesian universal subject as concealing a political position, Nietzsche's dismissive attitude toward anything like a Cartesian unity of person, linguistic objections that situate the Cartesian ego as a grammatical category, and now Lacanian objections according to which the Cartesian ego merely personifies the embeddedness of the self in language and a symbolic order that paradoxically instantiate its ontic failures. And one could continue to cite countless other objections to the Cartesian self.

[9] See Rorty 1979, pp. 50–1 and ff. for self-transparency as the mark of the mental. Rorty, for example, demonstrates that the ancient Greek conceptions of intellect (*nous*) or soul (*psyche*) do not specify a similar distinction between the mental and the non-mental. As Rorty says of the Cartesian subject: "the novelty was the notion of a single inner space in which bodily and perceptual sensations, mathematical truths, moral values, the idea of God, moods of depressions, and all the rest of what we now call 'mental' were objects of quasi-observation" (Rorty 1979, p. 55).

cal construct precedes Descartes and is perhaps most readily visible in a whole genre of literature that no doubt inspired Descartes with its emphasis on subjective psychology. The Stoic *meditatio* and the confessional epistle, the structured self-examination of a Marcus Aurelius in his εἰς ἑαυτὸν βίβλιον, Seneca's *Letters to Lucilius*, and the Christian version of the Stoic meditation, Augustine's *Confessions*, all form an important background to the *Meditations on First Philosophy*.

We know that the Stoics developed a genre of meditative literature, arranged around specific exercises or thought experiments, in which the reader is allowed to become a spectator of his own life through the act of reading.[10] The confessional letters and dialogues of Seneca, for example, trade on the premise of self-regard, whether that involves taking stock of one's vices or envisioning untimely ills.[11] As Hadot writes of the Stoic *meditatio*, preserved for us in the writings of Seneca, Cicero, Epictetus, and Marcus Aurelius:

> The exercise of meditation is an attempt to control inner discourse, in an effort to render it coherent. The goal is to arrange it around a simple universal principle: the distinction between what does and does not depend on us, or between freedom and nature. Whoever wishes to make progress strives, by means of dialogue within himself or with others, as well as by writing, to "carry on his reflections in due order" and finally to arrive at a complete transformation of his representation of the world.

Examples of the readerly *meditatio* found in works such as the Senecan moral epistles involve injunctions to readers to examine their consciences, investigate memories, and use the imagination as means of distancing the self from the immediacy of a given emotional or mental state. Thus in Epistle 99, Seneca enjoins the audience to "place before your mind's eye the vast spread of time's abyss and

---

[10] On the Stoic meditation and the confessional literature it spawned, see Newman, pp. 1473–1517.

[11] Indeed, the Stoic use of the meditation as a literary genre seems to have done not a little to inspire the spiritual exercises of the Christian tradition that seem to be the model for that modernist avatar of subjectivity, the Cartesian *res cogitans*. This statement does not imply that the Cartesian meditation is essentially a replica of the Augustinian meditation. In fact, the process of introspection developed in Augustine's own explorations of self-knowledge is decidedly modified by Descartes through the latter's applications of the method of introspection as a foundation for science. On this notion of foundations in Descartes' philosopy, see Menn, chapter 2, section B.

embrace the universe; and then compare what we call human life with infinity."[12] Another meditation on time involves a calculation of how much of one's allotted span has been wasted through meaningless distractions:

> Calculate how much of that span was subtracted by a creditor, a mistress, a patron, a client, quarreling with your wife, punishing your slaves, gadding about the city on social duties. Add to the subtrahend self-caused diseases and the time left an idle blank. You will see that you possess fewer years than the calendar shows. Search your memory: how seldom you have had a consistent plan, how few days worked out as you intended, how seldom you have enjoyed full use of yourself, how seldom your face wore an inartificial expression, how seldom your mind was unflurried.[13]

Here the practice of self-regard or mindfulness is illustrated through a list of contrasting states, including appetites, emotions, distractions, a generally scattered condition of the mind (*animus intrepidus*), and concern about one's image. Self-presence as a way of life is treated here as an ascetic practice that involves primarily adjusting habits of thinking. As Hadot writes of this virtue: "the fundamental attitude of the Stoic philosopher was *prosoche*: attention to oneself and vigilance at every instant."[14] Later, this kind of examination of conscience and detailed inquiry into the nature of time as a subjective flow measured by the quality of the mind's attention and concentration becomes part of monastic practice, becoming formalized within the Christian tradition of spiritual exercises that help shape the Cartesian meditations.[15] Just as the act of reading the Stoic *meditatio* creates a reflexive space for the reader that brings about a

---

[12] Seneca, Epistle 99.10, quoted by Hadot 1995, p. 182: "Propone temporis profund vastitatem et universam complectere, deinde hoc, quod aetatem vocamus humanam, conpara immenso."

[13] Seneca, *De Brevitate Vitae*, 3.17–30. Translated by Moses Hadas in *The Stoic Philosoph of Seneca*, p. 50.

> Duc quantum ex isto tempore creditor, quantum amica, quantum rex, quan tum cliens abstulerit, quantum lis uxoria, quantum servorum coercito, quantun officiosa per urbem discursatio; adice morbos quos manu fecimus, adice e quod sine usu iacuit: videbis te pauciores annos habere quam numeras. Repet memoria tecum quando certus consilii fueris, quotus quisque dies ut desti naueras cesserit, quando tibi usus tui fuerit, quando in statu suo vultus, quand animus intrepidus . . .

[14] Hadot 1995, p. 130.

[15] On the history of Stoic *meditatio* as transmitted to the monastic disciplines of th early Church, see Hadot 1995, chapter 4, "Ancient Spiritual Exercises."

delineation of what belongs properly to the self, so Descartes uses this stance of self-regard to delineate what can and cannot be known with certainty.[16] Again, whereas the Stoic *meditatio* encompasses a dialogue between one's reason and one's subjective states and entails a scrutiny of how one represents the world to oneself, the Cartesian meditation provides a rational strategy for accepting the majority of one's representations against the alternative of overwhelming doubt. It seems that Descartes muddied the ancient category of criterion of truth with his newly deployed method of introspection. Thus indubitability, or self-transparency, becomes both the final answer to skeptical doubts as well as the mark of the distinctively mental. The Cartesian subject was born in the throes of an epistemological dilemma, but the philosophical necessity that attends the Cartesian inference tells us nothing about the nature of the subject whose existence is inferred. What is the *res cogitans?* Can it be apprehended alongside the indubitable states that evince its existence, or does it remain elusive? What is the content of this Cartesian "ego"? Descartes' answer, "a thing that thinks," tells us both too much and too little. If thinking is the act that characterizes this newly discovered substance, how is it that this activity becomes a thing at all? How can we circumscribe this individual spirit, the transcendental thing that is posited but never apprehended by the inner gaze?[17]

The substantive view of the *res cogitans* is problematic because it

---

[16] On the Stoic *meditatio* as a readerly practice, see Newman, and on Augustine's use of *meditatio* as the source of his introspection, see Stock 1996. Stock's work is important because it shows that the act of reading, valorized by Augustine as a means of access to the word of God incorporated in Scripture, is a ready-to-hand introspective structure employed by pagan authors and adapted to its Christian use from the role it played in pagan self-examination.

[17] Early critics of the Cartesian project were highly sensitive to this pitfall and took pains to distinguish the positing of subjectivity from the category metaphysics of the *res cogitans*. Fichte's self-positing principle of identity, to mention one modern example, represents a rejection of the Cartesian fallacy of the substantive subject. For Fichte, "the act of self-establishment or self-positing constitutes the essence of the I, which is thereby understood not as some thing or object, but as primordial activity" (Redding, p. 54). Cf. also Gillespie's chapter entitled "Fichte and the Dark Night of the Noumenal I." Fichte is concerned to critique the notion of self-knowledge implicit in Cartesian self-awareness when Descartes writes: "what am I then, a thing that thinks?" In other words, Fichte shows that one cannot make an inference from the nature of one's interior states to the nature of the self that undergoes such states. He asks if the self that knows its own projections is known in the same manner as those projections.

personifies the introspective gaze in a move that seems entirely un-justified. We are left with several questions. First, what dialectical possibilities does a philosophical appeal to the subjective, or intro-spective stance, offer outside the realm of epistemology? Second, how cogent can such an appeal be, if it relies on introspection, or posits a rhetoric of immediacy, for its dialectical force? These are questions that I attempt to answer in this book through detailed investigation of Neoplatonic methodologies. Nevertheless, here I would like to offer a provisional response that situates Plotinus' views on self-apprehension within a larger philosophical framework.

Self-perception in the *Enneads* – A Non-discursive Approach

In the philosophy of the Ancient Commentators, self-perception becomes an increasingly important topic within the larger project of interpreting Aristotle's *De anima*. However we should keep in mind that although Aristotle does raise the puzzle about how it is that we perceive that we perceive, this topic does not (in Aristotle's text) imply a theory of self-consciousness.[18] Rather, at the beginning of *De anima* 3.2, Aristotle tries to show that the faculty of perception must itself be responsible for the perception of perception. Modern com-mentators differ over whether, in this passage, Aristotle affirms that each sense is also responsible for perceiving its own perception, or whether he here continues to believe, as he says in the *De somno*, that there is a faculty of common perception that accounts for this abil-ity.[19]

For our purposes, what is interesting is that several Neoplatonic authors came to interpret this passage of the *De anima* as a reference to self-awareness, and not to the simple perceptual awareness that Aristotle rather clearly had in mind. Certain of the later Commenta-tors[20] on the *De anima* recognized a sixth sense, beyond the five senses that each has its proper sense objects, which either did or did not coincide with an Aristotelian "common sense." The name for

---

[18] For this conclusion, see Kosman 1975.
[19] On this topic, see Everson 1997, pp. 141–4. He contrasts his position with Modrak 1987.
[20] For the identity of this group, see both Bernard and Lautner (who identifies the "group" as the Neoplatonist, Damascius!).

this additional mental faculty was *prosektikon*, from the noun *prosoche* (to pay attention to, to be aware of). Again, in his commentary on Plato's *Phaedo*, the sixth-century philosopher Damascius describes the *prosektikon* as the witness of the soul, as a self-awareness that simply records the presence of any experience that the subject undergoes. As such, it transcends the usual classification according to lower and higher faculties that many Neoplatonic psychological elements must fit,[21] and instead is said to extend through the rational soul as well as the irrational soul. As we will see in more detail, for some Aristotelian Commentators, perception of perception was no longer a perceptual function.[22] As a result, they also sometimes interpreted perceptual awareness as a kind of cognition.

In the later Neoplatonic tradition, commentators on Aristotle's *De anima* seized upon III.2 (425b12 ff.), where Aristotle discusses the issue of perceiving that one perceives. Although several of these Commentators may be seen today as predecessors of the so-called spiritualist interpretation of Aristotle's theory of perception,[23] as for example, Philoponus, who holds that perception consists in a "cognitive apprehension of the perceptible form,"[24] what matters for my purposes is what they had to say about self-perception. Philoponus tells us of a group of interpreters[25] who

say that it is the task of the attentive part of the rational soul to apprehend the acts of the senses. For the rational soul has not only five faculties, noetic thought, discursive thought, judgment, will and choice, they add an additional sixth faculty to the rational soul, which they call the attentive. This attentive part, they say, attends to what is going on in the person and says "I

---

[21] For this notion of classification, see Blumenthal's earlier book and the remarks of Sheppard, "Phantasia and Mental Images: Neoplatonist Interpretations of Deanima 3.3," in *Oxford Studies in Ancient Philosophy* Suppl. vol. 1991, pp. 165–74.

[22] For this conclusion, see the conclusion to Lautner's article.

[23] For this somewhat stigmatizing terminology, see Everson 1997, which is an exposition of Aristotle's theory of perception that sets out to show that physical explanations play an important role in this theory.

[24] Bernard, p. 158.

[25] Lautner 1994 identifies this "group" as Damascius, with the following passage in mind: *In Phaedonem* I.271: "What is that which recollects that it is recollecting? This is a faculty which is different from all the others and is always attached to some of them as a kind of witness: as conscious of the appetitive faculties, as attentive to the cognitive ones." This translation was distributed by Lautner at the BICS 1997 Summer Institute.

have thought noetically," "I have thought discursively," "I have been angry." So, if the attentive part is to go through all the parts of the soul, then let it pass through the sense as well and let it say, "I have seen," . . . [26]

Another approach is that of Pseudo-Simplicius:[27] What we find in his *Commentary on the De anima* is a kind of rationalization of the perceptual faculty, so that perceiving that we perceive is distinctive of human perception Perhaps the idea is that perception of perception involves a judgment of whether or not one's perception is correct, or perhaps the idea is that a propositional representation of one's perceptions is involved. But if perception of perception is propositional, then it is rational. Again, as a result of these internally uttered propositions, self-consciousness follows from this perception of perception. Consequently, self-consciousness is characteristic of the rational mind only: "Therefore to perceive that one perceives does not belong to every faculty of perception, but rather to the rational faculty alone" (Ps.-Simpl. 290.6–8).[28]

In this later material, we see a general reworking of the Aristotelian source; the Commentators tend to assimilate *aisthesis*, or the perceptual structure that characterizes specifically non-intellectual perception, to cases of *noesis* of *noesis*, or to the intellectual structure of knowledge. For the later Commentators, perceiving that one perceives becomes the basis for distinguishing the human soul in toto from the animal soul. It also serves as a more general argument against the Aristotelian notion of the soul as the first actuality of a living body,[29] by becoming associated with a notion of self-reflection that specifically entails an incorporeal subject. For example, Philoponus tries to demonstrate that Aristotle fails to account for percep-

---

[26] Translated and quoted by Bernard, p. 156. Cf. Lautner 1994 who also comments on this passage.

[27] By Pseudo-Simplicius, I mean the author of Simplicius' *Commentary on the De anima*. Many scholars think the author is Priscianus. For the debate over the identity of the author of *CAG* IX, see the 1978 monograph of Carlos Steel, *The Changing Self*. Blumenthal criticizes identifying Pseudo-Simplicius with Priscianus (*Soul and the Structure of Being in Late Neoplatonism*, ed. Lloyd, Liverpool, 1982).

[28] For a summary of Pseudo-Simplicius' views on self-consciousness, see Blumenthal 1996.

[29] That is, perception of perception is a topic that can create the kind of interpretive dissonance that one sees in the Commentators, since as Neoplatonists, they will also hold that the soul is essentially disembodied.

tion of perception in the *De anima*, because *any* self-reflexivity must belong to a mental and not to a physical substance:

the common sense apprehends nothing but perceptibles and all perceptibles are in a body, that is, they subsist as compounds together with matter, whereas the act of perception is not in a body and therefore is not a perceptible.[30]

Finally, perception of perception in the later tradition more generally becomes associated with a faculty of self-consciousness that relies on a unified subject of awareness. This later tradition still falls short of attributing to Aristotle something like a Cartesian mental self, or *res cogitans*; nevertheless, perception of perception is philosophically significant because it becomes a foundation for notions of self-identity. In Philoponus, for example, there is an argument that self-perception is uniquely grounded in the unity of the perceiving subject: "For if one part apprehended this, and another that, that would be equivalent as he himself [sc. Aristotle] says in a different context, to your perceiving this and my perceiving that. Hence the attentive [part] must be one" (Philoponus 465, 1, ff.).

The promotion of empirical self-awareness to a philosophically significant issue allowed the tradition to formulate the concept of rational perception or of a transcendent faculty of awareness. But it stopped short of the strong Cartesian sense of the *res cogitans*, no doubt because indubitability was not attributed to this new faculty. Descartes' substantive view of the *res cogitans* is problematic because it personifies the introspective gaze–the mind is simply that which reports on states of mind. The notion of the mind has become hostage to this privileged introspective stance that has left us with the notion of a subjectively discoverable self and, consequently, an insuperable mind-body dualism. In the terms of this dualism, "I appear to myself as a single, unified subjective self, faced by a multifarious composite objective world."[31]

---

[30] Bernard paraphrasing Philoponus. On the argument from self-reflection to incorporeal nature of the self, see Gerson 1997. Also, for Aristotle's own difficulties in accounting for the possibility of self-perception as a feature of the *aisithetikon*, especially if his theory of sensation is taken to be grounded in physical explanations, see Everson 1997, chapter 4, "The Perceptual System."

[31] Priest, p. 82.

To summarize, if the self can be apprehended as the subject of all mental states, that is, if the self is introspectively available, then we are dealing with a self-reflexive theory of identity. As Gasché describes the process:

> The theory of reflection is characterized by the assumption that the cognitive subject becomes a self-relating subject by making itself an object for itself. The identity that springs forth from such an activity is a result of turning that kind of attention originally directed upon objects back upon the knowing subject itself.[32]

Now the problem with this way of formulating self-reflection is that it posits the self that knows as itself an object of self-consciousness. Thus, the self itself becomes an object for the self. But the subjectively apprehending self cannot be an object of perception in the same way that objects of perception are. To think this is to equate self-knowledge with self-perception, and this is a mistake, at least according to Plotinus (see the next section). In the *Enneads*, Plotinus explicitly proscribes this tendency to make the self an object of the self. Plotinus does not think that self-knowledge has the same structure as self-perception.[33]

Self-perception versus Self-knowledge: The *Enneads*

Turning now to the *Enneads*, it is worth attempting to sort out the difference between perception of perception and self-knowledge. One strong motivation for doing so is the difficulty of Plotinus' somewhat inconsistent, but highly distinctive, vocabulary of self-reflection. Plotinus does use the word *"sunaisthesis"* when referring to the intellect's knowledge of its own contents.[34] The Aristotelian Commentators used this word to describe self-perception, following the Stoic tradition. But Plotinus also has developed a very precise vocabulary of reflection and tends to use the word *parakolouthesis*

---

[32] Gasché, p. 61.

[33] Here I acknowledge the conclusion to Gerson 1997. Gerson also makes the point that self-knowledge is not, in the *Enneads*, primarily the knowledge of [an empirically available] self.

[34] Cf. V.8.11.24: "If therefore sight is of something external we must not have sight or only that which is identical with its object. This is a sort of intimate understanding and perception of a self that is careful not to depart from itself by wanting to perceive too much." On Plotinus' use of *sunaisthesis*, see Graeser 1972, chapter 7.

when he refers specifically to self-consciousness, or being aware that one is aware.[35] In ordinary consciousness, the mind is simply engaged with knowing its object. The thought, "I am now engaged in knowing this object," seems to be a superfluous event, as if to split the mind's focus between the object of awareness and an intentional state that captures the features of this awareness. Hence, Plotinus uses *parakolouthesis* both of this kind of superfluous intentionality and of any kind of accidental predication. In other words, for Plotinus self-consciousness is more or less an accident of awareness. As has been frequently pointed out, Plotinus seems to think that ordinary consciousness entails self-consciousness, but that the act of turning one's ordinary consciousness into a further intentional object is a kind of falling short of awareness. To be aware that one is engaged in the act of knowing an object is to be distracted by a different object of awareness as well as to be excessively removed from the object with which one is engaged.[36]

In treatise V.3 Plotinus articulates the structure of self-knowledge along the lines of a response to Skeptic attacks that attempt to drive a wedge between the self's identity as either subject or object in the act of self-apprehension. That is, Plotinus refutes the Skeptics' argument against self-knowledge by refusing to grant the major premise of their argument, that is, that self-knowledge is a case of self-perception. Plotinus overturns the Skeptical objections by refusing to grant that the self can be an object of any kind.

> Self-division is impossible. How will it divide itself? It cannot do so randomly. In fact who is it that does the dividing? Is it the person identifying with the subject of vision or the person identifying with the object? Then again how will the subject recognize himself as the object if he identifies himself as the subject? (V.3.3)

It is important to see that self-knowledge cannot be equated with perception, since the self is not an *object of knowledge*, according to Plotinus. Plotinus' intellect is not directed toward any intentional states and has no intentional object: "the being of intellect consists in an activity that is not directed toward anything" (V.3.7.19)[37] Moreover, it is neither the subject nor the predicate within any

---

[35] See Smith 1978.
[36] See Smith 1978 for all of this.
[37] On Plotinus' critique of intentionality, see Emilsson and Rappe in Gerson 1996.

ordinary grammatical structure:[38] when it affirms, "I am this," if the word "this" refers to something other than the self, it will be saying what is false.

Again, it is important to emphasize the difference between Plotinus' views on self-reflection and the stance that results from the phenomenological *epoche* of the modern, subjectivist self. For Brentano and his influential student, Husserl, intentionality just is the predominant characteristic of the mental:

> Every mental phenomenon is characterized by what the scholastics of the Middle Ages called the intentional (or mental) inexistence of an object, and what we might call, though not wholly unambiguously, reference to a content, direction toward an object or immanent objectivity. (Brentano, *Philosophy from an Empirical Standpoint*, p. 88)[39]

By contrast, what emerges in Plotinus' representation of the self is the difficulty of demarcating a realm of the mind, a realm in which the subject, or "I," finds itself clearly delineated as a self-contained space that is over against an object or objects. The reason for this difficulty is that Plotinus does not admit that the intellect's thoughts are intentional, that is, directed toward objects:

> We allocated to [discursive reason the ability to] reflect upon what is external to it and to meddle in external matters, but we take it that it is basic to intellect to reflect upon its own nature and what belongs to its own nature. (V.2.3.17)

To summarize, then, Plotinus does admit that self-knowledge is possible and even necessary (cf. V.3 and V.5), but he does not think that self-knowledge is equivalent to self-perception or to self-consciousness. Not only is it the case that the self cannot be an intentional object for the self, it is also the case that the intellect does not engage in intentional thinking.

One perhaps surprising starting point for getting at Plotinus' views on the nature of self-awareness, is to examine Plotinus' concept of *apatheia*. Recently a scholar has written that *apatheia* cannot be considered the telos of Plotinian ethics in the way that it can be for Stoic ethics.[40] Stoic *apatheia* refers to a lack of emotional reactivity

---

[38] On the Cartesian subject as a grammatical place holder, see Kenny and Zizek.
[39] Quoted in Priest, p. 59.
[40] Bussanich, 1992.

and so it coincides with the optimal rational response to the world that is the province of the sage's special knowledge. Plotinus' version of *apatheia* implies the negation of more than simply the emotions. Although it does continue to have some ethical force (the mind is to be purified of emotions, passions, and false opinions), *apatheia* becomes part of Plotinus' vocabulary of self-reflection. Indeed, the notion of *apatheia* is central to Plotinus' formulation of the problem of subjective identity. This concept does not capture the difference between emotional and rational states of mind, but rather between the mind conceived as insular, or self-enclosed, and the mind conceived as intersubjective, or public. For Plotinus, far from being an emotion, a *pathos* is an event that renders the mind subject to conditions imposed from without. Such a condition erodes or infringes on the autonomy of the mind, its self-determination, self-awareness, and self-attention. Hence *apatheia* refers to the original condition of the mind, before it comes to be occupied with the transitory objects of awareness that concern it in its embodied state. Again, *apatheia* is not only a moral condition of the mind, since a *pathos* is any event or experience to which the mind is subject. *Apatheia* seems to imply a mind not subject to experience, one that undergoes no conditioning.

What is it that makes an experience a *pathos*, an event to which the mind is subject? The Stoic distinction between a representation and assent to that representation (between *phantasia* and *katathesis*) would be one way of capturing the difference between a *pathos* and an action, or rather activity, the latter being presumably a mental event that is not caused by any external source. In Stoic psychology,[41] the mind is passively subject to presentations when something appears to be the case. However, the rational mind is uniquely responsible for agreeing to or withholding assent from the content of that appearance. *Apatheia* for the Stoics involves vigilance in the process of testing the truth values of one's representations. Yet Plotinus' formulation of the concept is still more radical.

In treatise III.6.5, Plotinus raises the question that his successors eventually found unsurmountable given the terms of Plotinus' formulations: if the soul is originally not subject to passions (as Plotinus maintains, despite all empirical evidence to the contrary) then why

---

[41] See Long, "Representation and the Self in Stoicism," in Everson 1991.

does it need to be purified by means of philosophy? Plotinus' (typically paradoxical) answer is that the soul does not need to be purified, if we mean that the mind can truly be subject to passion. A state of mind that initially functions as a passion (that is, seems to come from outside the mind and has a force that brings about other states of a mind as a result of its own presence) can be re-investigated. This state that seems to arise from an external source (the *legomenon*, or "so-called passion," as Plotinus puts it) is actually an activity of the soul. Thus it can be redescribed as an *energeia*, an activity.[42]

In the first part of III.6.5, Plotinus alludes to a Stoic notion, according to which a *pathos* is a disturbance that is caused by a presentation, as for example the appearance of an expected evil that can give rise to the passion fear. Now, according to Plotinus, the role of reason is to eradicate, not the passion (as per the Stoic position), but the presentation altogether, since if the presentation is removed, the emotion it triggers will no longer be able to arise. As Plotinus theorizes: "it is as if someone, wishing to remove the images that arise from a dream should cause the dreaming mind to wake up, and should then say that the mind caused the passions, meaning that whatever the soul saw [in its dream] was only apparently external" (III.6.5.10). Plotinus concludes that one should just "leave the soul alone" and not allow it "to gaze at another."

Elsewhere, Plotinus suggests that anytime the mind simply looks at another thing, it is necessarily either enthralled by that object or subject to it. Thus to be aware of an external object is to be subject to passion, in the sense that a *pathos* is an adventitious event. In VI.1., "On the Kinds of Being," Plotinus describes passion as a state that is characterized by its displacement by another state. We might say

---

[42] For a much fuller discussion of the differences between *energeia* and *pathos* in Plotinus' theory of perception, see Emilsson 1988, chap. 7. Emilsson considers Plotinus' rejection of the Aristotelian notion, which has sense-perception involving a passive potential, on the part of the percipient, to become the object perceived. This rejection follows from Plotinus' denial that there is such a thing as a passive potency (Emilsson 1988, p. 127; *Enneads* II.5.1.21–24). Emilsson goes on to consider why perception is conceived of as purely active; why, for example, does Plotinus think that an agent is not affected by his own act of perception? Emilsson quotes *Enneads* III.6.2.35–6, "the act [of vision] is not an alteration but simultaneously approaches what it has," in support of his interpretation, according to which the soul's prior possession of the Forms is required for sense-perception (Emilsson 1988 p. 135).

that a passion is ontologically fungible. Although the Stoic conception of *pathos* also involves a distinction between what happens to a person and what a person actually does,[43] Plotinus seems to insist on an indifference to ordinary objects of awareness that goes beyond the Stoic conception. Thus, for example, in V.3.6.36, Plotinus scorns the practical intellect because, being practical, it "looks to the outside and does not stay in itself." In V.3.7, in the course of explaining what the activity of intellect is like, Plotinus gives us a gloss on the meaning of the word *energeia* (activity) since the function of intellect is pure *energeia*:

For those for whom the essence is not potential, but actual, there is a unique and appropriate activity that consists in a resting from other things. Therefore, the essence of such things is activity, and yet it is an *activity directed toward nothing.*

In this very striking statement, we get an equation between *energeia*, as activity that has no direction or object, and knowing, which is self-directed. Plotinus here demands a radical segregation of the mind from any external object and yet, at the same time, denies that the mind can really be present to an external object. An object that is apparently external is somewhat like a dream image. Just as the dreamer is the source of all the impressions that appear to be outside the self represented in the dream, so all objects encountered by the mind are only apparently external. The way to achieve *apatheia* is described by Plotinus as "turning away" from external images, or as

---

[43] For an excellent discussion of the difficulties implicit within the Stoic definition of *pathos*, see Hankinson 1992. Hankinson notes that Galen, who dissented from Chrysippus' definition of *pathos*, recognized a certain flexibility in the concept. He cites Galen's example of cutting. Note Plotinus at VI.1.19.15 also uses this stock example and finds that the Peripatetic categories of action and passion are inherently confusing: "In the case of cutting, the cutting that comes from the one doing the cutting and the cutting that is present in the one who is being cut, are one, and yet cutting and being cut are different." Plotinus applies this difficulty to cases of passive affection when the agent is apparently affected by his own activities: "what happens if someone becomes heated as a result of a thought being entertained by him, or becomes angered by an opinion held by him, and there is no external influence?" (VI.1.21.10–11). The conclusion to this discussion in treatise VI.1 seems to anticipate the interpretation I have presented here, namely, that often the same alteration can be considered either a passive affection or an activity: "being the self-same motion, from one point of view, it will be an action, while from another point of view it will be an affection" (VI.1.22.12–13).

"refusing to see them," or as "not paying attention to them," or as "waking up" (III.6.5.15.ff.).

Are we here encountering a kind of phenomenological *epoche*? What does it mean for Plotinus to insist that the mind not be allowed to look at any objects? Plotinus does call intellect "the seer" – is he suggesting that the self is some kind of watchful, "fleshless eye"? I think not, but here one needs a bit of background on Plotinus' own theory of perception.[44] Plotinus was followed by subsequent Neoplatonists in holding that that the mind actually projects the forms encountered in sense-perception.

As Priscianus has it:

the soul has the form of the perceived object by the projecting of its logos, but not as receiving from it [the object] some shape or impression as from a seal.

Or again, as we read in Simplicius:[45]

The other cognitive activities obtain their perfection from ther own being and project the form of their object of themselves, but that of sensation requires also the object sensed which lies outside in order to project actively the form of that object. (*In De anima* 165, 29)

For Plotinus as well as for the later Neoplatonists, what appears to be external is due to the projective activity of the soul. Hence a *pathos*, insofar as it can be defined as an event whose cause is exterior to the person, can be redefined as *energeia*, as an event whose cause is the person, that is, her act. Thus the mind exercises its projective powers even when engaged in perception and should more correctly be described as acting rather than as suffering. However, to the extent that its object is *conceived* of as external, the mind will continue to suffer.

In Plotinus' example of the dream, the dreamer realizes that the dreamer himself projects the *phantasmata* seen in the dream. Once he realizes this fact about his own creations, he is no longer subject to them. What goes on is the assimilation of experience to self

---

[44] See again Emilsson's monograph for a thorough discussion of this theory of perception.

[45] Cf. also Proclus: "Therefore, there is a capacity of the soul which is superior to the sense and does not cognize the sense-object through the sense organs but through itself and thus rectifies the dullness of the sense" (*IT* 250, 12, Lautner trans.).

awareness: I seem to be undergoing an experience, but a certain kind of self-awareness on my part, namely, wakefulness, makes it clear that I underwent no such experience and indeed precludes my undergoing the experiences to which I am subject in the dream state.

In the conclusion to this chapter, I will suggest that self-reflection can refer to a "reversal of thought," as Plotinus is accustomed to saying (V.5.11.11). In the example of the dream, the dreamer on awaking discovers that objects are projected in the dream state. One can say that to discover oneself as the dreamer, or source of the dream images, is equivalent to self-awareness. It is in this sense that Plotinus can say that the activity of nous is not directed toward any object and is instead directed toward itself. That is, the mind has a kind of awareness about the nature of its objects. At the same time, Plotinus displays no tendency to conflate awareness of perception with intellectual self-knowledge. Ordinary awareness does not equate with self-knowledge, even though such ordinary awareness carries with it as an accidental feature an aspect that might be called self-consciousness. Rather, his discussion of *apatheia* allows Plotinus to suggest that the mind often has a tendency to become lost in the objects of awareness. And this tendency distracts the mind from true self-knowledge.

Still we must ask, how cogent is Plotinus' theory of self-reflection? We have already seen that Plotinus does not succumb to a reductive theory, according to which the self can be defined as a transparent substance that accurately reports all of its states. Again, Plotinus finds that some of these states are inherently uninteresting, and he also finds that certain states do escape notice and do so on a regular basis.[46] More telling however, is the objection that self-transparency would not be coherent if defined in this way. For to be aware of the self as an object is not true self-transparency. Thus although Plotinus does say that the intellect is self-transparent, he can not mean that this self-transparency equates with the subjective awareness of the contents of one's mind.

---

[46] See Smith for the topic of degrees of self-awareness in Plotinus' thinking. The idea that one can be more or less self-conscious and that this kind of experience is adventitious to the cognitive activities of intellection and discursive thinking is highly developed in *Enneads*.

What kind of self-transparency is in question here? How does the mind come to self-knowledge? Later Neoplatonists distinguished between *probole*, the projective power of the mind, and *prosbole*, the unitive power of the mind. Thus *prosbole* is a type of attention that brings the mind back to its origins and hence to its own contents. Plotinus demands a kind of ultimate privacy from the person who wishes to gain self-knowledge. He demands an activity of the mind that is entirely self-directed. "We have no *perception* of what is our own, and since we are like this we understand ourselves best when we have made our self-knowledge one with ourselves" (V.8.11). Perception and intellection, it turns out, will not be analogous, which is why there is no such thing as self-perception, for Plotinus. If anything, self-knowledge will involve an entirely different kind of activity than that involved in perception. Primarily, Plotinus characterizes intellectual activity as *objectless* knowing.

> We allocated to [discursive reason the ability to] reflect upon what is external to it and to meddle in external matters, but we take it that it is basic to intellect to reflect upon its own nature and what belongs to its own nature. (V.2.3.17)

Thus even if intellect is primarily oriented toward the Good, and only secondarily toward the Forms, Plotinus tells us that the perfection of intellectual activity consists in achieving a kind of knowledge that is entirely free of objects: "It must see that light by which it is enlightened: for we do not see the sun by another light than his own. How then can this happen? Take away everything!" (V.3.17.35).

One problem with my emphasis in this chapter on the objectless awareness of nous is its incompleteness; I have not given due consideration to the objects of intellect, the *noemata*, that are identical with the acts of intellect. The subject-object dichotomy is to some extent maintained in the intelligible world, as many texts in the *Enneads* remind us that the nous in fact contemplates an object that is multifaceted, complex, and endlessly diverse.[47] Nevertheless, the intellec-

---

[47] *Enneads*, V.3.1.1–15; VI.7.12; V.9.6.8. On the problem of whether or not the intellectual object involves intentionality, see Emilsson 1996. I tend to think that the concept of intentionality, as developed by Searle in the book of that title, applies to states of mind, that is, mental constructs, that are analogous to language in important ways. Searle defines intentional states as directed toward states of affairs in the

tual object is not outside the intellect: "Grant that intellect contains the real beings and contains all within itself, not as if they were in a place, but as containing itself and being one with them" (V.9.6.1–5). These remarks constitute a succinct account of Plotinus' epistemology, a theory that posits an intersubjective world of autonomous minds, each contemplating all the Ideas as well as the other minds.[48] I have not here been concerned with the epistemological consequences of this doctrine, nor have I treated it as a theoretical construct that answers epistemological questions, such as how to account for the infallibility of intellectual activity.[49] Instead, I have been concerned with Plotinus' psychology of contemplation, which is to say, the activity of the human psyche as it engages in *theoria*.

Plotinus sometimes speaks about the soul's "native activity":

> when soul looks into intellect, it possesses what it has from within and its thoughts and activities are native to it. And these alone are what one should call the activities of the soul, namely those that are intellectual and from within the soul. But the inferior states of the soul are *pathe*, received from outside; [they belong to the] soul when it [undergoes] this kind of experience. (*Enneads* V.1.3.16–20)[50]

Soul attains to its native activity in the process of detaching from external objects, as we just saw. Therefore, in this chapter, the concept of objectless awareness contrasts primarily with the more usual

world, thus rejecting a referential theory of language based on simple notions of naming. As Emilsson writes in his 1996 article, speaking of the "thoughts" (*noemata*) that intellect has:

> These thoughts are not thoughts of something else nor are they true because they agree with some other reality against which they may be tested. On the contrary, they constitute reality. Hence, they are not true in the ordinary sense which takes truth to consist in a correspondence between a proposition or thoughts and reality. Nevertheless, these thoughts may also be said to be true in the sense that through them something is known, namely these thoughts themselves. So if forced to explicate what the thoughts "say" and "to whom," the answer must be that they make their own content known to Intellect. But Intellect, we have seen, is just these thought acts.

[48] For an account of Plotinus' intersubjective epistemology see Gerson 1994, chapter 4, "Truth and the Forms."

[49] For the epistemological implications of Plotinus' identity thesis, see Emilsson 1993.

[50] On this passage, see the commentary of Atkinson 1983, who contrasts the "native" activity of the soul, for which Plotinus uses the word *oikeion*, denoting likeness to the object, with the identity of knower and known in actual intellectual contemplation.

activity of the soul in which the soul pays attention to various intentional objects, to *pathe*, or conditioned states of consciousness. Objectless awareness allows the soul to "look into intellect," to engage in introspection by setting aside its discursive activities. In his treatise "On Well-Being," *Enneads* I.4, Plotinus once more discusses the natural state of mind that arises when thought "turns back on itself"[51] in a self-reflexive activity that is characterized by stability or freedom from objects of thought.[52] This activity allows the mind to perceive "directly . . . that intellect and thought are active."[53] Here the mind looks into intellect, into its own nature, rather than pay attention to or be absorbed by external conditions; it withholds attention from any discursive objects. My purpose in this chapter has been to suggest that the introspective stance invoked within Plotinus' contemplative psychology does not presage the Cartesian reification of the self qua thinker, for Plotinus cannot, unlike Descartes, reify the introspective stance. Quite the opposite actually occurs, since Plotinus wishes the mind to desist from its usual activity, that is, to desist from thinking discursively. As a result of this change in the direction of awareness, far from reifying the thinker, the subject of thought discovers that it is not a thing at all. The next chapter will be concerned with this contemplative psychology, focusing particularly on the topic of introspection.

---

[51] *Enneads* I.4.10.8: ἀνακάμπτοντς τοῦ νοήματος.

[52] *Enneads* I.4.10.13–14: περὶ ψυχὴν ἡσυχίαν μὲν ἄγοντος τοῦ ἐν ἡμῖν τοιούτου, ᾧ ἐμφαίνεται τὰ τῆς διανοίας.

[53] *Enneads* I.4.10.16–17: καὶ οἷον αἰσθητῶς γινώσκεται μετὰ τῆς προτέρας γνώσεως, ὅτι ὁ νοῦς καὶ ἡ διάνοια ἐνεργεῖ.

4

Introspection in the Dialectic of the *Enneads*

In this chapter, my theme is introspection: how does it function in Plotinus' dialectic, what are some of the philosophical issues associated with it, and most importantly, how does Plotinus think it can be practiced? Plotinus anticipates Descartes in arguing both that the soul as subject of perception cannot be an extended substance and that the mind necessarily knows itself.[1] Like Descartes, Plotinus also invokes an introspective stance within his dialectical procedure.[2] Methodologically, it will be seen, Plotinus shares with Descartes in a tradition of philosophy of mind that employs thought experiments as a method of persuasion.[3] The special nature of this persuasion is effected through the textual representation of a highly structured form of self-reflection. I will be looking at the philosophical appeal to self-reflection, and asking whether and how it informs the contemplative pedagogy of Plotinus. In particular, in order to discuss his views about self-consciousness and self-reflection, I will concentrate upon Plotinus' use of thought experiments.

What does it mean to for someone to be a person – what is the essence of the human self? In the modern, Cartesian tradition, one answer to this question is that the self is the mind, whereas the mind

---

[1] For possible historical or philosophical connections between the thought of Plotinus and Descartes in regard to the issue of self-knowledge, see Lloyd 1964 and Emilsson 1991. See also chapter 3 of Menn.

[2] The seminal work on whether or not there was anything like a notion of the subjective and whether or not there was any claim to knowledge of subjective states is, of course, Burnyeat 1982. See also Everson 1991a for a rejoinder to Burnyeat's discussion of Cyrenaic subjectivity.

[3] On Cartesian thought experiments, see Wilkes 1988, chapter 1, and also McDowell 1986. For the Cartesian method of self-representation, see Judovitz 1988.

in its turn is a substance uniquely endowed with reflexive consciousness.[4] Recently, historicist challenges to this mentalistic conception of personhood have argued that the ancient Greek philosophers managed their psychology and epistemology quite well without the concept of consciousness.

Richard Rorty, in his book, *Philosophy and the Mirror of Nature*,[5] claims that Descartes invented the modern notion of mind. Prior to Descartes, people had intellects capable of grasping immaterial, universal truths, but ever since Descartes, people have had minds. The Cartesian mind's great virtue consists in its incorrigibility: it is indubitably aware of any given experience as evidenced within consciousness.

This concept of personhood privileges two features of the mental life, that is, the mind's self-transparency and the privacy of mental states. For any state that the mind is in, the subject of consciousness, upon introspection, cannot doubt the existence of that state. Moreover, the access that the subject of consciousness enjoys with regard to her own inner states is private: only the subject can know with certainty that she is in a particular mental state.[6] Cartesian subjectivity and self-consciousness are the two pillars upon which epistemology in the modern era has been reconstructed: along with this privileging of the subjective point of view coincides the invention of subjective truth.[7]

Prior to Descartes, the ancient Skeptical tradition capitalized upon strategies that maximized the opacity of the the external world vis-à-vis the perceiving subject. In their ad hoc replies to the positivistic epistemological constructions of the Stoa, academic Skeptics regularly argued as follows: how each of the external objects appears we can perhaps say, but how it is in its nature we cannot assert.[8] Descartes' *Meditations*, for the first time in history, presents us with a

---

[4] For these two criteria as the defining attributes of personhood, see Gill. See also David Wiggens, "Locke, Butler, and the Stream of Consciousness," in A. Rorty 1976

[5] R. Rorty 1979.

[6] This is a summary of Gill 1991.

[7] On the notion of subjective truth and its invention, see Burnyeat 1982 and McDowell.

[8] On Skeptical strategies the literature is vast. Primary sources are of course Cicero' *Lucullus* and Sextus Empiricus, *Against the Dogmatists*, for the debate between Skeptic and Stoics on the criterion of truth. For an excellent summary of this debate, se Frede.

text in which the isolation of the perceiving subject from the cognized object became a locus of epistemological certainty. The way to *remove* epistemological doubt was discovered *via* the method of subjective truth: how things *seemed* counted as an instance of the way things actually *were*:

> I am the same who feels, that is to say, who perceives certain things, as by organs of sense, since in truth I see light, I hear noise, I feel heat. But it will be said that these phenomena are false and that I am dreaming. Let it be so: still it is at least quite certain that it seems to me that I see light, that I hear noise, and that I feel heat. This cannot be false, properly speaking it is what in me is called feeling; and used in this precise sense that is no other thinking.[9]

As one scholar, trying to account for the notion of subjective truth, perspicuously puts the matter: "This permits a novel response to arguments which conclude that we know nothing from the fact that we are fallible about the external world. Whatever such arguments show about knowledge of external reality, we can retreat to the newly recognized inner reality, and refute the claim that we know nothing on the ground that at least we know these newly recognized facts about subjective appearances."[10] For modern critics of the Cartesian project, Descartes' problem lay in his confusion between employing the criterion of incorrigibility (that is, using the *cogito*) to prove the existence of the person and employing this same criterion to determine the essence of the person as mental.

We also find that in the Neoplatonic tradition, the possibility of self-knowledge is treated as a proof or demonstration that the self is incorporeal. For example, Proposition 15 of Proclus' *Elements of Theology* states that "everything that is capable of reverting upon itself is incorporeal." Now despite the parallelism of this text to the Cartesian distinction between *res extensa* and *res cogitans* as resting upon the criterion of self-transparency, the meaning of "reversion" in the Neoplatonic tradition does not share the Cartesian conceit of mental states that are incorrigibly transparent.

Plotinus does think that, at the highest level of identity, self-knowledge is not only certain, but actually necessary. But unlike

---

[9] Descartes, *Meditatio Secunda*, paragraph 9.
[10] McDowell 1986.

the case of Descartes' *res cogitans*, this subjective certainty does not hold for any act of cognition: instead, it holds only in extraordinary circumstances at the highest summit of intellectual absorption.

This disparity in the epistemological valuation of mental states occurs for two reasons. First, Plotinus is sensitive to the empirical falsity of the claim that mental states are apprehended incorrigibly within consciousness; he recognizes that there can be a fairly wide gulf between mental processes and the conscious awareness of those processes.[11] Second, for Plotinus, Cartesian incorrigibility is fundamentally representational in nature, since all discursive activity of the mind, such as thought or perception, introduces a representational gap between the knower and the object known.

The intellect, as the subject or seat of all such representations, cannot fathom itself as an object of thought or of perception: self-awareness does not constitute self-knowledge *eo ipso*.[12] If self-knowledge is to be valid, it must be able to circumvent the intentional structure in which objects are normally represented to consciousness. For Plotinus, any *conceptual* representation of the self or subject of consciousness can never be complete and can never succeed in conveying the self that it purports to represent. The fallibilism of any such conveyance is a consequence of Plotinus' more general theory of knowledge according to which truth cannot be ascertained by means of linguistic or conceptual representations. It can be apprehended only when there is an identity between the knower and the known.[13]

---

[11] This is a topic that I will not be exploring in this chapter, since much excellent work on the ideas of consciousness and quasi-consciousness has been done by Warren. But cf. *Enneads* IV.4.5.20 for an instance of Plotinus pointing out that self-consciousness does not necessarily attend the various thoughts or experiences that the mind might entertain at a given time.

[12] On the association of incorrigibility with the Cartesian subject of consciousness, see Gill 1991 and Wilkes 1991.

[13] An interesting parallel to the critique of self-representation as equivalent to self-knowledge developed here may be found in Kant: "the simple representation I, for itself empty of all content, which can never be said to be a concept, but only a pure consciousness which accompanies all concepts" (*Critique of Pure Reason*, A346. Quoted in Marion, p. 57).

Incorrigible Arguments

In the last section, I considered incorrigibility as the foundation of Cartesian epistemology. Descartes triumphs over Skeptical doubt concerning the existence of the self by resorting to an ancient strategy: he insists upon the self-evidence of the thing in question. According to Descartes, if we are aware of our states of mind, then we are aware of or know ourselves. I also suggested that Plotinus does not invoke the incorrigibility of self-awareness in order to sustain a *conception* of the immaterial self, since the self cannot be known discursively. In what follows I will show that, contrary to the opinion of many scholars, Plotinus does develop an argument from incorrigibility in defending the possibility of self-knowledge, although he does not do so for the sake of an epistemological project. In fact, Plotinus' interest in subjectivity stems more from the aspiration for self-realization than from the aspiration for certainty.[14]

The problem for Plotinus is not simply whether the self can be known, but more importantly, how can the self be known? If the mind attempts to represent itself to itself, then it is still trading in an epistemological distance brought about by the distinction between mind as subject and any of its possible objects. This is a problem that Plotinus explores in his treatise V.2.(49), "On the Knowing Hypostases and On What Is Beyond."

The very first line of the treatise begins by asking whether or not a simple entity can know itself, and this is a loaded question. It looks forward to Plotinus' theory of noetic unity, but it also is couched as a reply to Skeptical arguments against the possibility of self-

---

[14] Commentators often acknowledge Lloyd 1964 in their footnotes when they wish to dismiss Plotinus as a progenitor of the modern mental person, but in doing so, they often fail to notice that Lloyd rightly distinguishes between two different notions of self-knowledge. One of them he calls the doctrine of *conscientia*, which is a formal account or proof of the incorrigibility of consciousness. Thus Descartes, according to Lloyd, would have us believe that "the proposition that I know I am sad and the proposition that I am aware it is I who am sad are deducible from the proposition that I am sad." Now Lloyd differentiates this from another notion of self-knowledge, self-knowledge as a kind of inner sense, which primarily has psychological force. This second notion is associated in the Platonic tradition with *gnothi seauton*, and is tied to the doctrine of the "god within," in religious texts. The upshot is this: philosophical reasoning would like to present us with a formal, reasoned, demonstration for self-knowledge, while religion would like us to dive within and find ourselves or god, or both.

knowledge. In chapter 2, lines 2–5, for example, we encounter the familiar Skeptical complaint that sensation encounters only the external world. Plotinus here would admit that mental states such as perception are subject to correction, since perceptual objects are outside of the perceiving faculty. But what is especially interesting is that the body now becomes quite explicitly a part of the external world: even when the soul perceives the body's internal processes, these are still external to the perceiving subject.

This delineation of the person as the soul, and more specifically, as the subject of awareness, is in keeping with Plotinus' enunciation elsewhere of what belongs properly to the body of the world soul, the physical universe. Plotinus clearly states that the individual ensouled body is a part of the cosmos whose growth and decay are controlled by the soul of nature, or by the world soul. For example, the nutritive power of the soul is actually a contribution to the embodied human being from the world soul.[15]

Now the ancient Skeptics not only denied that there could be knowledge of the external world, they also denied the possibility of self-knowledge. We find in Sextus Empiricus a series of arguments designed to impugn the possibility of self-knowledge: the soul cannot know itself as a whole or as a part, for either the subjective side or the objective side would have to disappear.[16] Plotinus, in refuting these arguments,[17] proceeds by means of a hierarchy of increasing self-awareness, beginning with sense-perception and ending with intellectual self-knowledge.

Can the faculty of discursive thought have knowledge of itself? Is the thinker, *qua* thinker, self-transparent? This question is of great importance if we want to know whether or not Plotinus thinks that we can construct an argument that proves that the self can know itself. Can we use reason to demonstrate that we are, by nature rational beings, that we are, in Descartes' words, "things that think"?

Definitely not, according to Plotinus. Self-knowledge, if it exists at all, must be prior to the deliverances of discursive thought. Here we

---

[15] *Enneads* V.9.3.27. On this passage, see Blumenthal, p. 29.

[16] Sextus Empiricus, *Against the Dogmatists*, I sections 310 and 311. Wallis 1987 was the first scholar to call attention to V.2 as a response to the Skeptical attack on the possibility of self-knowledge.

[17] Here I am very much indebted to the work of Wallis 1987 on Skepticism and Neoplatonism.

find Plotinus enlarging upon the representational gap that he admits in the case of sense-perception by extending it to all modes of mental representation whatsoever: "[intellect's thoughts] are certainly not premises or theorems or propositions. These are about things other [than themselves] and are not identical with the realities [that they signify]." (V.5.1.38–40)

Thought, in representing states of affairs, may specify exactly which states of affairs are necessary for the veridicality of its assertions, although it obviously fails as a guarantor for such conditions. Of course thinking that things are thus-and-so is not identical to their being thus-and-so, in most circumstances. The point seems almost too obvious to belabor, and yet it is a point that Plotinus repeatedly stresses when discussing the ontological concomitants of discursive thought. Apparently, what crucially distinguishes mental states from acts of the intellect is that the former are directed toward particulars in the world, while the latter are not. To borrow a bit of modern jargon, one might say that one of the most salient characteristics of discursive thought is its intentionality, the fact that it is about objects that are other than itself.[18]

Actually, when Plotinus describes discursive thinking he associates it with two distinctive modes of alterity: conceptual alterity, or transition from one concept to another, and ontological alterity, or the non-identity of the thinking subject with the object of thought. The latter dominates his discussion of the topic. In III.8.6, for example, Plotinus again contrasts intellectual knowledge, in which the identity between knower and known prevails, with discursive thinking: "[Soul] is other than its object, and has a discursive awareness that sees as if it were one thing gazing at another." (1.24)

As has been frequently pointed out, Plotinus borrows the language of Aristotle's discussion at *De anima* III.8 concerning the identity of knowledge and its objects,[19] where Aristotle delineates two possible ways in which the mind can be identical with its objects. It can be identical with the object itself *qua* hylomorphic compound, or it can be identical with the Form, abstracted from the composite

---

[18] Cf. Searle 1983, p. 1: "Intentionality is that property of many mental states and events by which they are directed at or about objects and states of affairs in the world."

[19] *De anima* 431a1: τὸ δ'αὐτό ἐστιν ἡ κατ'ἐνέργειαν ἐπιστήμη τῷ πράγματι.

substance. Aristotle chooses the latter possibility.[20] He further stipulates that the mind "thinks the forms by means of mental images"[21] in order to represent its objects (whether they be perceptual or conceptual). Plotinus, following Aristotle, agrees that thinking in the ordinary sense involves mental representations of the Forms: "the discursive mind making a judgment about sense impressions has a simultaneous awareness of the Forms" (I. 1.9.17–21). Nevertheless, Plotinus' account of epistemic identity diverges from Aristotle's. According to Plotinus, the mind's ability to entertain a representation of the Form does not render the mind identical with its intelligible object. Discursive thought still sees its objects as substantively distinct from itself. It either gazes outside at the world and discovers the sensible object or gazes within toward the Forms and discovers the conceptual object. At its best, to be sure, the mind provides, in Plotinus' words, a kind of "partnership" between the inner and the outer,[22] but discursive thinking is always inherently directed toward some object.

In treatise V.2, Plotinus denies that this same discursive structure is present when the intellect knows its objects. The question then becomes, does intellect know only its objects, or does it also (necessarily) know itself?[23] Plotinus' answer to this question is a resounding yes, but our task is to trace the path by which he arrives at it.

Initially it seems that Plotinus has just raised more problems than he is able to solve. We have already seen how eager Plotinus is to admit the Skeptical strategy of denying that there can be knowledge of an object that is external to the knower. In chapters 1 and 3 of our treatise, we learn that the intellect does not have these problems: it is aware of "what is in it" and, presumably, whatever is in intellect,

---

[20] τῆς δὲ ψυχῆς τὸ αἰσθητικὸν καὶ τὸ ἐπιστημονικὸν δυνάμει ταὐτά ἐστι, τὸ μὲν ἐπιστητὸν τὸ δὲ αἰσθητόν. ἀνάγκη δ᾽ ἢ αὐτὰ ἢ τὰ εἴδη εἶναι. αὐτὰ μὲν δὴ οὔ.

[21] *De anima* 431 b5 (Hicks's translation): τὰ μὲν οὖν εἴδη τὸ νοητικὸν ἐν τοῖς φαντάσμασι νοεῖ. "It is the forms which the faculty of thought thinks in mental images."

[22] τήν γε κυρίως τῆς ψυχῆς τῆς ἀληθοῦς διάνοιαν. νοήσεων γὰρ ἐνεργεία ἡ διάνοια ἡ ἀληθὴς καὶ τῶν ἔξω πολλάκις πρὸς τἄνδον ὁμοιότης καὶ κοινωνία (II.1.9). "[We are talking about the] discursive intelligence proper, which belongs to the genuine soul. Genuine discursive intelligence in fact is an actualization of the intelligibles and often a samenesss or partnership of the inner and the outer."

[23] "Nous has knowledge of as many things as are objects of intellect. But does the intellect that knows these objects also know itself?" (V.3.1.22).

is intellect.[24] There is every reason to believe that intellect *can* know itself, given that its objects are internal. But why, one could insist, is it *necessary* that it know itself? Plotinus takes up this question in a very early treatise, V.9(4), where, according to one commentator, he invokes an Aristotelian conception of *energeia* to demonstrate the necessity for the mind's self-knowledge. According to this Aristotelian doctrine, intellect *is* pure intellectual activity; hence, intellect necessarily engages in knowing: τῇ οὐσίᾳ ὧν ἐνέργεια (*De anima* 430a 18). At V.9.5.5 and following, Plotinus apparently alludes to this Aristotelian description of nous as pure actuality: τὸν ενεργείᾳ καὶ ἀεὶ νοῦν ὄντα.

So far, this dialectical approach to Plotinus' arguments for self-knowledge has yielded a structure that rests upon formal ontological principles.[25] There appear to be no ancestral traces of Cartesian incorrigibility, which rests upon an appeal to the self-evidence of the *cogito.* Nevertheless, it is generally accepted that a hallmark of Plotinus' procedure for solving epistemological questions especially, is the largely introspective nature of his arguments.[26]

At V.3.6 Plotinus associates his demonstration of the mind's self-knowledge with some form of philosophical necessity: "Has then our

---

[24] For this strategy, see Lloyd 1964: "Neoplatonists argued regularly that the mind or thought can think of itself because the identity of *nous* and *noeton* implies that every *nous* is also an *on*, or *noeton*; and they were only repeating Aristotle's unsatisfactory solution in *De anima* III of the traditional *aporia.*"

[25] According to Lloyd, the Neoplatonic demonstration of the necessity for mind's self-knowledge rests upon the metaphysical commitment that thought and its object are one in intellect and so is a formal account.

[26] See Smith 1978, pp. 104–5: Smith discusses the concept of *enhorasis*, an intuitive approach to metaphysical thinking, and in particular the appeal to intuition in III.7.5: "The verb (*enhoratai*) is a favorite with Plotinus to express the way in which we may find the relationship of elements within the intelligible. It may be found in the treatise, 'On *Time and Eternity*,' where too we are told the normal reasoning will not adequately grasp the nature of the eternal and its relationship to Being. We must employ 'the eternal in us.' "

See also Warren 1964, an article that cites numerous Plotinian examples of introspection as a method of philosophic investigation. Warren raises the issue of whether or not the many instances Plotinus cites of human conscious activity are actually intended to represent the states Plotinus is investigating. Plotinus appeals to such examples as the lack of self-consciousness associated with either intense concentration or with habitual actions as evidence for questions concerning the origins of perception, memory, and imagination within the human soul.

argument demonstrated something of a kind which has the power to inspire confidence? No, it has necessity, not persuasive force, for necessity is in intellect but persuasion in the soul" (V.3.6.8–10). How can he think he has succeeded in an argument that has the force of necessity? It is a question of how one follows the argument.[27] The argument takes the form of a *reductio*: he first assumes that the intellect can be in contact, not with reality directly, but only with an impression of some kind. Plotinus then goes on to say that if this is the case, the same doubts about intellectual knowledge will arise as arise in the case of sense-perception. But if we have an intellect that cannot vouchsafe that it knows, then we will have to posit another intellect to oversee the first, and so on. Either we lack knowledge entirely, or we are capable of knowing that we know. Intellect must be the primary instance of self-knowledge.

Plotinus has pointed out the necessity of self-knowledge and also that soul knows by means of intellect. So if soul knows anything, it participates in a kind of subsidiary self-knowledge: in knowing that knowledge is present, the mind recognizes that its knowledge is owing to the self-knowledge present in intellect, that is, the mind affirms its own ability to know. This affirmation is a partial self-knowledge that constitutes a demonstration of the principle of intellect, whose very nature is to know itself. Otherwise we would have intellect that is unintelligent, and this is sheer impossibility.

And yet it hardly seems plausible that this reductio could count as a demonstration at all, much less as an irrefutable one, for it seems merely to beg the question. The Skeptic's riposte will be, "That's just what I mean; there is an infinite regress of knowers, and intellect, the very principle of knowledge, can't guarantee anything, since it doesn't even know itself." In other words, Plotinus is not entitled here to assume an incorrigible principle.

This demonstration of the principle of self-knowledge, if it is one, cannot be said to be a formal account. Instead, its purpose is to ready the student for an intellectual affirmation on her own part.

---

[27] For a detailed discussion of the dialectical context of *Ennead* V.3.5.1–15, see Wallis 1987. Wallis identifies this passage as a response to standard Pyrrhonist strategies that attempted to eliminate both of the disjuncts, that the self knows itself either as a whole or as a part. In either case, according to the skeptics, the subjective or objective side must disappear in the moment of self-apprehension.

Plotinus is convinced that it is not by rational argument that the principle of knowledge can be established, but only by a self-recognition on the part of the soul of this indubitable fact of awareness itself.

> How could one apprehend an image of intellect? Every image will be constituted from that which is inferior to it. Rather, the image must come from intellect, so that it is no longer [grasped] by means of an image. Instead, it is as if one took a sample of gold [to represent] all gold, and then (if the sample were not pure) one purified it, and then could show either by gesturing or by indication, that this is gold, only not all gold, but rather just this gold that exists in the quantity [on display]. So it is in this case as well: intellect as it exists in the divine can be apprehended when we have purified the intellect in ourselves. (V.8.3.12ff.)[28]

Likewise, in treatise I.4, *"Peri Eudaimonias,"* we find a description of self-reflexive awareness in which thought, projected back onto itself, is likened to a calm reflective surface, a *katoptron*. Because Plotinus is focusing upon the self as self-reflective consciousness, though not upon the self as discursive thinker, there is both a continuity as well as a divergence from the Cartesian argument from incorrigibility.

Direct insight into the nature of the cognitive moment as such is the method that Plotinus employs. The mind attains self-knowledge, not by developing a conception of what it is to be a knower, but by uncovering self-knowledge through a process of gradual detachment from the objects of consciousness:

> If someone is unable to discover the soul in this detached state, first let him grasp the discursive soul, and then ascend from there. But if he cannot even do this, then [let him grasp] the faculty of sense-perception that conveys the intelligibles still more distantly, or even sense-perception by itself (with its faculties) since sense-perception has its nature [determined] by the Forms. (V.3.9.28ff.)

To summarize this section, we can say that self-knowledge involves the realization that the mind or self is not an object of any kind. In this sense, self-awareness does not automatically yield self-knowledge. Rather, the mind can *become* self-transparent by concentration upon itself, and the self that it thereby discovers will no longer be any of the intentional structures that occupy the mind when directed to-

---

[28] My translation.

ward an external object. Nevertheless, Plotinus is not content to let this rest as an item of doctrine. He makes use of thought experiments as a means of illustrating his recommended method for cultivating self-knowledge. These experiments also convey his radical insistence upon a specific orientation to the truth under consideration: the student must not consider herself as separate from the reality that she seeks to comprehend.

Thought Experiments

It has been argued that Descartes, writing in the tradition of the meditation manual, a genre designed for an introspective audience, uses his provisional doubt as a cathartic method, thus imitating the progression of a penitential meditation, in which his soul is purged of the error of doubt by undergoing sensory deprivation.[29] Descartes writes in the meditative tradition previously shared by authors whose intention was to foster a mental state that could become receptive to divine grace, or to the light of divine knowledge. In the *Meditations*, these exercises are also coupled with a theoretical approach to epistemology, intended to be illustrated by the self-reflective practice of the reader. As Gary Hatfield writes of the *cogito*, the briefly sketched argument to the conclusion "that the proposition 'I am,' 'I exist,' is necessarily true" is ultimately presented as resting on the direct apprehension of the meditator's own thinking.[30]

Hatfield stresses that Descartes is keenly aware of his selection of the meditative mode of discourse. He insists upon the need for a practical basis for the metaphysical inquiry whose conclusions often run counter to the testimony of the senses and the ontological assumptions fostered by long habit. Descartes writes concerning the primary notions of metaphysics, that "though in their own nature they are as intelligible as, or even more intelligible than those the geometricians study, yet, being contradicted by the preconceptions of the senses to which we have since our earliest years been accustomed, they cannot be perfectly apprehended except by those who give strenuous attention to them." And in the reply to the second

[29] A. Rorty, "The Structure of Descartes' *Meditations*," in A. Rorty 1976.
[30] Hatifield 1986.

set of objections, he writes, "I counsel no one to read this work, except those who are willing to meditate seriously with me." The notion of the subjective self that Plotinus shares with the modern world is the self that presents itself in the introspective stance. For the development of this introspective communication between author and reader, Plotinus relies upon a series of thought experiments embedded within the text, whose purpose is to foster the potential for self-awareness and so orient the student upon a path of self-knowledge. In *Enneads* V.8 Plotinus presents a thought experiment involving visualization of the sphere: "So far as possible, try to conceive of this world as one unified whole, with each of its parts remaining self-identical and distinct . . ."

Here Plotinus suggests that the reader try to perceive the world as unified within thought, to think of the world as a single object of thought, yet as retaining all of the features of its different members. Consider, he tells the reader, how any conditions of awareness whatsoever are confronted by you, the knower. These directions are a way of calling attention to the most general features involved in any encounter with the world, any possible object of awareness. We might paraphrase these instructions as follows: consider the total possible field of objects of awareness – that same field is simply what I mean by "world."

It is fair to call this passage a meditation because it involves two features often employed in meditation techniques: the active but directed use of the imagination, and the sustained presence of this imaginative construction as a method of changing habitual modes of thought or self-awareness:

So that whatever part of, for example, the outer sphere is shown forth, there immediately follows the image of the sun together with all of the other stars, and earth and sea and all sentient beings are seen, as if upon a transparent sphere. (V.8.9.3, Armstrong's translation)

This meditation involves a very careful direction of the mind and imagination of the student. Holding the simple image, the sphere, before the mind's eye, the reader is to fill up the space of that image entirely, exerting herself to the utmost to picture the entire universe of sentient and non-sentient beings in all of their diversity. Certainly one would need at least some practice and effort to carry out all of the conditions of the meditation successfully.

All of these components of the picture must be held in an even gaze. All sentient beings are visible within the diaphanous sphere at a single glance: *euthus*. An important feature of the meditation is the training of the student's concentration and attention. The practice of this exercise leads both to a focusing capacity, an intense direction of the mind's eye to a single object, without letting any feature of that object dominate in the moment, and to a detachment. None of the beings, either animate or inanimate, either human or non-human, is to have priority within the meditation. All are equally and completely subsumed within the general category of content of the sphere. All are, we might say, equidistant from the center. This equidistance is what Plotinus is hinting at by saying that the elements are, as it were, upon the surface of the sphere.

Actually, the passage we have just examined is one of numerous texts in which Plotinus uses the symbolism of the sphere to illustrate the relationship between consciousness and its contents. We find these texts broadly divided into two different types, one macrocosmic, the other microcosmic. Under the first type, the vision is described as planetary, and the contents of the vision include an enumeration of the parts of the cosmos and their respective inhabitants.[31] Under the second type, Plotinus uses a more abstract description of a geometrical object, a simple illuminated sphere, although at times, this shape can represent an individual head, or a head peering out by means of the faces of all sentient beings.[32]

This variation between the microcosmic and macrocosmic perspectives is Plotinus' way of illustrating two different ways of conceiving the world. The macrocosm is a publicly available world, inhabited and experienced by countless sentient beings, each with a diverse perspective. The microcosm is that same world, seen from within the confines of an individual consciousness. Above all, these texts suggest that Plotinus was grappling with the issue of how to represent subjectivity as a philosophical construct, as well as with the methodological issue of how to couch a dialectical appeal to the subjective.

At this point it is time to recap and to take stock of where we are in terms of the historical question with which we began. Starting

---

[31] Cf. *Enneads* V.8.9; VI.7.12; V.1.2.
[32] Cf. *Enneads* VI.5.8; VI.5.7; VI.7.15

with the general question, what use does Plotinus make of the appeal to incorrigibility in arguing for the necessity of self-knowledge, we found that there were texts in which the self-evidence of consciousness forms the last step of a dialectical progression. Furthermore, these texts were complemented by a series of thought experiments in which a highly structured form of subjectivity is represented as immediately present to the reader. In effect, the thought experiments offer the reader a mirror in which to observe his own inner life. These texts provide a reply to the historical question, "When and why did philosophers first lay claim to knowledge of their own subjective states,"[33] even as they raise other questions. First, can we compare any of the tenets or implications of Cartesian subjectivity with elements of Plotinus' appeal to the subjectivity of consciousness? Second, what philosophical work are Plotinus' thought experiments designed to do? Are they an elaboration of his arguments, or are they supposed to provide an element of persuasion quite apart from the metaphysical assumptions upon which they rely?

Internalism, Phenomenalism, and the Limitations of the Subjective

Plotinus begins VI.5.9 with a kind of psychological experiment: let us say that someone imagines a given number of elements as forming a sphere within his thought. Now Plotinus wants us to look at the relationship between the maker of the sphere, *to poioun,* and the content of that sphere, *ta mere:*

> If in a thought [experiment] someone should gather all the elements, once they had come into being, into a single spherical shape, he could not then claim that many agents made the sphere in a piecemeal fashion, with [each agent] cutting off a different content for himself and isolating it for the purpose of production. Rather, [he should admit] that the cause of the sphere's production is single. (VI.5.9.1–5)

Suppose the hypothetical thinker in our passage to be considering any group of *stoicheia,* any possible content for the sphere, for the purposes of argument. No matter how diverse the causes that initially produced these elements in the external world, for the contents of

---

[33] Burnyeat.

the sphere considered solely as objects of thought, it is true to say that their productive cause is singular, namely, the hypothetical thinker himself.

This thought experiment relies crucially upon an appeal to the introspective stance to secure the strong form of internalism expressed in the conclusion to the argument, a conclusion that bears close comparison to the internalist position of contemporary philosophy:

> an individual person or animal's mental states and event kinds – including the individual's intentional or representational kinds – can in principle be individuated in complete independence of the natures of empirical objects, properties, or relations.[34]

In our passage, the contents of the sphere (the *stoicheia*) or, as we might say, the contents of consciousness (consisting in simultaneous mental events or states) have only one unique cause at the time in which they are thought, namely, the hypothetical thinker. Now since the thinker is not a separate substance apart from his own thoughts, the mental events/states of this thinker are in some sense a part of the thinker. Therefore, the contents of consciousness belong to an intelligent and not to a physical substance. This conclusion both resembles Cartesian internalism and rests upon a methodology that recalls Descartes': the argument turns upon an appeal to introspection. Only the thinker as he is thinking can confirm that he is the cause of his thoughts. Someone else, to whom the perceiver is reporting his thoughts, might have occasion to remark that the cause of a particular perception was, for example, the man, Socrates.[35]

Following on this experiment, Plotinus briefly attempts, to address the problem of intersubjectivity, that is, the public availability of a self-consistent world to a plurality of knowers. The causal independence of mental states from the physical environment must now be treated as an analogy: just as the mind is the source and cause of its own contents, so the world soul is the source and cause of *its* own

---

[34] Burge, p. 118–9. He continues: "The mental nature of all an individual's mental states and events are such that there is no necessary or other deep individuative relation between the individual's being in states, or undergoing events, with those natures, and the nature of the individuals' physical and social environments."

[35] Cf. *Enneads* V.3.3.1–5.

contents. Hence, the world soul contains the physical cosmos, while universal soul contains the plurality of individual souls.[36] The question is, what justifies this transition from treating the individual mind as an example of the causal independence of the mental with respect to the physical, to the larger inference, that there must be some universal mind that exercises causal independence with respect to the physical macrocosm? And more importantly for our purposes, how does Plotinus' appeal to introspection enter into the structure of the argument? On the surface, this appeal seems a crudely deceptive attempt at persuasion. Starting from an internalist position, Plotinus ends by invoking the metaphysical principle that underlies his experiment, the doctrine of panpsychism. In fact, however, Plotinus needs his doctrine of panpsychism to account for the intersubjective consistency of the world. The argument appears to exhibit a circularity masked by the ingenuity of an appeal to the immediacy of consciousness.

To understand this transition, we turn to another thought experiment. Here we consider the analogies between Plotinus' exploration of subjectivity and the *esse est percipi* variety of idealism upon which modern-day philosophers heap so much scorn. The passage we are about to consider seems to introduce a form of phenomenalism as a step in the argument, which is intended to show that there are Forms for all sentient beings, or that all sentient beings exist within the hypostasis nous.

We have already seen this text in chapter 2. There I suggested that the text invites the reader to unify all sentient beings and to see them as existing in the mind, in much the same manner as the previously discussed thought experiment. In the context of the present passage, objectively all sentient beings constitute one world body; subjectively, they constitute a single phenomenal presentation. As a result of this first step, the unification of all sentient beings, the

---

[36] For thorough discussion of the causal relations between the individual embodied soul and the world soul, see Helleman-Elgersma, pp. 42–52. There is a distinction between the hypostasis soul (universal soul) and the world soul, which governs the cosmos as a whole. Elgersma calls attention to the work of Blumenthal, who demonstrates the inadequacy of the prevailing assumption in scholarship, introduced by Zeller, that these two souls should be equated. If the individual soul is simply a part of the world soul, and not directly related to the universal hypostasis, soul, then the cosmos would entirely subsume the autonomy of the individual.

reader now envisions a purely qualitative world, a world consisting of pure experience. These presentations intimately belong within the consciousness of the person who is conducting, so to speak, this experiment:

> The emergence of [all things] is from a single source, so to speak, but the source is not like some one particular breath or like a single feeling of warmth. Rather, it is as if a single quality contained all qualities in itself, and actually preserved them, so that [the quality of] sweetness [would be preserved] together with the [quality of] fragrance, and this single quality were [to become] simultaneously the taste of wine, and of all the modes of taste, and sights of colors, and all the sensations of touch. The quality would bring about whatever sounds are heard, all songs and every rhythm.

Thus the progress of the passage is from the objective description of the quality, as sweetness or smell, to its fundamental nature as a kind of awareness on the part of the perceiver.

This text presents a thought experiment in which the objective world dissolves before the mind, leaving in its wake what might literally be described as a stream of consciousness. In our passage, individual substances are shown to consist in qualia, and these qualia in turn are simply modifications of consciousness, or nous, which, I take it, is the "single source" described in the text. In both of these experiments, Plotinus shows us how the soul constructs a contracted sense of self when it conceives the world as outside of the self; this notion of externality is a result of habitually identifying with the body. The thought experiments reveal a way of conceiving the world as not external to the self. Gradually the boundary that separates self and world is erased, when the demarcations of selfhood are no longer around the body, but around the totality of any given phenomenal presentation.

So far, we have encountered thought experiments in which the subjective stance has been used as a support for some very weighty metaphysical tenets, including the doctrine of panpsychism and the doctrine of the Platonic world exemplar. In both passages, a structural puzzle crops up. A supposedly unmediated and hence, unbiased, appeal to consciousness becomes a method of securing credibility for what are obviously entrenched dogmas within the Platonic school. Why bother to employ such a circuitous method? Do we stand in danger of being fooled by the text and its rhetoric of immediacy? Persuasion is not the final goal of this experiment; participation is. The success of the thought experiment means for Plotinus a validation of the contemplative journey.

In fact, one of the strongest motivations that Plotinus has for approaching subjectivity by means of these thought experiments is to point out the limitations of the subjective. The appeal to introspection invites a scrutiny of the assumptions that the knower makes about himself. Instead of singling oneself out as possessing a privileged epistemic status, these texts encourage the reader both to doubt his own identity and to recognize his own cognitive limitations.

In the thought experiments we have discussed, one of the most important configurations presented is the relationship between the sphere and its contents. The person, *qua* knower, or subject of consciousness, will identify with the sphere, rather than with any of its contents. Immediately, definitions of the self that are appropriate for the knower considered as a sensible particular are no longer appropriate for the person undergoing the exercise. The purpose of this exercise is to sustain an insight into the nature of the individual insofar as he is a knower, by suggesting a contrast between his knowledge of himself, *qua* individual, and his identity as a knower, *qua* knower. The very stance that is assumed if one identifies, not with the contents of consciousness, but with consciousness apart from its contents, immediately begins to erode the identity of the knower. The center of consciousness is infinitely expansive, including within itself any individual identity that the knower may possess as an unremarkable feature of the total interior landscape. That is, every cognizable fact about the knower's identity as subject is converted to the status of an external condition: body, personality, life history, passions, and so forth. This detachment from the narrow confines of a historical selfhood, while it does not consist in a denial of the empirical self, allows the larger selfhood of soul to emerge from behind the veil of the objective domain.

Subjectivity and Its Transcendence

In chapter 18 of the *Vita*, Porphyry relates how he had once tried to "show that the object of thought existed outside the intellect"[37] and

---

[37] δεικνύναι πειρώμενος ὅτι ἔξω τοῦ νοῦ ὑφέστηκε τὸ νόημα (18.10).

that this belief formed the chief obstacle to his embracing the teaching of Plotinus,[38] who taught that the intelligibles, or forms, existed within nous. Porphyry's difficulty seems to be founded upon an assumption that characterizes ordinary as opposed to intellective cognition, namely, that the world, or real being, must exist outside of the knower. This assumption is in turn founded upon the need to withstand the subjectivism that would apparently result from saying that intellect cannot discover an object that exists prior to it.

Porphyry's objections may serve as an introduction to a key difficulty in the conception of self-knowledge that I have been developing here. The path of introspection should result in the belief that the empirical self is not the true self. But it is hard to see how the individual subject of consciousness, which contains but is not identical to any of its contents, can ever overcome the solipsism that threatens to engulf it. The creations of the individual mind are entirely subjective; the objects of intellect, nous, are preeminently objective.

The problem of discontinuity between the individual mind along with the individual's thinking, and the intellect as such, together with its extensionality as the eternal forms, formed the basis of "worst difficulty" argument already in the Platonic *Parmenides*, which is generated from the subjectivist implications of treating the ideas as the *noemata*, or thought objects, of an individual mind.

But, Parmenides, said Socrates, may it not be that each of these forms is a thought, which cannot properly exist anywhere but in a mind . . . (132b7) And besides, said Parmenides, according to the way in which you assert that the other things have a share in the forms, must you not hold either that each of those things consists of thoughts, so that all things think, or else that they are thoughts which nevertheless do not think? (132c5)

So, far from continuing in the thought productions that limit and condition the knower with an overlay of opinion, however true, or scientific knowledge, however coherent, there must be some use of

---

[38] Many scholars have done an exemplary job in pointing to the connections between this central tenet and the historical developments of the Stoic, Peripatetic, and Middle Platonic interpretations of the Demiurgic creation combined with the self thinking Aristotelian divinity. One of the most interesting treatments of the problem is that of Rich 1954, pp. 123–33, who discusses the Platonic Forms as thought in a human mind, a pattern evidenced already in the *Parmenides*, as part of the "worst difficulty" *aporia*.

the human intelligence which can lead to an insight that frees the knower from the narrow confines of her own thought, from the confines of her own intellect, and permits access to intellect as such.

Plotinus' methodology attempts to stand outside of the conditions of particular thought and to grasp the total occasion of awareness that includes both subject and object of intellection as its terms of reference. He expects that this fundamental condition of conscious experience, the reality of the knower as engaged in the confrontation with the world as given to consciousness, will provide the best opportunity for an exploration of the nature of intelligible reality.

Plotinus relies upon a method of directly pointing to the very primacy of cognition or awareness in its most general aspect, the very consciousness that is the basis for any mode of cognition. This method assumes at the outset that intellect in us is intellect as such, but we do not yet recognize it. Plotinus tells us: "And to put it another way, *nous* does not belong to the individual, but it is rather universal" (III.8.8.41). The soul attains to identification with intellect through the practice of concentration, but not concentration upon anything external to it, for this attachment to and distraction by the conception of an external, ontologically separate reality, is precisely the habit that obstructs the mind's progression in knowledge.

Conclusion

One of the questions we started with when undertaking this study of Plotinus' presentation of subjectivity was "what does it mean for someone to be a person?" In the thought experiments considered, Plotinus treats the empirical self as an object of consciousness rather than as the subject of consciousness:

> It seems that one who intends to know the nature of intellect must [first] catch sight of the soul, and the most divine part of soul. And this could happen in the following way, if you first removed the body from humanity and so also from yourself, of course, and then [you removed] the soul that gives rise to the body, together with sense-perception, which definitely [has to go], as well as desires, passions and all the remaining nonsense, since all that inclines us to the empirical self. What remains of soul is what we were calling the "image of intellect."

The empirical self is no longer the self with which the knower identifies, whereas the authentic self emerges as the pure subject of awareness, only uncovered when the various modes and objects of cognition are progressively shed.[39] What gives the person in this experiment the right to demarcate her selfhood as if it existed outside of the boundaries of any mode of cognition or any of the psychological parameters that normally characterize a personality or possessor of a life history? The detachment recommended here seems at odds with a requisite self-honesty that would admit passions, sense experiences, and bodily states as all belonging to the self.

To put this issue into sharper focus, we borrow from a complaint lodged against the Cartesian *res cogitans*, the pure subject of consciousness enshrined within the empiricist tradition:

> For empiricism, the self is an unobjectifiable subject, just as the eye is an invisible organ. But . . . the empiricist self vanishes when subjected to empiricist scrutiny. The self is not discoverable by any sense, whether inner or outer; and therefore it is to be rejected as a metaphysical monster.[40]

The thought experiments that Plotinus engages in continually refer the reader to this self that can never be grasped as a definite object, as this or as that. Indeed, the most that such a "witness" self, or subject of consciousness, would have to say for itself would be, "am, am," or "I, I."[41]

This speculative self, the watchful fleshless eye that has been repeatedly denounced in the post-modern era as an artificial attempt to reify a linguistic convention,[42] is easily discoverable within the premodern tradition. But for the modern tradition, this self was part of an elaborate epistemological construction that introduced an enormous amount of excess metaphysical baggage, to wit, Cartesian dualism and its internalist consequences.

Plotinus' motivations lay in another direction entirely. In fact, it would be difficult to overemphasize the affinities that Plotinus shares

---

[39] Cf. the acute study of Plotinus' recommendations for contemplative detachment from the empirical self by Schroeder 1989.

[40] Kenny 1992.

[41] *Enneads* V.3.10.36.

[42] That is, reifying the first person pronoun, which, as subject of all self-referring predicates, is a linguistic device to indicate the presence of an ego-substance, but is according to some theorists, a metaphysical cipher. See Kenny.

with Descartes in terms of textual allusions to a religious tradition. The most significant feature of Plotinus' thought experiments is their association with prayer or invocation, a usage we can see by returning to the treatise "On the Intelligible Beauty":

Keeping watch over this image, place another next to it, taking away its mass. Remove both space and the imaginary conception of matter in you [altogether]; do not simply try to get hold of another sphere, smaller in mass than [the first]. *And calling upon the god whose imaginary conception you have, pray for him to come.* (V.8.9.11; Armstrong's translation; my italics)

Here the sphere is obviously treated as an icon of deity. But more than the sphere itself, the world as a whole, since it is contained within the sphere, is conceived as an icon, a sacred image of the god who can be encountered face to face within his shrine.[43] This meditation then is also a Cletic prayer, an invocation that depends upon making the world as a whole both one's offering and one's object of worship. The exercise helps the student to treat the world as a theophany, as an image of the deity whose real presence is yet to be recognized.[44] This recognition is best attained, according to Plotinus, within an introspective search: Plotinian prayers employ the formula, "alone to the alone."[45]

This introspective practice involves simplifying and clarifying the relationship that the soul as knower has with all possible objects of awareness. One of the consequences of this clarification is the restoration of the soul's proper fullness, an appreciation of the rich and creative intellectual potential that is available to every human being

---

[43] There are many passages in the *Enneads* where the image of the sphere is associated with the activity of contemplative meditation or prayer. Often Plotinus uses the language of solar worship to discuss this kind of meditation, but as often he uses the language of cult and celebration, employing dance imagery as an application of the same spherical model. Cf. especially *Enneads* V.5.8 (Armstrong's translation): "So one must not chase after it [the One], but wait quietly till it appears, preparing oneself to contemplate it, as the eye awaits the rising of the sun; and the sun rising over the horizon ('from Ocean,' the poets say) gives itself to the eyes to see." Or again, *Enneads* VI.9.8.35 ff. for dance imagery. For explicit uses of shrine imagery, see VI.9.11.19–30 and V.1.6.10. This last passage is again a very pointed discussion of prayer and invocation.

[44] For an excellent discussion of the worship of the cosmos as either itself divine or an image of the divine, see Pépin 1986.

[45] Dodds 1960, pp. 16–17, discusses the history of this phrase and cites evidence of Numenius, who seems to have employed it in fragment 11 of his *Peri Agathou*, and whether or not the phrase was actually part of an Egyptian cult formula.

as a birthright. No longer circumscribed by its historical, temporal, and emotional limitations, the Plotinian self embraces a vast domain whose boundaries extend to the fullness of what is encountered in every knowing moment. In this respect, the reconstructed self of Plotinus is met with in a moment of attention that can be reenacted at any point within history.

5

The Symbolism of the *Enneads*

The significance of imagery or symbolism in the *Enneads* has long been a source of scholary contention.[1] In 1961 Beierwaltes published his well-known article, "Plotins Metaphysik des Lichtes,"[2] in which he studied Plotinus' extensive employment of the image of light. Beierwaltes starts out with an assumption that governs the way he looks at the metaphors in the *Enneads*. He assumes that figures of speech can be more or less adequate to the task of representation, and that representational adequacy depends upon the ontological approximation of image and archetype. Since it is incorporeal, light turns out to be the most appropriate image for the task of representing philosophical truth.

In Beierwaltes's view, light is not merely a metaphor when it is used to describe intellect, since it can succeed as an image of the intellect only when "there is a presence of the original in the image."[3] Visual seeing differs from intellectual seeing because the visual object is external to the subject whereas the intellectual object is internal to the subject. Thus vision can be either intellectual or perceptual, but light, as the medium of vision, remains the same entity in either mode.[4]

Replies to Beierwaltes have been both numerous and extensive, but most interpreters believe that in the *Enneads* symbols have no

---

[1] For concise histories of this controversy, see Schroeder 1992, p. 37, and Blumenthal 1987.

[2] Beierwaltes 1961.

[3] Beierwaltes 1991.

[4] Beierwaltes 1961, p. 342: "Thinking and realization are actually a mode of seeing."

independent value.[5] The majority of scholars insist that, far from speaking of the adequacy of symbols, one should speak of the subordination of symbols, since metaphor only redescribes doctrine.

In my reassessment of the *Enneads'* metaphors, I show that previous approaches have been hampered by their adoption of a lexical rather than a rhetorical understanding of metaphorical language. My claim is that although metaphor in the *Enneads* provides pragmatic variation upon already established themes, it does not compete with literal language as a means of conveying doctrine. Instead, its purpose is to assist the reader in assimilating doctrine. At least some metaphors in the *Enneads* can be read for their rhetorical function as directive utterances, designed to tell us not how things are, but how to see things.

How does metaphor accomplish this? To answer this question, one has to be familiar with what Plotinus sees as the major drawback besetting doctrinal deliverances.[6] Plotinus holds that language fails

---

[5] Perhaps the first response came in the form of Ferwerda's monograph (Ferwerda 1965), whose view can be summarized from the following paragraph taken from his introduction (p. 7): "Nous pouvons donc conclure que l'image chez Plotin tout comme chez Platon ne vaut jamais en soi; elle vaut ce que vaut la connaissance de celui qui s'en sert; elle ne vaut que si elle est vraie et, ce qui est extrèmement important, si elle est verifiée. Sa fonction est donc purement illustrative et pedagogique, parce qu'elle constitue un procède dialectique et non pas la description adequate de l'unité rétablie entre les Formes et le monde sensible." See also Cilento and Blumenthal 1987.

Recently, Schroeder 1992, pp. 24–39, has come to the defense of Beierwaltes's views. He reiterates his position in Schroeder 1994, p. 473.

[6] A minor flurry of scholarship has arisen over the issue of whether Plotinus equates non-discursive with non-propositional thought. For the controversy and its history see Lloyd 1969–70, Sorabji 1983, Lloyd 1986, Alfino 1990, and Lloyd 1990. Sorabji's argument is that non-propositional thought is a concept at odds with Plotinus account of nous's activity, since the latter involves complexity. Alfino and Lloyd respond by countering that nous's thoughts cannot be propositional since in that case they would be assimilable to language and so possess a signifying function. However, they argue, nous's thoughts are not representational and do not signify.

A lack of standard terminology makes this debate difficult to resolve. When Plotinus explicitly denies propositional thought to nous, the terms he actually uses are προτάσεις, ἀξιώματα, λεκτά. This vocabulary is eclectic, comprised of the Aristotelian and Stoic words denoting "propositions." In short, Plotinus might be taken to exclude Stoic or Aristotelian accounts of propositional thought from nous, without thereby precluding propositional thought *eo ipso*. For this point, I am indebted to the written remarks of Steven K. Strange. In this chapter I attempt to locate a non-discursive methodology in the the texts of the *Enneads* rather than reviewing the

---

as a vehicle for conveying metaphysical truth since words necessarily refer to entities standing outside of the linguistic system, whereas truth is both self-certifying and self-revealing.[7] Truth cannot be ascertained by linguistic or conceptual representations; it can be apprehended only when there is an identity between the knower and the known.[8] Of course, the major problem with such a theory is that it appears necessarily to elude both verification and experience.

Metaphor enters as one way in which Plotinus, holding to this theory of truth, tries to bring the possibility of the identity of the knower and the known into the sphere of experience. He employs metaphorical expressions to point out features of accessible experiences that exhibit, more or less perfectly, some degree of unity between the knowing subject and the object known. In this way, he uses metaphor to guide the reader to a better understanding of what knowing, in the most proper sense, is and is like.

Plotinus employs the image of the diaphanous earth to contrast two ways of looking at the world. The first way of looking at things he describes as "looking outside" (τὰ ἔξω σκοπεῖσθαι; the second way of looking at things he sometimes calls "seeing inside."[9] My concern will be to show that when Plotinus wants to contrast discursive thinking with non-discursive thinking (or intellectual knowledge) he invokes this distinction between looking outside and seeing inside. To give his readers a sense of what seeing inside might be like, Plotinus employs the image of the transparent world.

The chapter develops in four stages. First, I elaborate a rhetorical reading of the metaphorical utterances in the *Enneads*. Next I review some of the distinctions between discursive and non-discursive thinking relevant to the discussion in part three, where I apply a

grounds for positing the existence of non-propositional thinking as a construct of Plotinus' philosophy.

[7] Sorabji 1983, p. 152; Lloyd 1986, p. 259; Alfino 1990, pp. 274–5.
[8] At V.5 1, for example, Plotinus disparages discursive reasoning because it deals only with things that exist outside of itself (V.5.1.30): οὐ γὰρ δὴ προτάσεις οὐδὲ ἀξιώματα οὐδὲ λεκτά· ἤδη γὰρ ἂν καὶ αὐτά περὶ ἑτέρων λέγοι, καὶ οὐκ αὐτὰ τὰ ὄντα εἴη. [Intellect's thoughts] are certainly not premises or theorems or propositions. These are about things other [than themselves] and are not identical with the realities [that they signify].
[9] Cf. *Enneads* V.8.4.26, οἷος ὁ Λυγκεὺς ἐλέγετο καὶ τα εἴσω τῆς γῆς ὁρᾶν . . . Just as Lynkeus was said to see the inside of the earth . . .

rhetorical reading of the metaphor of the transparent earth. I conclude with some remarks on Plotinus' philosophy of metaphor.

Metaphorical Deixis in the *Enneads*

Earlier we saw that Plotinus criticized discursive thought for misrepresenting reality: true being does not exist externally to the knower. The unity of the knower and the known is the condition *sine qua non* for intellectual apprehension; discursive thought involves the severance of this unity.[10] How does Plotinus' own linguistic praxis conform with his views on the limitations of discursive thought? We might aver that, practically, the consequences of Plotinus' critique leave us no better off than does Skepticism – deserted by an author who becomes almost willfully inscrutable and taunted by a text that becomes almost instantly displaced.

One scholar who has raised this issue is Steven Strange.[11] He writes:

Plotinus' critique is metaphysically important, because it requires a new view of the status of the language of metaphysics. Terms of ordinary language, the normal use of which is to speak about everyday sensible experience, must have new meanings if they are to be applied to Forms. Plotinus thinks that the highest and most important kind of reality can only be spoken of using metaphors.

Strange's remarks are relevant because they consider how Plotinus' theoretical constraints operate upon his own discourse. But Strange does not consider why it is that metaphor is any less vulnerable to Plotinus' criticisms. Is not metaphorical thinking – the obvious objection – itself discursive? It has been far more common for scholars to argue that symbolic language in the *Enneads* should enjoy no such privileged status. We find this opinion expressed in Ferwerda's monograph and echoed in Blumenthal's bibliographic survey.[12] Plotinus never uses a symbol without a surrounding context that expli-

---

[10] Alfino 1990; Lloyd 1990. Actually, Plotinus employs more than one tack for the purpose of criticizing discursive thought. Another strategy, equally pervasive throughout the *Enneads*, is to demonstrate the indeterminacy of discursive thinking with regard to the expression of necessary truths. This second type is squarely grounded in Plotinus' anti-essentialist analysis of individuation.

[11] Strange 1987.

[12] Ferwerda 1965, p. 7. See also Blumenthal 1987a, p. 572.

cates the contents of that symbol, presenting it in a discursive form. Ferwerda concludes that symbols in effect only redescribe the doctrinal content and are used as a cap, functionally insignificant as vehicles of meaning. They have no independent value.

Metaphor here is thought to have a purely derivative status because it must be interpreted in the light of statements of fact or of doctrine. This is to discover the meaning of the metaphor in the cognitive content that it is purported to have and to say that, as a vehicle of this content, the metaphor depends upon a literal statement of fact, which accurately describes, one might say, the way things are. Metaphor is thereby disparaged on the philosophical grounds that any representation equates with derogation, in accordance with standard Platonic ontology.[13] Whereas Strange's remarks hinted at a role that metaphor might be able to play in the exposition of Plotinus' philosophy by circumventing the strictures of ordinary literal usage, the majority of Plotinus scholars are doubtful that such a role would be consonant with the cautionary views that any Platonist is bound to hold concerning the status of images in general.

How one responds to the use of metaphor in Plotinus' text may be conditoned by one's understanding of the nature of metaphorical utterances. Thus before looking at metaphorical language in Plotinus, I would like to sketch more precisely what I have in mind by a rhetorical conception of metaphor.

The traditional comparison theory of metaphor is most familiar to classicists from Aristotle's *Rhetoric*.[14] It simply asserts that all metaphors are elliptical usages for similes, or imply similes. Thus the metaphor can be explained in terms of other, literal species of language use, in the sense that once a comparison is stated, it may be literally true that certain objects share features in common.[15]

---

[13] Cf. Blumenthal 1987a, p. 542: "This view is required by the many texts where Plotinus speaks of likeness as a relation of inferiority."

[14] Classicists are most familiar with the substitution theory of metaphor, a theory purportedly extending all the way back to Aristotle's *Poetics*, chapter 21, and *Rhetoric*, chapter 11. Black 1977 summarizes this theory as follows: "The substitution view regards the entire sentence that is the locus of the metaphor as replacing some set of literal sentences." For modern explication of this theory, see Searle 1979, and for recent criticism, see Lakoff and Turner 1989, p. 123. For extensive discussion of Aristotle's views of metaphor, see Ricoeur 1977, pp. 9–43.

[15] See Searle 1979.

If Thrasymachus says to Socrates, "You need a wet nurse," he is using the metaphor of infancy to describe Socrates' behavior and is suggesting that Socrates and infants share some behavioral features. Thrasymachus' Socrates and babies both snivel, and so the metaphor is simply an elliptical way of asserting some real property of Socrates.

An objection to this theory is that often the comparison itself seems to carry a feature that is either irreducibly metaphorical or would not count as a literal use of the term.[16] For example, although young children may be said to whine, this usage of "whine" is perhaps itself metaphorical since it refers only secondarily to a noise and primarily to some kind of behavior that has certain psychological features not captured in the physical act of whining.

The comparison theory has recently given way to various pragmatic views of metaphor. According to these views, the sentence or literal meaning of the statement diverges from the utterance meaning of the sentence, or the way that the sentence is being used, such that the literal reading of the metaphor has a false truth value, whereas the metaphorical reading of the metaphor has a true truth value.[17]

When Thrasymachus says "Socrates needs a wet nurse," that is not literally true, because in fact Socrates has long been taking solid food. Nor would any serious listener berate Thrasymachus for having failed to notice this about Socrates. We would, however, seriously fault the truth of Thrasymachus' statement if it turned out that Socrates was behaving appropriately in the course of his argument and was responding in a judicious way to his interlocutor.

The literal falsity of this metaphor suggests to his audience that Thrasymachus is using language (a) not literally and (b) with some other objectives. Perhaps he wants to say that Socrates is caviling unnecessarily. Finally, though, he intends his assertion to have some effect on Socrates. Thrasymachus will be trying to change the format of the conversation by getting Socrates to concede that Socrates is

---

[16] Searle 1979.

[17] Needless to say, this chapter does not offer a complete survey of all pragmatic theories of metaphor. In particular, it omits the recent work of Lakoff and Turner 1989, which holds that metaphor is a process of cognitive enhancement in which concepts from one semantic domain are mapped onto another domain (Lakoff and Turner 1989, p. 112).

expecting Thrasymachus to be too punctilious in his speaking style. He is therefore positively asserting that he is not going to be the wet nurse that Socrates seems to demand as his interlocutor. Moreover, Thrasymachus' very use of this wet nurse metaphor shows that he refuses to be a wet nurse. By insulting Socrates in this way, he exhibits non-compliance with Socrates' strictures. So metaphor here is like a dialect that speaker and listener share,[18] used to encourage the interlocutor to expect changes in the conversational dynamics.

The views of Beierwaltes and Blumenthal depend upon a comparison theory of metaphor: for both scholars, the literal resemblance between the *comparanda* (whether this resemblance be construed as ontological, *pace* Beierwaltes, or doctrinal, *pace* Blumethal) is the source of the metaphor's meaning. In short, these interpreters view Plotinus' metaphors as straightforwardly lexical.[19] The meaning of the metaphor must be recovered by looking at what we take it to be asserting, that is, at its paraphrased cognitive content, according to the majority view, or by keeping in mind the true ontological reference of the symbol, according to Beierwaltes.

What these interpretations have left out is a pragmatic account of metaphorical language.[20] A pragmatic view might reveal that Plotinus' metaphors are irreducible to literal language because of the cognitive enhancement they lend to the process of communication.[21] The heuristic value of metaphorical language in the *Enneads* cannot

---

[18] Skulsky 1986.

[19] On the lexical interpretation of Aristotle's theory, see Ricoeur 1977, pp. 9–43. Aristotle defines metaphor (*Poetics* 1475b) as "the application [*epiphora*] of an alien name."

[20] I am using the word "pragmatic" here as a means of introducing a semantic/pragmatic distinction. Pragmatics considers the contextual background of word usage or conversational implicatures associated with an utterance, as distinct from the lexical denotation the word is commonly understood to have. Cf. Lakoff and Turner 1989, pp. 125–6.

[21] Ricoeur 1977 and Laks 1992 have attempted to assimilate Aristotle's theory to more recent cognitive approaches to metaphor. According to Laks, Aristotle tells us in the *Poetics* that good metaphors actually help us to perceive likenesses and that one species of metaphor, metaphor by analogy, can even produce likenesses between the objects under comparison. Thus Laks finds no real contradiction between substitution and cognitive views of metaphor when it comes to the interpretation of Aristotle's text.

be measured by its doctrinal equivalent, in the sense that one might abstract a propositional content existing independently of any contextual considerations.

In fact the often abrupt, often subtle, perspectival shift that metaphor effects in an audience is garnered by Plotinus as a means of interrupting, then helping us to distance and even to abandon, habitual ways of thinking. Plotinus' metaphors attempt at once to describe how things are, so that they succeed in being reality depicting, and at the same time to diverge from normal descriptive use by telling us how to see things.[22] His metaphors push us outside of the semantic system, in which a word is exchanged for some conceptual equivalent, by partially denoting some feature of the world or indeed of experience itself.[23] Plotinus relies on metaphor to communicate ostensively; he uses it to pick out features from within his own cognitive environment, in the belief that the same kind of experience or object may become apparent to his audience as well. Communication, essentially the awareness shared between speaker and audience resulting from the intentions of the speaker to bring this state of affairs about, is facilitated by means of metaphorical utterance.[24]

By using the metaphor of the transparent world, Plotinus pushes us to the limits of language's signifying function, forcing us to ask ourselves *how* we should be looking if we wish to follow the argu-

---

[22] This view of metaphor is often called the "strong creative theory" (Black 1977). According to this theory, metaphors function by mapping some semantic domain (the focus) onto a literal frame. This view has it that by conceptualizing the frame in terms of the focus, we increase our ability to comprehend the frame. Such cognitive enhancement occurs maximally when the set of correspondences noticed between frame and focus are created by the metaphor. When we see something as something else, then we create a likeness in certain respects between the objects insofar as we are considering them: "Some metaphors enable us to see aspects of reality that the metaphor's production helps to constitute."

[23] Cf. Soskice 1991, for the idea of metaphor as accomplishing its work through an indeterminacy or refusal to specify fully the conceptual frame with which it is involved.

[24] Davidson 1978 in this line of thought writes:
> We imagine that there is a content to be captured when all the while we are in fact focusing on what the metaphor makes us notice. If what the metaphor makes us notice were finite in scope and propositional in nature, this would not in itself make trouble; we would simply project the content the metaphor brought to mind onto the metaphor. But in fact there is no limit to what a metaphor calls to our attention, and much of what we are caused to notice is not propositional in character.

ment. His metaphor is designed to make the reader reflect upon the question of how the world is seen, and whether or not the world is as it is seen:

> as if someone should have the sight that Lynkeus is said to have had, and to see the inside of the earth, as the myth riddles about the eyes they have there. (V.8.4.26)

The self-repudiating feature of Plotinus' most prominent metaphor does more than convey a sense of the mythical. By means of this image, an experiential component is infused into the text. Seeing through the earth is not possible for human beings, and yet Plotinus returns to this image as the basis for establishing communication between himself and the reader.

Discursivity and Its Discontents

Let us now turn to Plotinus' typology for discursive thinking. My central point is that for Plotinus, one of the most salient characteristics of discursive thought is its intentional structure: discursive states exhibit directedness by being about objects that are ontologically independent of those states:

> We allocated to [discursive reason the ability to] reflect upon what is external to it and to meddle in external matters, but we take it that it is basic to intellect to reflect upon its own nature and what belongs to its own nature. (V.2.3.17)

Of course, thinking or saying that things are thus-and-so is not identical to their being thus-and-so, in most circumstances. The point seems almost too obvious to belabor, and yet it is a point that Plotinus repeatedly stresses when discussing the ontological concomitants of discursive thought.

How is it that discursive states are directed toward particulars in the world? Here Plotinus' account is informed by the Aristotelian doctrine of isomorphism, enunciated at *De anima* III.8, according to which the mind, when comprehending or perceiving an object, becomes identical with the form of that object. Aristotle stipulates that the mind "thinks the forms by means of mental images" (*De anima*, 43165; Hicks) in order to represent its objects (whether they be perceptual or conceptual). Finally, he employs a strong analogy between sense-perception and mental perception, describing ordinary thought as a kind of mental receptivity to form.[25] Here is the relevant passage from the *De anima*:[26]

But if thought is like perception, then the mind must be acted upon by the thought object or something else must [happen] which is analogous to this. Therefore, the mind must be impassive, but must be capable of receiving the form.

Following Aristotle, Plotinus preserves this analogy between mental and physical perception. Discursive thinking involves mental representation of the forms:

the soul . . . is other than its object, and has a discursive awareness that sees as if it were one thing gazing at another. (III.8.6.22–25 [with omissions])

Having appropriated the Aristotelian terminology, Plotinus sets himself the task of making a clear distinction between *noesis* and *dianoesis*, or non-discursive and discursive thought, a distinction that is absent in the Aristotelian discussion. In *Enneads* V.5, we see him groping toward an account of *noesis* that departs from the intentional model that Aristotle uses.

In the opening chapter of this treatise, we encounter the well-worn Plotinian formulation of discursive thought as that which is "cognizant of what is external" (τῶν μὲν ἔξω . . . ἀντιλήψεται). Plotinus etymologizes the word, δόχα, "opinion," from the verb δέχομαι, "to receive," in keeping with Aristotelian isomorphism:[27]

Opinion receives, indeed, that is why it is opinion, because it receives something from an object that is substantially different from that which receives it.

---

[25] Again, in V.3., Plotinus employs the *aisthesis*/noesis analogy, but at the same time he tries to modify it by refining his vocabulary, using the terms ὅράσις (sight) and βλέπει (look at) as contrasting terms: "if [sc. discursive mind] looks, it looks at an object different from itself that becomes complete in something different from itself. But in the intelligible order none of this takes place: the seer and the seen are in the same place."

[26] *De anima* III.4.13–16; 429a3.

[27] *Enneads* V.5.1.62. The actual details of Aristotelian noetic isomorphism are open to interpretation. Whether the form of the noeton is numerically one and the same as the form within intellect, or whether the intellect is caused to become like in form to the noeton is a question that remains problematic, whichever horn of the dilemma one chooses to grasp.

In the case of non-discursive thought, Plotinus breaks with the Aristotelian conception of *noesis* by rejecting its criterion for the identity of the knower and the known as too weak: the mind's coming into contact with the νοητόν is not enough to render the mind identical with its intelligible object.[28] Although it is true that Aristotle distinguishes between perception and thinking on the grounds that the latter is "up to us" because the objects of thought are internal to nous, nevertheless, as we have seen, Aristotle indicates that "thinking is [a case of] being affected, or of being acted upon."[29] Aristotle thinks that, for human beings, using one's nous involves representing (already acquired) concepts by means of mental images.[30]

By contrast, Plotinus' account of thinking at the highest level is that such thought is precisely non-representational, whereas discursive thinking is always inherently representational.[31] Discursive thought gazes outside at the world and discovers the sensible object, or gazes within toward the Forms and represents them by means of

[28] In cases of non-perceptual thought, it is extremely difficult to get at what Aristotle means when he asserts the identity thesis, that mind is identical to its thoughts. On the mechanics of Aristotelian thought, see Wedin 1992. Wedin holds that the productive intellect contains a repository of concepts and that the passive intellect recalls these concepts when actualizing its capacity to know.

[29] *De anima* 429b24: νοεῖν πάσχειν τί ἐστιν

[30] Aristotle *De anima* 431b4: τὰ εἴδη τὸ νοητικὸν ἐν τοῖς φαντάσμασι νοεῖ. Cf. also *De memoria* 450a1–7: νοεῖν οὐκ ἔστιν ἄνευ φαντάσματος. On both of these passages, see Wedin 1992. See also Frede 1991 and Kahn 1991 for the role of *phantasmata*, or images, in the act of thinking.

[31] Plotinus finds that this same intentional structure operates in cases of sense-perception. Visual experience is subject to evaluation as true or false because it is a mental state directed toward particulars in the world. At V.3.3 Plotinus narrates a kind of script in which he spells out what is taking place mentally when a perceiver recognizes a visual object: "One might ask oneself, 'Who is this?' if he has met the person on a previous occasion, and answer with the aid of memory that it is Socrates. So too when someone pays attention to the details of what he sees, he analyses the [visual] presentation."

The experience as a whole, designated by the phrase ἃ ἡ φαντασία ἔδωκεν, literally, "what the imagination presents," is associated by the percipient with a propositional content. When we think or perceive, we represent to ourselves a certain propositional content that "unfolds" (we might say unpacks) the intuition or describes what has been apprehended in perception. This logos, or propositional content, goes hand in hand with the intentional object, telling us what the mental state is about.

concepts.[32] Absent from intellectual activity, *noesis,* is the intentional structure of discursive thought in which there is a discrete subject that stands apart from the object known. No longer can it be said that the mind exhibits directedness toward an object in the act of *noesis.* Rather, the subject discovers that it is its own object: "when something knows itself, [this] is the proper meaning of knowing" (V.3.13.15).

Plotinus derails the Aristotelian analogy between perception and knowledge by introducing Platonic language to describe the act of νόησις, invoking in particular Plato's μέγιστα γένη. They show up in V.3 as a countermeasure to Aristotelian isomorphism. Here the Platonic categories of sameness and difference violate the unilateral direction of intentionality:

> That which contemplates must be [divided] into two things and each of these must be external [sc. to each other] or both must be internal. Contemplation must constantly [take place] within identity and difference. (V.3.10.23–26)

But what does this experience of difference within identity amount to? One answer is that it amounts to a paradox. Plotinus exploits the fact that the Platonic categories are a series of paired opposites to demonstrate the paradoxical nature of intellect's activity: the intellect knows an object that is simultaneously not grasped as an object. Moreover, this object is both unitary and inherently multiple.[33] These contradictions cause Plotinus' difficulties to proliferate as he tries to describe the nature of intellectual thought.[34] This "knowledge which is not one thing different from that in which it is"[35] is enigmatic by Plotinus' own admission: "just *how* [this form of thought can exist] Plato left for us to investigate . . ." (V.8.4.54).

---

[32] The representation of Forms by means of concepts or *logoi* is obviously an enormous topic and one that cannot be discussed here. See Emilsson 1988, especially chapter 7.

[33] V.3.10.39.

[34] Cf. VI.7, where the reader encounters an aitiology for the complexity of the intelligible world: οὐδέν ἐστιν αὐτοῦ, ὅ τι μὴ ἄλλο, ἵνα ἄλλο ὂν καὶ τοῦτο συντελῇ (VI.7.13.55). There is nothing in it which is not other, so that in its otherness it may contribute this too.

[35] Plotinus quoting *Phaedrus* 247d7–e1.

The Metaphor of the Transparent World

The problem with Plotinus' formulation in *Enneads* V is that it would seem to posit a solipsistic activity that is a far cry from what ordinarily takes place in human cognition. At this juncture, Plotinus turns to the metaphor of the transparent world.[36] He uses this metaphor in an effort to represent a methodology that can escape from the limitations of discursivity, because it circumvents or modifies the subject/object dichotomy that characterizes ordinary thought. At the opening of V.8.9 there is an extended meditation upon the relationship between wisdom and the products whose creation it governs. The beauty of our cosmos, Plotinus tells us, can best be appreciated if we conceive of the cosmos as transparent. We can see the beauty of the world only if we are capable of seeing through the world. Although the remarks in chapter 1 may seem elusive, falling somewhere in between metaphor and cosmological speculation, it quickly becomes apparent that Plotinus expects the reader/audience to be following very closely indeed.

He offers us nothing less than instruction in how to recreate this image of the transparent world for ourselves, describing an exercise involving visualization of the world as situated within a diaphanous sphere: "So far as possible, try to conceive of this world as one unified whole, with each of its parts remaining self-identical and distinct . . ." (VI.8.9.1–3.)

Here Plotinus suggests that the reader try to perceive the world as unified within thought, to think of the world as a single object of thought, yet as retaining all of the features of its different members. At this point we might do well to ask, why does Plotinus want his reader to think of this world as a whole?

Plotinus attempts to fine-tune the manner in which we normally comprehend the world by opening up the field of awareness to include all possible objects of awareness. His purpose is to restore the natural fullness that is available to the human intellect as a birthright but has been obscured due to the dominance of discursive thinking. Normally he discursive mind focuses its attention upon a

---

[36] For a very lucid discussion of the metaphor of transparency in V.3.9 and V.8, see Beierwaltes 1961 and Beierwaltes 1991.

succession of objects in an unceasing temporal flow: "discursive thought, in order to make a statement, must grasp its objects one [after] another."[37] This concentration upon the objects of discursive thinking leads to a forgetfulness of the full resources of consciousness, a condition that Plotinus refers to as "bewitchment" or "falling under the spell" of the objects of consciousness: "everything that is directed toward another thing is under the spell of the other" (IV.4.43.16).

By contrast, Plotinus describes non-discursive thinking as the ability to see the objects of awareness "all together together at once."[38] The first step in the visualization presented in our text, then, is intended to develop the reader's ability to unify the objects of consciousness. This will be the first step that Plotinus wishes the reader to follow in order to gain some sense of what Plotinus means by non-discursive awareness. Another feature of the image now emerges into view:[39]

So that whatever part of, for example, the outer sphere is shown forth, there immediately follows the image of the sun together with all of the other stars, and earth and sea and all sentient beings are seen, as if upon a transparent sphere.

Although the sphere is envisioned as transparent, it is not empty. Holding the simple image, the sphere, before the mind's eye, the reader is to fill up the space of that image entirely, to picture the entire universe of sentient and non-sentient beings in all of their diversity. The reader has before the mind's eye a vast field consisting in the panoramic sweep of the entire cosmos that is simultaneously intricate in its detail and specification. The purpose of this interior visualization is to call attention to the quality of interior vision itself and in particular, to its capacity to be at once unitary and multi faceted in a way that exterior vision is not.

This facet of the image, its appearance as an integral totality functions as a balance upon the monolithic quality of the initial visualization. It also introduces a third stage in the developing vision

---

[37] V.3.17.23. Cf. V.1.4.19–21: "Indeed, there is a succession of things involved with soul, at one moment Socrates, at another a horse, always one particular thing whereas Intellect is all things" (Atkinson's translation).

[38] V.8.6.9: ἀθρόον

[39] V.8.9.3. Armstrong's translation.

Let the luminous sphere pictured in the mind contain all things within it, whether in motion or at a standstill, or rather both in motion and at a standstill. Keeping watch over this image, place another next to it, taking away its mass. Remove both space and the imaginary conception of matter in you [altogether]; do not simply try to get hold of another sphere, smaller in mass than [the first]. (V.8.9.9–14).

The reader, trying to contract the teeming morass of all sentient beings into this tiny sphere, must ruthlessly compress the entire universe. Instructions for this form of imaginary compression are included in the exhortation to "remove space." Here Plotinus suggests that the student try to picture the world as existing within his imagination, that is, to confront the world solely as it is apprehended in awareness.

A parallel image is developed in VI.4.7.22–6:

If you were to make a small luminous mass a kind of center and then to place a spherical body around it so that the light inside illuminated the entire container, there being no other source of light for the outer mass . . .

The image is very similar in structure and content to the one developed in V.8. The subject of consciousness, represented by the center, is described as pervading the entire field of light, which represents consciousness. From the viewpoint of this subject, there is no source of light for the outer mass other than that which originates in the center. That is to say, the objects of awareness are and must be available for a conscious subject. Although this state of affairs may seem quite obvious and not altogether interesting, it is a state of affairs to which Plotinus is very concerned to alert the reader: Plotinus is communicating a way of looking at the objects of awareness such that one sees them as pervaded by, or not other than, the subject of awareness.

The sustained practice of this visualization leads to a state of greater detachment from the objects of awareness. None of the beings, either animate or inanimate, either human or non-human, is to have priority within the vision. All are equidistant from the subject of consciousness, an equidistance that Plotinus signals by using the word "center" in VI.4.7.23. Similarly, the objective status of the knower herself or himself is now open for investigation.

Any objective fact about this knower, as for example his or her location in time or place, now becomes one more component of the integral vision that includes all beings, even the knower himself or herself. Given this initial confrontation with the world in all of its vastness as experienced within consciousness, the identity of knower itself becomes an issue, since the knower is discovered to be outside of the contents of the sphere, and yet related to it as its cause and source.

One obvious feature of these images is their fluid dynamism, the precision and clarity of an extremely vivid picture that undergoes a sudden shift of perspective.[40] Such a combination of sustained observation together with abrupt displacement reflects two primary mental components that accompany the non-discursive thinking conveyed in these texts: concentration and insight. The contemplative practice that is meant to underlie these images is designed to strengthen these intellectual qualities within the student and employs a non-discursive approach to that end. The self-disciplined effort of focusing the mind upon its object with intensity and attention is a feature of non-discursive thinking, since in this state, the subject and object of awareness must merge.

Heuresis and Didaxis in the *Enneads*

Now it is time to cast our gaze back toward the subject/object dichotomy that characterizes discursive thinking and to ask whether there has been any modification of the intentional structure noticed earlier. In ordinary visual experience and for that matter, in ordinary discursive experience of any kind, we find ourselves looking outside the mind. Plotinus contemplates the possibility of entering into these same discursive states with a kind of readjusted gaze, directing the attention inward and looking, not at the visual or conceptual object as situated outside of the intentional state, but at the intentional

---

[40] For some comments that confirm the meditational quality of VI.4.7.23–40, see Armstrong's and Dodd's discussion in *Entretiens Hardt V*, pp. 338–9: (Dodds) "This very striking passage of which Armstrong has reminded us suggests the exercise that are sometimes prescribed for contemplatives: the novice must first visualise an image, then correct it step by step in order to make his contemplation more perfect I have wondered whether Plotinus is not here prescribing such an exercise. One finds similar things in the discipline of the Indian Yogis and I think also sometime in some of the Christian mystics."

structure of the mind, which includes both the subject and the object of knowledge. Once this perspective is adopted, the knower is no longer looking outside of the mind. Gazing outside of the mind, one also gazes into the mind. This metaphor of the transparent world is designed to give the reader some indication of an experience that, although it cannot be viewed as approximating the unity of intellection, is nevertheless a relative unity that can be recalled with respect to intentional states.

Plotinus would have us contemplate not simply visual experience, but the entirety of the objective world – any possible object available for representation – and ask, how is it present to us? The reader, looking simultaneously into his or her own experience and out at the world, interprets the text fully only when thought turns back upon itself. In this respect, these texts may remind us of the identity of word and object that characterizes the kind of speech that Plotinus posits as an ideal philosophical language:

The wise men of Egypt . . . did not use the forms of letters which follow the order of words . . . but by . . . inscribing in their temples one particular image of one particular thing they manifested the non-discursiveness of the intelligible world. (V.8.6, Armstrong's translation)

Not everyone agrees that there may be a self-referential element embedded within this allusion. One scholar, concluding his article with a glance at the Egyptian sages, comments:[41]

This is the prelapsarian language which, had it ever existed, might be recovered to supply the words the mystic lacks. But the passage is poignant precisely because its author knows that such a language signifies only to the wise and that between theirs and ours lies an (almost) unbridgeable chasm.

This assessment of sagacious discourse may leave us with an excessively pessimistic view about the possibility of coming to understand the philosophy of the *Enneads*. For what happens when, in contemplating the visual field as such, the reader is looking into his or her own thought? Surely it could be argued that just this self-awareness is an example of the subject and object of consciousness approach-

---

[41] Alfino 1990.

ing a unity. The transparent world is a metaphor for what is actually present to consciousness, and Plotinus directs us to our own consciousness to discover what he is trying to communicate by means of this image. The exercise that he prescribes is an appreciation of the simultaneous presence of all beings together as a unified objective field for consciousness to experience. This experience of the unity of consciousness, which neither excludes the outside world nor isolates the mental apart from its intentional content, becomes a reference point for the reader as he or she attempts to follow Plotinus in his investigations. Above all, Plotinus would remind us that we can truly enter into the life of philosophy, not by virtue of an individual claim to philosophical expertise, but by virtue of the reality of our essential nature as intellect. For the discovery of this nature, we have to begin in the midst of our own cognitive life.

Pragmatics of Metaphor Reconsidered

Here I commence to argue for a rhetorical reading of the metaphors in the *Enneads* by meeting some methodological objections: are all of Plotinus' metaphors to be read in a strong creative sense, or is only the metaphor of the transparent earth to be so read? Are there any linguistic criteria by which we can justify this reading? I am going to suggest that Plotinus approximates ritual language as a signal to his audience that his metaphors are meant to be creative in the sense outlined earlier.

To capture the ritual features of Plotinus' metaphorical language, we turn briefly to a body of Alexandrian religious literature that antedates the *Enneads,* the *Corpus Hermeticum (CH).*[42] The *CH* is a group of treatises couched as dialogues between Hellenized Egyptian deities (Hermes, Tat, Asclepius/Imhotep, Ammon, and Agathos Daimon, with the addition of Nous, who also functions as an interlocutor) broadly informed by an eclectic mixture of Greek philosophical

---

[42] For a modern English translation of the *CH,* see Brian Copenhaver, *Hermetica: The Greek Corpus Hermeticum and the Latin Asclepius in a new English translation,* with notes and introduction (Cambridge; New York, 1992). For a Critical edition of the text of the treatises II-XII of the *Hermetica,* see *Corpus Hermeticum,* Tome I, Traités II-XII, texte établi par A. D. Nock et traduit par A. Festugière, Septième edition (Paris, 1991).

schools, and framed as either revelatory or initiatory in tone.[43] Much could be said about the possible influences of Hermetic literature in the *Enneads*, given its probable development during the first to third centuries C.E. What especially concerns me is the linguistic marking that designates the dialogic and initiatory aspects of this literature.

In what follows I suggest that there is a dialogic element present in some of the imagistic sequences in the *Enneads* that may recall the Hermetic tradition. Linguistic phenomena such as intimate address, real time intruding upon the narrative voice, the presence of technical prayer formulae or invocations, and the heavy use of epithets as well as anaphora feature significantly in Hermetic initiatory texts. These same elements are self-consciously adopted and prominently displayed in those texts of Plotinus that appropriate the ritualistic milieu of his Alexandrian predecessors. Syntactically, the grammar exhibits a shift from the indicative to the imperative, subjunctive, or optative moods. This shift in the mood of the verb is often accompanied by a shift in the person of the verb, from third to second.[44]

Turning now to a lexical item, in the opening lines of V.8.9, two terms, κόσμος and πᾶν, are used in a way that recalls ascent formulae found within the *Hermetica*.[45] Plotinus' exercises actually recall the hymnic quality of many of the Hermetic ascent sequences, which in the *CH* may appear coupled with an epiphany or declaration of enlightenment on behalf of the student. Such is the case with *CH* XI, an initiatory dialogue between Nous and Hermes, in which Hermes asks for clarification concerning the relationship between God and the universe. The first part of the dialogue is conceived as a hymn by at least some editors, and hence I use Scott's translation and presentation of the opening series of formulae:[46]

⟨ὁ⟩ θεός, ὁ αἰών, ὁ κόσμος ὁ χρόνος, ἡ
γένεσις.
ὁ θεὸς ⟨τὸν⟩ αἰῶνα ποιεῖ,
ὁ αἰὼν δὲ τὸν κόσμον,

---

[43] On the nature and history of Hermetic literature, see Fowden 1986.

[44] Cf. V.1.2.11: λογιζέσθω, σκοπείσθω; V.8.9.2: λάβωμεν; VI.4.7.24: περιθείης.

[45] Cf. Festugière, vol. IV. pp. 156–7.

[46] Walter Scott, *Hermetica.* The ancient Greek and Latin writings which contain religious or philosophical teachings ascribed to Hermes Trismegistus. Introduction, texts, and translation. Vol. I (Boulder. 1982), pp. 206–207, *CH* XI.

ὁ κόσμος δὲ τὸν χρόνον,
ὁ χρόνος δὲ τὴν γένεσιν.

τοῦ δὲ θεοῦ [ὥσπερ] οὐσία ἐστὶ τὸ
ἀγαθόν, [τὸ καλόν, ἡ εὐδαιμονία, ἡ
σοφία,]
τοῦ δὲ αἰῶνος, ἡ ταυτότης,
τοῦ δὲ κόσμου, ἡ τάξις,
τοῦ δὲ χρόνου, ἡ μεταβολή,
τῆς δὲ γενέσεως, ἡ ζωή [καί ὁ
θάνατος].

ἐνέργειαι δὲ τοῦ θεοῦ νοῦς καὶ ψυχὴ,
τοῦ δὲ αἰῶνος, διαμονὴ καὶ ἀθανάσια,[47]
τοῦ δὲ κόσμου, ἀποκατάστασις καὶ
ἀνταποκατάστασις,
τοῦ δὲ χρόνου, αὔξησις καὶ μείωσις,
τῆς δὲ γενέσεως, ποιότης ⟨καὶ
ποσότης⟩.

ὁ οὖν αἰὼν ἐν θεῷ,
ὁ δὲ κόσμος ἐν τῷ αἰῶνι,
ὁ χρόνος ἐν τῷ κόσμῳ,
ἡ δὲ γένεσις ἐν τῷ χρόνῳ.

God, Aeon, Kosmos, Time, Coming-to-be.
God makes the Aeon,
the Aeon makes the Kosmos,
the Kosmos makes Time,
and Time makes Coming-to-be.

The essence of God is the Good,
the essence of the Aeon is sameness,
the essence of the Kosmos is order,
the essence of Time is change,
and the essence of Coming-to-be is life.

The workings of God are mind and soul,
the workings of the Aeon are immortality and duration,
the workings of the Kosmos are
reinstatement in identity and
reinstatement by substitution,
the workings of Time are increase and decrease,
and the workings of Coming-to-be are quality and quantity.

The Aeon then is in God,
the Kosmos is in the Aeon,

---

[47] Following the edition of Nock here.

Time is in the Kosmos,
and Coming-to-be is in Time.

The visionary passage at V.8.9 forms a similar sequence, beginning with the body of the universe, moving on to the cosmos, then to soul, and finally to *nous* or *theos*. Anaphora accentuates the ritualistic element of the texts, so that there is an iconic relationship between the form of the language and its pragmatic function.[48] The sense of transformation is graphically conveyed through the repetition of key words in slightly different collocations, and by the end of the passage, a given image can become the inverse of its initial presentation. For example, in VI.7.12, the vision moves from a tiny point of light to the unbounded light of the sun and, beyond that, to a light that is coextensive with all things. Again, in V.1.2 the adjective ἥσυχος (tranquil) is repeated in a series that begins with the individual body and terminates in the surrounding heavens.[49]

As an example of an ascent text in which these same features are conveyed by an authoritative wisdom voice transmitting instruction in gnosis, we can turn to the roughly contemporaneous Hermetic treatise twelve:

> Gather all of the opposites into yourself, such qualities as fire, water, heat and cold, dry and wet. And realize that you are everywhere at once, in the earth, in the sea, in heaven. You are not yet born, you are in the womb, you are old, a youth, dead, in an afterlife. Realize all of these things simultaneously, all times, places, things, qualities, and you can realize God.[50]

The conceit of the world within the mind is a central element of the Hermetic corpus that becomes the fulcrum of the religious experience promulgated in these texts: rebirth of the self as the world soul.[51]

---

[48] Janowitz 1989, pp. 12–14.

[49] V.1.2.14–20. ἥσυχον δὲ αὐτῇ ἔστω μὴ μόνος τὸ περικείμενον σῶμα καὶ τοῦ σώματος κλύδων, ἀλλὰ καὶ πᾶν τὸ περιέχον ἥσυχος μὲν γῆ, ἥσυχος δὲ θάλασσα καὶ ἀὴρ καὶ αὐτὸς οὐρανὸς ἀμείνων. Let the body now become still for the soul, not just body enveloping [soul] and the body's turmoil, but the entire body that surrounds it. The earth must become still, the sea and sky, and the heaven itself, still greater, must become still (V.1.2.14–17).

[50] *CH* XII, 10b, Scott's translation.

[51] *CH* XIII 11b,: ἐν οὐράνῳ εἰμι, ἐν γῆ, ἐν ὕδατι, ἐν ἀέρι, and *CH* XI 20: καὶ ὁμοῦ πανταχῇ εἶναι, ἐν γῆ, ἐν θαλάττη, ἐν οὐράνῳ, Festugière, vol. IV, p. 143, cites these parallel passages from the *CH*.

The image of the sphere is also frequent in the *Hermetica,* appearing as a cosmic head in more anthropomorphized versions,[52] and elsewhere as the great krater, the cosmic mixing bowl of Plato's *Timaeus,* into which the divine mind has been poured as into a baptismal font.

> He filled a great basin with mind and sent it down to earth; and he appointed a herald and bade him make proclamation to the hearts of men: hearken each human heart; dip yourself in this basin if you can, recognizing for what purpose you have been made, and believing that you shall ascend to him who sent the basin down. (*CH* IV.4, Scott's translation)

By now it should be clear that Plotinus has recast a tradition of gnosis within a framework of classicizing dialectic, thereby developing a unique philosophical dialect that speaks not to different audiences, but rather with varying voices. Pragmatically, these texts are marked as belonging to an initiatory *askesis.*

Conclusion: Metaphor and Metaphysics

I have been discussing the use of metaphor in a highly eclectic and perhaps even syncretistic text. Although the path of least resistance might prompt us to view this text solely within the cultural amalgam of Alexandrian gnosis, there is some merit in viewing the text as Plotinus' unique contribution to a theory about the language of metaphysics and perhaps as a critique of philosophical discourse within the Platonic tradition. I would suggest that Plotinus has attempted to invert the usual relationship that exists between metaphor and metaphysics.

Rather often, critics charge metaphysicians with subverting natural language for their own purposes,[53] inventing a parasitic orthodoxy that thrives at the expense of usual semantic relationships. The language of metaphysics is typically the language of unsaying, of the unseen and insensible. Perhaps Derrida best captures the suspicion that metaphysical discourse arouses precisely because of the meta

---

[52] *CH* X.103, Scott's translation: "Since the kosmos is a sphere, that is to say a head, whatever is connected to the membrane of the head is soul and is by nature immortal."

[53] The critics' number is legion, but I am thinking especially of Wittgenstein, of Derrida, and of Ayer.

phorical subterfuge with which it engages its audience: "Presence disappearing into its own radiance, the hidden source of light, of truth and of meaning, the erasure of the veils of being – such must be the insistent return of that which subjects metaphysics to metaphor."[54] In Platonic metaphysics, Form, or *eidos*, is metaphorized to become precisely the opposite of what it signifies. The *eidos* of an object is no longer what it appears to be, nor can a given Form signify or refer to any object in the world. In this way, Plato constructs a language far removed from the semantics of natural language.

A practical way of envisioning Plotinus' metaphors is to see that they constitute a reversal of the Platonic strategy. Plotinus represents the language of metaphysics as preeminently concrete and as securely grounding its references in that which is immediately accessible. In this respect, he employs what we might term a rhetoric of immediacy, in contrast to the Platonic tendency toward the ontological deferment of meaning.

Occasionally, we catch glimmers of Plotinus' critique of linguistic practices that characterized or even became the hallmark of the prior philosophical tradition. Here for example Plotinus criticizes the Platonic language of abstraction and along with it the entire Platonic dualist ontology.[55] Here Plotinus is quoting Plato's *Timaeus* with respect to the Platonic concept of participation in the Forms.

I am afraid that this manner of speaking is vacuous. What would the words, "far off" or "separate" mean in this context? If not for this way of speaking, there would in turn be no difficulty or puzzle about the concept of participation . . . (VI.5.8.6)

By contrast, Plotinus will sometimes bestow a didactic largesse upon his readers, insisting that they too have access to being, that the universe is but an imbrication of the intelligible forms, and that even the lowest possible mode of consciousness, sense-perception, cannot finally veil higher truths:

If someone is unable to discover the soul in this detached state, first let him grasp the discursive soul, and then ascend from there. But if he cannot even

---

[54] Derrida 1982, p. 268.
[55] For recent work on this passage, as well as on Plotinus' interpretation of Plato's participation metaphor, readers are referred to Strange 1992.

do this, then [let him grasp] the faculty of sense-perception that conveys the intelligibles still more distantly, or even sense-perception by itself (with its faculties) since sense-perception has its nature [determined] by the Forms. (V.3.9.28 ff.)

PART TWO

Text and Tradition in Neoplatonism

6

History of an Enigma: Mathematical Symbolism in the Neoplatonic Tradition

Pythagoreanism, Oral Teachings, and Neoplatonic Textuality

The language of Neoplatonism is the language of symbols. In the next chapters I want to discuss two different systems that are quite pervasive within Neoplatonism: Orphic symbolism and Pythagorean symbolism.[1] These systems are tied together historically, inasmuch as the traditions that their names represent are often conflated among ancient authors. Nevertheless, two distinctive series of metaphors are associated respectively with Orphism and Pythagoreanism. Whereas the Orphic tradition is cosmological (Orpheus sings about the birth of the cosmos, and so narrates a cosmogony), Pythagorean symbolism is essentially nonnarrative and involves mathematical and geometric concepts. Disparate as ways of framing the world, both these systems are central to Neoplatonic texts and become important vehicles through which the Neoplatonists attempt to convey their nondiscursive methodologies.

The thought exercises that have been the subject of the previous pages involve mathematical and geometric symbolism. In this chapter, I show that the history of this symbolism in Neoplatonic texts helps us to enter into a reconstruction of Neoplatonic self-representation precisely because these symbols are so powerfully charged by their historical eminence and also by their traditional weight.[2] Within the history of Platonism, oscillation between a ten-

---

[1] For the connections between Orphism and Pythagoreanism, see Burkert 1972, 125–33; West 1983, 7215, and now Kingsley 1995, pp. 115–16. Kingsley shows that Pythagoreans attributed their own cosmological poems to Orpheus.

[2] Throughout this chapter, my debt to the Gadamer-Habermas debate about tradition

dency to Platonize and a tendency to Pythagoreanize forms the basis of an ongoing dialogue concerning the nature of philosophical purity and authenticity.[3] By engaging with the Pythagorean tradition, the Neoplatonists bring about their own insertion into a tradition that they perceive as primordial or as a pristine form of philosophy. In his introduction to the *Platonic Theology*, Proclus can say:

> All of Greek theology is the child of Orphic mystagogy: Pythagoras was the first to receive initiation from Aglaophamos, Plato in turn received from the Pythagorean and Orphic doctrines perfect knowledge concerning the gods. (Proclus *PT* I.5, 25–26)[4]

This comment at once confirms how important it is for us to understand the Neoplatonist position vis-à-vis Pythagoreanism and underscores the labyrinthine complexity of the Neoplatonic appeal to tradition. Once more, Proclus looks back to Plato as an antecedent for his own appropriation of Pythagoreanism:

> Plato used mathematical language as a cloaking device, casting it as it were over the terms, and [veiling] the true nature of things, just as the Theologians used myths, and Pythagoreans employed symbols for the same purpose. (Proclus *IT* II 246)

Perhaps the scholar who has come closest to understanding and conveying this complexity is O'Meara, whose hypothesis, that Pythagoreanism did not begin to dominate in Platonizing texts until Iamblichus, is certainly a useful guide for charting what we might call the ideological ascendancy of Pythagoreanism within Platonism. As O'Meara tells us:

and its necessary distortions will be obvious. Indeed, I see the Pythagorean-Platonic dichotomy as a textbook case of the difficulties that beset a tradition from within when that tradition defines itself as essentially exegetical or interpretive.

[3] Hierocles' *Commentary on the Golden Verses of Pythagoras* also evinces this strategy. For the topic of tradition switching and the intersection between philosophy and theology, see Saffrey 1992.

[4] Evidently, the importance of Orpheus for the exposition of Platonic theology was under dispute during Proclus' days at the Academy. We read in Marinus' *Vita Procli* that Proclus' teacher, Syrianus, cherished a desire to introduce a formal lecture series, either on the Chaldean Oracles or on the Orphic poems. But Domminos, a colleague of Proclus, favored Orpheus, whereas Proclus favored the Oracles. At any rate, Syrianus' death prevented this course of instruction.

A tendency to Pythagoreanize is common in the history of Platonism and is represented in different forms and to different degrees among Iamblichus' immediate philosophical predecessors, Numenius, Nicomachus of Gerasa, Anatolius, and Porphyry. However, Iamblichus' program to Pythagoreanize Platonic philosophy was more systematic and far-reaching.[5]

According to O'Meara, the Pythagoreanizing tendencies of later Athenian Neoplatonism followed in the trail of Iamblichean innovations. This influence is especially significant in the work of Proclus, who, however, subordinated Pythagoreanism to Platonism contra Iamblichus, while preserving the form of Pythagoreanism by a pseudo-geometrical method in the organization of his *Elements of Theology*. By contrast, for Iamblichus, Plato stripped of historical accidents turns out to be Pythagoras; all that is ancient, pristine, and aboriginal to the Greek tradition belongs in the lineage of Pythagoras. And yet, as O'Meara also acknowledges through his survey of Iamblichus' predecessors, Pythagoreanism was deeply influential in the second and early part of the third centuries as well. Within the *Enneads*, as we shall see, the presence of Pythagorean symbolism is impressive, even imposing.[6]

The question before us is, what purpose is served through this Neoplatonic conceit of pristine wisdom and the Neoplatonic invocation of Pythagoras? To answer this question, we must recognize the competing aspects of Platonizing and Pythagoreanizing as fulfilling different functions within Neoplatonic texts. To frame this tension, it will be helpful to observe that insofar as Neoplatonism is an exegetical tradition, it remains a school that defines itself through its affinity to or even appropriation of privileged texts, that is, the dialogues of Plato. But with the invocation of Pythagoras we have a different authority for this exegetical tradition, one that exists outside the authority of the text, and nevertheless authorizes the text. It would not be an exaggeration to say that Neoplatonism conceives itself as a tradition that is forced to allude to something like the principle of ineffability as the final authority for its exegetical authenticity. Absurd as this may seem at first glance, what the Neopla-

---

[5] O'Meara 1989.
[6] For an earlier but truly encyclopedic history of Pythagorean elements in Neoplatonic texts, cf. Krämer 1964, pp. 292–311. Krämer's earlier work complements that of O'Meara by emphasizing the Middle Platonist and Plotinian expressions of Pythagoreanism.

tonists attempt at all costs is no less than a textual incorporation of the ineffable. For Plotinus and the Neoplatonists, Pythagorean theory becomes an emblem of the non-discursive, perhaps allowing them to improvise a discourse that can thereby escape the dictates of the exegetical tradition. In this sense, the authority extracted from the prestige of these symbols allows an alternative to the authority of the texts themselves. It is this freedom or hermeneutic space occasioned by the appropriation of the Pythagorean elements that now allows for self-reflection, an extended inquiry into the meaning of the tradition, as the remarks of Proclus about the genealogy of Platonism reveal. This genealogical convolution that constitutes one of the most important features of Neoplatonic self-representation should help us to gauge the intricacies involved in the recovery of textual meaning within this tradition as well.

Previously we saw that Proclus' genealogical approach gave us a clue about the hesitations and difficulties that beset the Neoplatonic reception of Plato. Perhaps the anecdotal evidence concerning Plato's oral teachings and their links to the Pythagorean tradition is the first place to look for the origins of this approach. One might turn to the culture of their transmission to learn more about the meaning of these symbols within subsequent stages of the tradition. To trace the path of their deployment is to gain access to the hermeneutic strategies of Neoplatonists, especially that aspect of their hermeneutics that relies on orality or secrecy as an interpretive device. The early history of Pythagorean symbolism, reported in the fragments of Aristotle's lost dialogue, the *Peri Philosophias*, sets the stage for the subsequent appearances of Pythagorean allusions in Neoplatonic texts. As is well known, the *Peri Philosophias* relates the Pythagorean elements of Plato's philosophy to an unwritten doctrine. It is this unwritten doctrine to which the Neoplatonists appeal – a wisdom transmitted outside of the texts – in their own incorporation of Pythagoreanism. For our purposes, we need review only the essential elements reported in this dialogue, much of which is reconstructed from Aristotle's brief descriptions in both the *De anima* and the *Metaphysics* as well as in the Commentator tradition.

From the commentaries, we learn that Aristotle supposedly discussed the Pythagorean teachings that Plato disseminated during his disappointing lecture, "On the Good," in his lost dialogue, *Peri*

Philosophias. For example, Simplicius tells us, in *In De an.*,[7] "The *Peri philosophias* reports the contents of Plato's lecture, "On the Good," from Plato's unwritten teaching, in which he records Pythagorean doctrines and their Platonic interpretation."[8] Aristoxenus gives us a more complete account of the lecture:

Aristotle was wont to relate that most of those who heard Plato's discourse on the Good had the following experience. Each came thinking he would be told something about one of the recognized human goods, such as wealth, health or strength, or some marvelous happiness. But when it appeared that Plato was to talk on mathematics and numbers and geometry and astronomy, leading up to the statement that the good was unity, they were overwhelmed by the paradox of the whole matter. (*Elements of Harmony* II, 30–31, Meibom)

To summarize, we can see that a doxographic tradition associates Plato with an unwritten Pythagorean doctrine according to which the Pythagorean One is identical to the Platonic Good, and this principle together with the source of all multiplicity, the Indeterminate dyad, constitutes the foundation of reality. So much is clear, but after this point the doctrine becomes harder to trace. There seem to be two Pythagorean traditions operating, one a Platonizing tradition that links the primordial number series with a succession of *sxeseis*, or geometric shapes, and one a more strictly arithmetical tradition that does not attribute any spatial dimensions to the primordial numbers.

The fragment of *Peri Philosophias* preserved in the *De anima* tells us that each of the primordial numbers forms a geometric progression, starting with the One, or monad, represented by the point; the two, or dyad, associated with the line; the triad with a plane surface; and the tetrad with the solid.[9] The numerical, the linear, the super-

---

[7] Simplicius *In de an.* 404b18–30: ὁμοίως δὲ καὶ ἐν τοῖς Περὶ φιλοσοφίας λεγομένοις διωρίσθη. Περὶ φιλοσοφίας νῦν λέγει τὰ Περὶ τοῦ ἀγαθοῦ αὐτοῦ ἐκ τῆς Πλάτωνος ἀναγεγραμμένα συνουσίας, ἐν οἷς ἱστορεῖ τάς τε Πυθαγορείους καὶ Πλατωνικὰς περὶ τῶν ὄντων δόξας.

[8] Cf. also Philoponus *In de anima* 404b18, p. 76, Hayduck:
Τὰ Περὶ τἀγαθοῦ ἐπιγραφόμενα Περὶ φιλοσοφίας λέγει. ἐν ἐκείνοις δὲ τὰς ἀγράφους συνουσίας τοῦ Πλάτωνος ἱστορεῖ ὁ Ἀριστοτέλης. ἱστορεῖ οὖν ἐκεῖ τὴν Πλάτωνος καὶ τῶν Πυθαγορείων περὶ τῶν ὄντων καὶ τῶν ἀρχῶν δόξαν.

[9] Aristotle *De anima* 404b16–27:
In the same manner Plato in the *Timaeus* makes the Soul out of the Elements. For like is known by like, and things arise from their Principles. In the same

ficial, and the solid correspond to the primal four numbers, an arrangement also discoverable in the fragments of *Peri Philosophias*, according to which the Living Being of the *Timaeus* is composed out of the One and out of length, breadth, and depth. Sextus Empiricus also reports a tradition in which the four primal numbers correspond to four dimensions: one, two, three, and four points are respectively necessary to make up the monad, the line, the plane, and the solid. Finally, the latter figures are each associated with a mode of intelligence: perceptual, conceptual, intellectual. In the *De anima* passage, we find four species of thought, each associated with a dimension of space: to the point corresponds intellect, to the line corresponds knowledge, to the surface corresponds opinion, and to the solid corresponds sense-experience (nous, *episteme, doxa, aisthesis*).

So much is enough for us to see that there is a tradition associating Plato with what might be called a geometric representation of consciousness and its elements, a form of representation, moreover, that is anecdotally linked to the so-called unwritten doctrines. Fortunately, the goal here is not to establish the truth or falsity of the oral-teachings hypothesis.[10] Rather, the goal is to describe the path of a hermeneutic trajectory that embraces the Neoplatonic reception of Plato, in order to understand Neoplatonic self-representation. The esoteric Plato may or may not have existed, but the fact remains that the traditional attestation to an unwritten doctrine forms a central pillar of Neoplatonism, which fully endorses the paradoxes generated by Plato's written disparagement of writing.[11]

At this point in our story, however, hermeneutic distortions of Pythagorean symbolism begin to surface in the Neoplatonic interpretation. If Aristotle and the Commentator tradition associate Plato's

---

way in the discourse On Philosophy it was laid down that the Living Creature Itself came from the Idea of Unity Itself together with the first Length, Breadth and Depth, and other things in similar fashion. And in yet another fashion they make Mind or Intuition be the One, knowledge the Dyad (since it proceeds in a single line to one point), Opinion the number of the Surface, and Sensation the number of the Solid.

[10] On this controversy, see Findlay 1974 and Krämer 1990, who provides an impressive history of its vicissitudes in the scholarly community from Schleiermacher on.

[11] On this paradox, see of course Derrida's *Dissemination* and also Ferrari, who might be seen as formulating a pragmatist's response to Derrida's prioritization of Platonic writing. Also see Griswold 1988.

Pythagoreanism with an unwritten doctrine, how does such a history authorize the Neoplatonic appropriation of this symbolism in the sense that I have described it, to inform a textual strategy that supposedly invokes the ineffable? What is of interest is precisely that this interpretive distortion enables the Neoplatonists to rewrite the history of their own tradition under the guise of an almost elemental authenticity. The latter, Neoplatonic history of Pythagoreanism, could be accused of either simplicity or duplicity with almost equal justification. In fact, in their enthusiasm for Pythagorean schemas, Neoplatonists seem to forget the iconic nature of these signs and instead attempt to imbue them with an indexical force. In Plotinus' favorite image, for example, the center stands in for the geometer's point, which conceptually takes up no space. Likewise, this entire diagram serves to delineate the space of the intelligible world.

To put it another way, the use of Pythagorean symbolism in the Neoplatonic tradition constitutes something like a denial of the semiotic, despite that it is the most profound indication of the tradition's semiology. If anything, the Neoplatonists seem to hold that the geometric forms they favor overcome the need for semiotic interpretation. They subsist in an immediacy of contact with the reader because they purport to open up a space to which the text grants direct access. In a more modern jargon, one might say that Neoplatonic Pythagoreanism presents itself as phenomenological, as being about the unmediated space of consciousness and not about the tradition presenting or describing that space. Nevertheless, it remains, for all of this, intensely hermeneutic or intersubjective.[12] The history of Pythagoreanism is what allows these symbols to work textually in the way that the Neoplatonists would like them to work.

The Neoplatonists thus refer back to the Platonic tradition of mathematical intermediates (*Republic* 510–511) and thereby situate the mathematical objects in the soul. If soul is number, then by using mathematical imagery the Neoplatonists attempt to point out an interior space. Perhaps one could go so far as to suggest an equation between Pythagorean language and the self-conscious evasion of the discursive. One might fill out this equation in any number of ways, but Plotinus' diagrams involving the forms of point, line,

---

[12] On the differences between hermeneutic and phenomenological approaches to interpretation, see Silverman, chapter 1.

circle, and sphere offer a compelling example. It seems that within these diagrams, Plotinus sketches a geometry of perception, or of awareness more generally. At times these diagrams seem to schematize consciousness itself, as if offering a kind of ancient emblem for something like Hegel's *Phenomenology of Spirit.*

Plotinus and the Geometric Representation of Self-Reflection

For the sake of clarity, often the argument wishes to lead to a conception of the multiplicity which has come to be, by positing many lines from one center. (*Enneads* VI.5.5)

The opening lines of the fifth chapter of treatise VI.5 present us with some evidence about Plotinus' use of geometric symbolism in his philosophic enterprise: he frequently has recourse to a geometric representation of reality. This observation is confirmed by other internal evidence within the corpus of the *Enneads*, where the geometric representation described in this chapter recurs in an expanded format over a dozen times and, in brief compass, in at least a dozen more. Plotinus employs the diagram of a center, surrounded by one or more concentric circles, to represent the hypostatic view of reality. The One is symbolized by the center, and each of the circles stand respectively for nous and soul.[13]

Why and how did Plotinus develop his conception of the intelligible universe as rings of light around a central point? This system seems to compete within the *Enneads* themselves with another system that describes the One as a monad, intellect as the indefinite dyad, and soul as number or multiplicity.[14] Certainly, many of Plotinus' descriptions of the intelligible world are fundamentally borrowed from the world of mathematics or geometry, despite his being reputed not to have engaged in mathematical speculation per se.

The basic diagram that Plotinus employs is the simple model of a

---

[13] Again, one could easily cite any number of similar passages: "For there is a kind of center, and around this a circle shining out from it, and beyond these another light from light (IV.3.17.12), or "Lifting ourselves up by that part of ourselves not immersed in the body, with this we fasten our own centers to the center of all things, as if the centers of the great circles [are the same as] the center of the entire sphere that encompasses them. There we are at rest" (VI.9.8.19–21).

[14] On this competing arithmetical system, see Krämer 1990 and 1964.

center surrounded by one or more concentric circles, with radii projecting from the center to the circumference of these circles. The terminal points of the radii form the circumference of the circles and the lines described by the radii fill up the surface of the circles surrounding the center. The geometric figures representing the hypostases are often described by means of mathematical images: just as are numbers, these images are conceived of as generating, multiplying, being added and subtracted. In this system of imagery the basic Plotinian conception of deriving all things from unity takes on a literal character as a process of metaphysical subtraction and addition.[15]

This image of a radiant circle, a spider's web or vortex of possibility, a matrix of becoming, is repeated throughout the *Enneads* as a kind of visionary siglum, an index that Plotinus is reverting to an ancient wisdom whose voice can be heard only in the reverberations of a symbol that carries with it the aspect of authenticity. The image of the radiant circle is for Plotinus an emblem of visionary truth. Layer upon layer of meaning is woven into the fabric of the image. The details of its mathematical transformations are conveyed often by means of imperatives that seem at once precise and formulaic: remove, add, contract, subtract. This same language of mathematics surrounds Plotinus' descriptions of the emergence of the second hypostasis, as is well known.[16] Plotinus refers to the inchoate nous as the indefinite,[17] or as pure indefiniteness (*aoristia, apeiria, apeiron*), and incorporates the Pythagorean symbolism of monad and dyad as elements within his account of ontological proliferation:

Therefore this multiple intellect, when it wishes to intelligize that which is beyond, wishes to intelligize that itself as one, but wishing to apprehend it in its simplicity emerges continually grasping something else multiplied in itself.(V.3.11.1–4)

Before the Dyad is the One, and the Dyad is second and from the One, that has it as something indefinite, but this is indefinite of itself. It is otherness, movement, desire, and life. (V.1.5.6)

---

[15] Cf. also *Enneads* V.8.9.11; VI.2.4.13; VI.5.12.18.
[16] Readers interested in the topic of geometric symbolism and its applications in the derivational theory of Plotinus' metaphysics should consult Bussanich 1988 and the references Bussanich cites.
[17] Cf. VI.7.17.25: ἓν ὡρίσθη; VI.7.17.15: ἀόριστος ἦν, βλέψασα δ ἐκεῖ ὡρίζετο; V.4.2.6: ἀόριστον καὶ ἄπειρον.

A glance at any number of contemporaneous Pythagoreanizing texts easily settles the issue of Plotinus' reliance on Pythagoreanism.[18] The concept of emanation from the point flowing into a line is found in Sextus Empiricus,[19] and Theon of Smyrna (*Expositio* 27, 1 ff.) also confirms the Pythagorean background of Plotinus' language in describing the inchoate nous when he writes: "the principle of number is the monad that itself seeks out the dyad, or Otherness, which it brings about by replicating itself."[20]

Yet what are these pictures for Plotinus, ultimately? Plotinus purposefully associates his doctrines with particular images that possess an undeniable cultural prestige and immediately invoke an entire philosophical milieu. At the very least, this practice serves as a kind of textual mnemonics that brings to mind the ambiguous status of the text itself. This ambiguity is captured by the very appearance of a symbol that is associated with an explicit doctrinal content but that serves as well to disrupt the text. One scholar, speculating on the qualitatively different forms of textuality presented by these images, remarks:

The glyphs, however, are not merely the passive objects of this hermeneutic, but are also the constituents of the very exegetical methodology itself. If individual hieroglyphic words reveal essences, we might say that the total field of operation of the glyphs and their interrelations constitutes a kind of grammar of essences. The glyphs teach the very process of their own decipherment. Taken together, they reveal a system of acquiring knowledge both about them and through them.[21]

The central Neoplatonic metaphor for self-recollection or self-knowledge, reversion, is graphically captured in these diagrams. To understand Plotinus' obsession with the relationship of the center to the periphery of the circle, we must translate into our own language of self-reflection and see that, through this diagram, Plotinus means to describe certain aspects of the relationship between consciousness and its objects. The knower – the point – is hidden, unseen, even

---

[18] Porph. *In cat.* 118, 24; Alex. *In met.* 768, 25 ff.; Proc. *Tim.* I, p. 78 24e.

[19] Emp. III 19, 28, 77; VII (*Adv. dogm*) 99; *Ad. math.* IX 380, 381.

[20] ἡ γὰρ ἀρχὴ τὴν ἀριθμῶν... ἡ μονάς... τὴν ἑτερότητα ζητοῦσα τὴν δυάδα... τῷ αὐτῆς διπλασιασμῷ ἐποίησε.

[21] Peter Lamborn Wilson in *Alexandria* 3, "Speaking in Hieroglyphs" (Grand Rapids, 1995). Wilson uses the word "glyph" not to refer to hieroglyphs, but to refer to just these textual images.

buried or lost within the field constituted by the objects of awareness. Plotinus' geometry of recollection suggests the recovery of the knower from beneath the overwhelming presence of the objective side of reality. When Plotinus describes intellectual activity as reversion or epistrophe, he seems to invoke the priority of the knower over any of its cognitive objects. For Plotinus, the image of the sphere signifies reflexive self-knowledge:

> If then our circles were bodily, not soul-circles, they would be in touch with the center at a place; the center would be in some place and they would be around it; but since the souls themselves belong to the realm of Intellect and the One transcends Intellect, we must suppose that the contact takes place by other powers, in the way in which the thinker is naturally united to the thought . . . (VI.9.8.20–21)

This reflexivity of consciousness, if it is signified through Plotinus' geometry of reflection, is most importantly a dialectical stance inculcated in or offered to the reader. Although this reflexive viewpoint entails a metaphysical order into which the subject's identity perhaps collapses or disappears, Plotinus' metaphor is a dynamic model in which the fulcrum of consciousness is preserved throughout. Indeed, it would seem that Plotinus here adopts the strategy of underdetermining or saying as little as possible about the nature of the reality that embraces or pervades this reflexive moment. The thought experiments that Plotinus engages in do not specify an entity that can be picked out by means of this dialectical position, as this or as that.[22] As was said earlier, the most that such a "witness" self, or subject of consciousness, would have to say for itself would be, "am, am," or "I, I."[23]

Mathematics gives access to the notion of a spaceless and timeless

---

[22] For this reason, Plotinus' reflexive self does imply the contradictions entailed by the notion of a transcendent entity, or "thing that thinks." In other words, that which thinks, for Plotinus, is surely not a thing. Rather than offering the reader a kind of false door behind the limits of phenomena, Plotinus is interested in a form of apprehension that does not instantiate this reflexivity, but consists in a way of seeing that may be either embraced or rejected according to the proclivity of the person seeing. For the inherent contradictions in the Cartesian subject of consciousness as transcendent substance, see the extended discussion by Zizek 1993, chapter 1, "The Void Called Subject."

[23] *Enneads* V.3.10.36.

generation precisely because it is empirically obvious that this interior form of addition and subtraction does not affect or give rise to an exterior space or world. Mathematics allows the Platonist to confront a universe that is nevertheless wholly immaterial. This acosmic aspect of geometric symbolism circumvents the question of cosmology and with it, the question of the origins of the exterior world. Instead, the mathematics of timeless generation leaves room for everyone to function as the supreme mathematician. It is by subtracting and adding elements to our world that we come to participate in the genesis of vision. In this sense, the symbols that Plotinus uses are meant to carry the force of self-exegesis within them.

The Interior World and the Geometry of Recollection

Although it is difficult to reconstruct the meaning and purpose of the geometric diagrams in the *Enneads*, a speculative interpretation that points to parallels in the Hermetic tradition and its subsequent history at least suggests that these diagrams can be associated with the process of self-recollection. A parallel text from the *Corpus Hermeticum* can allow us more fully to discuss Plotinus' apparent interest in using the faculty of imagination as a kind of analogy for intellect. What I hope to show is that both Plotinus and the *Corpus Hermeticum* point the reader toward a conception of interiority in which the experience of imaginative production functions as a kind of middle ground or even metaphor for the self-reflexive nous.

In particular, certain of the *Hermetica* present a set of imaginative exercises that form the substance of an initiatory dialogue between teacher and disciple. As in the *Enneads*, so also within these texts, we observe a dialectical stance that operates at the level of a shared convention – the convention of active imagination, or structured fantasy. *Corpus Hermeticum* XI, for example, presents us with an initiatory sequence in which nous itself attempts to reveal its nature by prescribing a meditation, not on some specific imaginary object, but on the imagination as the object. Nous attempts to resituate the student with respect to the world by referring to the imagination and so says, "in incorporeal imagination things are located differently" (*CH XI*, 18). In the same dialogue, the self-revealing nous goes on to develop this notion of interior space, again emphasizing features of the imagination within this dialectics of transformation:

19. Consider this yourself: command your soul to travel to India, and it will be there faster than your command. Command it to cross over to the ocean, and again it will quickly be there, not as having passed from place to place, but simply as being there . . . 20. See what power you have, what quickness![24]

For subsequent interpreters of the Hermetic tradition, Pythagorean symbolism was thought to involve a technique of meditation in which the imagination figured heavily. The Renaissance Hermeticists elaborated a method for bringing about an imaginary world, claiming "that, in its approximation, this world was an imperfect equivalent of realities existing on an ontological level inaccessible to direct experience."[25] It is of some interest that the Renaissance Platonists also found this same self-reflexive pedagogy operating in the texts of the *Hermetica*, and that they associated the *Corpus Hermeticum* with their spiritualized art of memory.[26] The briefest glance at the Renaissance memory work can in turn provide a useful way to frame this tradition of imaginative pedagogy in the subsequent history of Neoplatonism.[27] Giordano Bruno, for example, places the Hermetic idea of the human microcosm who is able to contain the macrocosm, at the center of his occult memory work. In his visionary work, *Seals*, he writes, "As the world is said to be the image of God, so Trismegistus does not fear to call man the image of the world."[28] Yates, in her brilliant presentation of Camillo's Theater of Memory, discusses the Hermetic conception of the microcosm in the form of Camillo's claim that he is able to remember the universe by "looking down on it from above." As Yates says, "The microcosm can fully understand and fully remember the macrocosm, can hold it within his divine memory."[29]

Readers of Yates's pivotal work will perhaps recall Camillo's design for a cosmic 'Theater of Memory' – essentially, a composite surface designed to help the practitioner reflect the talismanic images employed in Renaissance magic. That the Hermetists derived or falsely

---

[24] *Corpus Hermeticum* XI, 19 and 20, Copenhaver translation.
[25] Garin 1960.
[26] See, most importantly, Yates 1966 and Garin 1961.
[27] For two much deeper treatments of the topic of imagination as a prelude to intellect, see Charles and Moutsopoulos.
[28] Bruno, *Seals*, pp. 129–30, translated and quoted in Yates 1966, p. 254.
[29] Yates 1966, p. 148.

imputed these images to Egyptian astrological works demonstrates their enthusiasm for an ancient mode of inducing vision as the expansion of a cosmic memory. As Yates points out in her magisterial work:

Such inner, or imaginative, use of talismanic imagery, would surely find a most suitable vehicle for its use in the occultised version of the art of memory. If the basic memory images used in such a memory system had, or were supposed to have, talismanic power, power to draw down the celestial influences and spiritus within the memory, such a memory would become that of the "divine" man in intimate association with the divine powers of the cosmos. And such a memory would also have, or be supposed to have, the power of unifying the contents of memory by basing it upon these images drawn from the celestial world. The images of Camillo's theater seem to have in them something of this power, enabling the "spectator" to read off at one glance, through "inspecting the images" the whole contents of the universe. . . . In this way, the cosmically based memory would be supposed, not only to draw power from the cosmos into the memory, but to unify memory. (Yates p. 155)

Once more, to invoke yet another Renaissance Hermetist's interest in the imagination, we can turn to the fifteenth-century translator and philosopher Marsilio Ficino. As Eugenio Garin tells us, Ficino's conception of philosophy as essentially initiatory involves the privileged place of the Hermetic writings in his own system. Ficino describes a method of intellectual ascent through the invocation of an imaginal vision. This vision was to be cultivated through intense meditation on the so-called *figurae* of the soul, that is, on the soul's own imaginary constructions. These Hermetists translate the Platonic notion of the "eye of the soul" (*Phaedrus* 247) into the faculty of the imagination, or *oculus Imaginationis*. This inner eye provides a glimpse into the nature of the intellect because it reveals an interior world and hints at the vast expanse of the soul itself.

It is important to observe that even within this historically remote tradition, the geometric representations used by the Hermetists in their memory work are meant to coincide with a technique of self-reflection. To this extent, the images are not systematic. Rather, for the Hermetists they are more deitic. They indicate a textual sleight of hand and are meant to suggest an anti-discursive or, rather, an interior, space. Present within the imagination, they both permeate this ground and, by calling attention to it, illuminate it after a fashion.

Hence it becomes appropriate to ask how the Neoplatonists make use of this space that opens up underneath the gaze of the subject in their own work on images and the faculty of the imagination. Once more this question surfaces when we turn to look at the fifth-century philosopher Proclus, who is arguably one the strongest proponents of what can be called a Neoplatonic geometry of recollection.

Geometry and Theurgy in Proclus and Iamblichus

Much work has already been done on Proclus' use of mathematics, on his cognitive theory of the imagination, and on the pervasiveness of mathematical or geometric analogies in Proclan metaphysics.[30] Thus for readers familiar with the work of Beierwaltes or of Moutsopoulos, the discussion that follows will provide perhaps no more than a gloss on the work of these scholars. Nevertheless, since we are tracing the history of interpretation, looking for the hermeneutic pathway of Neoplatonism, it is important to summarize Proclus' work on the geometric tradition, insofar as it reflects the non-discursive pedagogies embedded within the the larger exegetical enterprise of the Neoplatonists.

Proclus' *Commentary on the First Book of Euclid's Elements* is probably the most important ancient source for charting the Neoplatonic reconciliation of Platonic mathematical pedagogy, as outlined in Plato's *Republic*, and the neo-Pythagorean arithmology as celebrated, for example, in such texts as Nichomachus of Gerasa's *Theology of Arithmetic*. Proclus actually attaches two distinct prefaces to his Commentary; the first attempts to argue for the role of mathematics in the education of the understanding, and the second contains a more loosely argued history of geometry, emphasizing especially its significance in the Platonic curriculum.[31] Although Proclus does refer extensively to classical works, including the *Republic*'s doctrine of mathematical intermediaries as well as to the *De anima*'s doctrine of the imagination as passive intelligence, he also insinuates a seemingly more original geometry of recollection, first adumbrated

---

[30] Cf. Beierwaltes 1965, part II, "Kreis," pp. 165–217. Again, Moutsopoulos 1985.
[31] See also the much fuller discussion of Proclan mathematical symbolism in Charles-Saget 1982.

in Chapter III of his second preface (*IE* 62).[32] Here he suggests that geometry is not necessarily confined to the sublunar world and that the figures that count as its subject matter do not belong solely to the world of the material imagination. In fact, geometry as a science is "coextensive with all existing things, applies its reasonings to them all, and includes all their kinds in itself" (*IP* 62, 1–2). Hence it is capable of teaching us "through images the special properties of the divine orders" (*IP* 62, 5–6).

Behind this rather grandiose, for a Platonist, claim about the scope of geometry lies Proclus' theory of the imagination, which builds on the Platonic and Aristotelian models but again strikes out in a very original direction as evidenced in the Euclid commentary and elsewhere. To briefly review the central features of his theory of imagination, we find Proclus here suggesting that the imagination is a kind of intermediate ground between soul and intellect. In one passage, Proclus describes this intermediary function as a faculty that is capable of reflecting, by means of spatial realizations or renderings, the abstract ideas present in the discursive intellect.

For this is the reason also he [Euclid] gives his work the subtitle "plane geometry." And thus we must think of the plane as projected and lying before our eyes and the understanding as writing everything upon it, the imagination becoming something like a plane mirror to which the ideas of the understanding send down impressions of themselves. (*IE* 12.11–6)

This psychic space functions as a mirror and as a window to the intelligible space upon which the soul borders. But the imagination is, as it were, a two-way mirror; herein lies the innovation to be found in Proclus' theory of the imagination. Earlier we saw that the imagination translates the language of the ideas into a kind of pictogram, thus making it possible for the embodied soul to comprehend geometrical properties. Additionally, however, this same faculty of imagination also directs the soul's attention inward, away from its own representations.

Therefore just as nature stands creatively above the visible figures, so the soul, exercising her capacity to know, projects on the imagination, as on a mirror, the ideas of figures; and the imagination, receiving in pictorial form these impressions of the ideas within the soul, by their means affords the

---

[32] All quotes are from the Morrow translation (Morrow 1992).

soul an opportunity to turn inward from the pictures and attend to herself.
(*IE* 141)

Geometry in this sense becomes a form of self-disclosure: "as if a man looking at himself in a mirror should wish to look upon himself directly" (*IE* 141, 10). Thus in his own interpretations of the geometric figures of point, line, circle, and sphere, Proclus discovers a path of intellectual reversion that operates by means of a contemplative geometry. Proclus' geometry of cognition emphasizes the reflexivity of consciousness, its ability to recover its own origins through an investigation of this interior world. It seems to be something like an art of memory to which Proclus refers when he interprets the Pythagorean geometric tradition in his *Commentary on Euclid's Elements*. Here we find him meditating on the reflexive powers of the imagination:

[the soul] wants to enter within herself to see the circle and the triangle, there, all things without parts and all in one another, to become one with what she sees and enfold their plurality, to behold the secret and ineffable figures in the inaccessible places and shrines of the gods. (*IE* 141.22)

Proclus then links this geometry of self-recollection to the method of intellectual ascent, as when, for example, he discusses the series of objects that can be traced initially from the image of the circle:

Clearly then the self-moved figure is prior to that which is moved by another; the partless is prior to the self moved; and prior to the partless is the figure which is identical with unity. For all figures attain consummation in the Henads, the source from which they all entered into being (*IE* 142.2–5).

Proclus sees this kind of interior vision as a path to unity, proceeding from the act of unifying the mind by means of the imagination and then developing toward what might be described as an ever-deeper self-expansion within the horizons of interior vision. Although we find this extraordinary passage in his *Commentary on Euclid's Elements*, Proclus informs us that this geometry of vision belongs to the Pythagorean tradition when he writes, "we have drawn out at great length these matters of the Pythagorean doctrine."[33]

[33] For a much more thorough discussion of Proclan metaphysics and its relation to Iamblichan Pythagoreanizing, see the groundbreaking work of O'Meara, especially the chapter entitled "Proclus on Mathematics," section 8, "The Method of Geometry," pp. 171–73. O'Meara points out that Proclus in fact diverges from the Iam-

The circle then does not equate with a symbol in the sense of an image connected to a discursive series, but remains a symbol connected to a form of unitive vision. As such, it becomes in Proclus' hands an emblem of a non-discursive, or unitive, way of knowing. Proclus says later in the same work,

> If you divide bodiless things into soul and Nous, you will say that the circle has the character of nous, the straight line that of soul. That is why the soul, as she reverts to nous, is said to move in a circle. . . . Again, if you distinguish body and soul, you will put everything that is body on the side of the straight line and make everything psychical partake of the identity and homogeneity of the circle. (*IE* 147.15)

Elsewhere in his works, Proclus conceives of the circle especially as an icon of self-knowledge:

> To intelligent beings the circle gives the power of being continuously active in relation to themselves, enabling them to be filled with knowledge from their own store, to assemble the intelligibles in themselves and perfect their insights from within. For nous always gives itself the object of its thought, and this object, is as it were its center. (*IT* II 148)

Werner Beierwaltes, too, in his pioneering study of the geometric imagery employed by Proclus and Plotinus, develops an interpretation of this imagery that emphasizes its association with the non-discursive.[34] For Beierwaltes, the geometry of the radiant circle refers primarily to "thinking that thinks itself," or, in his words, to "the self-transparency of thought concerning the assimilation of the individual thought objects in itself to a reflexive oneness."[35] According to this commentator, this geometry of perception describes the transformation of the subject-object relationship within the act of knowing, involving a successful circumvention of the disruptive moment of intentionality.[36] The play of movement from center to periphery

---

blichean tradition that privileges arithmetic (a tradition that produced such works as the *Theologoumena Arithmetica*). Proclus reverts to a more Platonic emphasis on geometry, particularly working with the *Republic*'s assignment of a mediatory role to geometry (*Republic* 510b–511b, cited by O'Meara).

[34] This chapter can in no way do justice to the complexity and detail of Beierwaltes's magisterial study, to which we owe so much of what we know about Neoplatonic methodology.

[35] Beierwaltes 1965.

[36] For a discussion of intentionality and the Neoplatonic circumvention of intentionality, see above chapters 3 and 4.

traces the path of an "intuitive seeing without opposition and [alludes] to an oxymoronic not seeing."[37] By remetaphorizing the notion of epistrophe, the circle embodies or even becomes a kind of literal configuration of the non-discursive, a consummate emblem of self-knowledge:

The circle is an image of intellect, for it remains within and proceeds with its generated powers and turns toward itself in the gnosis that grasps itself equally in all directions. (*In Rem.* II 46, 18–21)

Finally, this geometric symbolism develops into an almost Hermetic meditation on the macrocosm, as not just the mind but the world itself is described as turning in the circle of intellect: "the world is the same as the eye and its vision and the ear and its object and the one *aisthesis* knows all things in itself" (*IT* II 85, 17–19). This world that is directly experienced as the content of soul is revealed in the imagination. Meditating on the world within the mind brings about a unified memory or awareness that seems to move about the soul as self-mover and lures that soul ever deeper into the stretches of its own infinity. In one way, awareness is like a line that projects from a center, stretching outward from the source of awareness, and in another way, the mind encloses itself and turns back on itself as Proclus is fond of telling us, like a living dance. As Beierwaltes says: "in the circular return and procession the soul transforms itself, becomes and takes back what it lost in the dimensions of time and otherness."[38]

For Beierwaltes, the dance of the soul about its center expresses the freedom and expansiveness that comes with a more developed sense of the interior. There is a detachment of consciousness, a separation of the soul from its objects. This same imagery of the soul's dance of awareness appears in the *Enneads*, where the experience of unity is likened to a circle or circumference with all the radii entirely filled in. The mnemonics of the self, the geometry of perception that describes and inscribes the space of consciousness, is a central part of Neoplatonic methodology. The space that arises within this sort of meditation functions as a counter space or interiority that balances one's experience of being immersed within the

---

[37] Beierwaltes 1965.
[38] Beierwaltes 1965.

world of objects. And yet, for all of this imagery's persuasive power, one must never lose sight of the fact that it is surrounded by paradox. It tells us of an expanse that has no dimensions and, paradoxically, of a knowing that knows no object. This constant meditation on the paradox of subjectivity and its transformation by what is apparently a geometry of recollection might appear repetitive, naive, or just impossible to the reader of today. But it comprises one of the richest and most expressive moments within the Neoplatonist language of vision.

This discussion of geometric symbolism, particularly the image of the sphere, has certainly not done justice to the rich Pythagorean tradition (or neo-Pythagorean tradition) that we find proliferating in the texts of Plotinus, Proclus, and Iamblichus. Nor have I even touched on the historical connections that link Proclus, for example, to the Pythagorean tradition, via Iamblichus (whose own work has been recently shown to reflect the neo-Pythagorean thought of Nichomachus).[39] Nevertheless, it is at least plausible to suggest that the arithmetic and the geometric function as very different conceptual systems, at any rate for Proclus.[40] Indeed, Proclus tells us as much in his *Commentary on the Timaeus*, where in a digression on the chiastic shape of the soul, he distinguishes between two different ways of representing reality, the arithmetic and the geometric (*IT I* 243).

In this same section, Proclus goes on to make his rather wellknown remark, that "Plato used mathematics as a method of concealing the true reality, just as the Theologians used myth, and the Pythagoreans used symbols." Since number represents division and is based primarily on the monad, and geometry represents continuity and is based primarily on the point, these two methods of describing reality are complementary: the soul partakes both in the discreet and the continuous. Perhaps hidden in these remarks Proclus suggests that the geometric method of representation can offer a clearer image of unity than the arithmetic method.[41] What is important for

---

[39] Again, see O'Meara's book for this fascinating bit of detective work linking Iamblichus and Nichomachus.

[40] O'Meara of course makes this very point in his chapter on Proclus and mathematics.

[41] Cf. also, Trouillard 1983, p. 234, cited in Shaw 1995, p. 195.

us is the singular contribution that this unique deployment of Pythagoreanism makes to Proclus' own articulation of a non-discursive methodology that is trapped so completely by the world and space of the texts it purports to overshadow. In the conclusion to this chapter, we turn briefly to the theurgic tradition. So far, I have been arguing that the Neoplatonic tradition shapes itself through appropriation of elements that accentuate its own emphasis on wisdom outside of texts. Self-recollection, non-discursive thinking, reflexive consciousness, and imaginal projection – all of these are tags that apply to the function of Pythagorean symbolism as found in the Neoplatonic context. And yet the ritual affiliations of this kind of symbolism outweigh its textual deployment. In other words, for the later Neoplatonists especially, mathematics forms part of theurgic operations.[42] To the extent that Proclus makes use of Pythagorean elements, he alludes to a pristine tradition and perhaps also suggests that these same elements possess a power that surpasses the intellectual context in which he presents them:

The unifying numbers, in themselves are unknowable. For they are more ancient than Beings and more unified than Forms, and since they are the generators of Forms they exist prior to those beings we call 'intelligibles.' The most august of theurgies demonstrate this, since they make use of numbers capable of acting ineffably, and by means of them, they effect the greatest and most ineffable of operations. (*PT* IV, 100.21–101)

Walter Burkert has pointed out the ritualistic dimensions of the Pythagorean Tetrakys, suggesting that the theurgical dimensions of number theory are a conscious replacement for traditional ritualism:

The Tetrakys, a "tetrad" made up of unequal members, is a cryptic formula, only comprehensible to the initiated. The word inevitably reminds of Trikys, the "triad" of different sacrificial animals. Is the sacrificial art of the seer, involving the shedding of blood, superseded by a "higher" bloodless secret?[43]

The ritual associations with Pythagorean mathematics are also seen in the Iamblichean formula, according to which the human being is made up of two numbers:

---

[42] For an extremely penetrating account of mathematics and theurgy, see Shaw 1995.
[43] Burkert, 1972, p. 187, quoted in Shaw 1995, p. 198.

For since animals are made up of soul and body, the Pythagoreans say soul and body are not produced from the same number, but soul from cubic number and body from the irregular volume.

As Shaw points out, the word *bomikos* (irregular volume) also describes the shape of an altar, and the very idea of volume seems to have had a role to play in the Chaldean conception of geometry. Lewy explains the Oracle, "do not deepen the plane,"[44] as referring to the successive stages of embodiment or material manifestation of reality. Thus the pyramid represents the first body, and, according to Lewy,

The number three is in the Oracles the measure of the noetic and therefore the purport of the Oracular warning is that the mortal should not "materialize his mental substance by extension into the realm of the somatic."[45]

The theurgic association with mathematics again forms part of the hermeneutic circle that we have been tracing with regard to the interpretation of Neoplatonic symbols.

Iamblichus venerated Pythagorean teaching as the source of a philosophical *askesis* designed to purify the mind; he also associated mathematics with forms of traditional psychology and worship. According to Iamblichus, Plato's successors identify the soul with number: Speusippus taught that the soul was a geometrical figure, Xenocrates that soul was a number, and Moderatus, a mathematical harmony.[46] Again, in the *Life of Pythagoras*, Iamblichus states that Pythagoras "practiced a marvelous divination and worship of the Gods according to the numbers most allied to them"(*VP* 147).

In chapter 22 of *On the Common Mathematical Science*, Iamblichus explains the significance of the Pythagorean tradition.[47] In this chapter, he speaks of a "mathematical *askesis*," aimed at the refinement of thought and purification of knowledge, affording human beings

---

[44] Hans Lewy, "Chaldean Oracles and Theurgy," pp. 394–6. Quoted by Shaw 1995. Cf. also Majericik.

[45] Lewy, p. 396. Quoted in Shaw, p. 210.

[46] Stobaeus I 364, 2–23. Referred to in Shaw's 1997 AAR paper, "Eros and Arithmos."

[47] "One must investigate the [origins of] the Pythagorean tradition. We propose to treat its precepts as fundamental elements, for the purpose of learning from them the symbolic and exotic meaning of mathematical expressions" (*DCMS* 22, p. 67, Festa).

an inner peace and harmony with the larger universe and leading finally to the apprehension of true reality.[48] The sphere is particularly venerated as a symbol of deity, since it "is both itself one and capable of containing multiplicity, which indeed makes it truly divine, in that while not departing from its oneness it dominates all the multiple."[49] Recently, Gregory Shaw has suggested that the sphere might have been the center of a theurgic rite or rites.[50] We know from the *De Mysteriis* that Iamblichus distinguished between grades or ontological levels of offering, levels that corresponded with the aspirant's predominant habits of self-identification, whether material, emotional, mental, or intellectual. In the *De Mysteriis*, Iamblichus treats in some detail the theory behind the theurgists' use of the ritual objects, or *symbola*, which lend efficacy to the rite. Nevertheless, he refrains from discussing procedures associated with theurgy practiced at the highest levels, for souls essentially identified with the intelligible order. Without wishing to repeat Shaw's careful discussion of Iamblichean mathematical theurgy, I think it important to cite his conclusions, since they shed a great deal of light on the traditional notion of a *symbolon*.

Briefly then, according to Iamblichus, theurgic ritual involves installing the deity in a receptacle (*hypodoche*), or *symbolon*, appropriate to the god. By connecting through ritual to this receptacle, the worshipper actually attains union with the god invoked: "the theurgic art discovers receptacles adapted to each of the gods" (*DM* 233). Because the goal of the rite is union with the god, part of its success depends on the displacement of self, or projection onto the receptacle. That is, the worshipper must somehow identify with the deity through the medium of the *symbolon*.

Perhaps concentration on an imaginary *symbolon* by fully absorbing one's attention in the object could be considered, in this sense, a form of theurgic worship, a displacement of self onto the symbol that leads to a unitive awareness. We saw earlier that Plotinus used the sphere in connection with an invocation or Cletic prayer to nous

---

[48] *DCMS* 22, p. 69, Festa.

[49] *In Timaeum* frag. 49, 27–29, in *Iamblichi Chalcidensis in Platonis dialogos commentariorium fragmenta*, translation and commentary by John Dillon (Leiden: Brill, 1973).

[50] Shaw's 1997 AAR paper, "Eros and Arithmos."

and that Proclus discusses the sphere in the soul's ascent to the intelligible order:

[the soul] wants to enter within herself to see the circle and the triangle there, all things without parts and all in one another, *to become one with what she sees* . . . (italics mine) (*IE* 141)

Becoming one with what the soul sees is the essence of non-discursive thinking. This dimension of theurgic worship, the displacement of a separate self that initially confronts the object of worship as external or as outside the self, relies on an erotic identification with the object for its completion. This identification comes about through an expansion of the boundaries of the self, a willingness to remove the veil of separation that distinguishes soul and deity. And this identification is represented in the Platonic-Pythagorean teaching that soul is a number.

Other references to theurgic worship are found in more theoretical texts, particularly in the Late Athenian Academy. Proclus and Damascius often allude to theurgic worship in the course of distinguishing different grades or stages of noesis. For example, they frequently cite verses from the Chaldean Oracles, a collection of fragments supposedly divinely revealed to Julian the Theurgist in the second century. The verses, written in hexameters, reflect a Middle Platonic theology akin to that of Numenius but also make use of a number of distinctions that become important for the later Athenian Neoplatonists, such as the triadic structures contained within the second hypostasis.[51] Damascius quotes fragment 1 in his chapter on the Unified (the third element of his Intelligible Triad) in his *Doubts and Solutions Concerning First Principles*. Here, in the midst of a technical discussion concerning the nature of the intelligible object, Damascius quotes the following verses:

There is something intelligible, which you should know in the flower of the intellect.

If you turn your own intellect toward it and know it as an object, then you will not know it.

---

[51] Standard editions of the Chaldean Oracles include *Oracles Chaldaïques*, ed. E. de Places (Paris: Belles Lettres, 1971). There is also an excellent English edition, *The Chaldean Oracles*, with translation and commentary by R. Majercik (Leiden: Brill 1989).

I ask you to know this without strain; turn back the sacred eye of your soul and bring the empty mind into the intelligible, until you comprehend it, since it is outside the intellect. (C-W I.105.3–5; 9–13; *Or. Ch.* Fr. 1)

This verse comes up when Damascius is discussing the problem of idealism or subjectivism in terms of how it might weaken the Neoplatonic identity thesis. His central question in this chapter is, how can we speak of knowing as a relationship that exists between the mind, on the one hand, and an object that is said to be unified (that is, unified with the mind), on the other. The identity thesis, if it posits this unity between mind and object, seems to disassemble itself from within, since how can this relationship obtain between two unified entities, if this relationship is construed as adventitious? Damascius' commentary is instructive in this regard:

The mind abandons itself to the object of knowledge in order to attain unity with it, desiring to be intelligible and no longer intellectual. For there is no distinction separating the [mind and that object] but wholly unified it presses on to dissolve itself and be unified with the unified and it denies all distinction, even that distinction between itself and the object known . . . (C-W II, 105, 18–21)

One point stands out in Damascius' interpretation of the Oracle. He seems to construe the phrase "backward turning eye," with the word "mind" (*psyche*). So in this form of knowing the mind should abandon itself and achieve complete identification with the object of contemplation. In many of the passages and exercises we have considered, self-displacement is a fundamental part of the process. Therefore, the exercise starts out from the position of introspection but ends up, as was already said, with a displacement of the self onto the object contemplated.

This is another example in which the psychology of contemplation informs a more general epistemology. In this case, the psychology is disclosed through reference to a contemplative object endowed with ritual and traditional associations. The hermeneutic complexities of this passage illustrate the importance of textuality as a medium through which the tradition can posit an extra-textual context. The Chaldean Oracles present themselves as a Babylonian wisdom tradition, but they gain in prestige through their appropriation of Homeric diction and vocabulary. Their Middle Platonic theology suggests that they already formed a part of the exegetical tradition even before their citation in theoretical texts such as the *Doubts and Solutions*. Here the Chaldean passage reminds the reader of the contemplative *askesis* informing the tradition as a whole, recasting theoretical issues in the light of ritual practice.

In a sense, the history of this enigma is overdetermined, having as its foundations the oral-teachings hypothesis, the ritualistic affiliations of mathematics, and above all the peculiar structure of Neoplatonic self-representation. Although the notions that Pythagorean symbolism was taught in a systematic or even consistent way, or that the geometry of recollection was *the central* pedagogic device used by Pythagoreanizing Neoplatonists,[52] are both beyond the scope of this chapter, this survey of Pythagorean symbols in Neoplatonic texts at the very least contributes to an overall theory of Neoplatonic textuality.

[52] Once more I refer the reader to the convincing and nuanced detective work of Gregory Shaw, in his two chapters "Mathematics and the Soul" and "Noetic Sunthemata – the Theurgy of Numbers," in which Professor Shaw argues for the preeminence of mathematical objects in the noetic stages of theurgy. For Iamblichus and Pythagoras, the reader should also consult the all-important work of O'Meara, the modern discoverer of the Iamblichean work "On Pythagoreanism," embedded in the text of Psellus.

7

Transmigrations of a Myth: Orphic Texts and Platonic Contexts

In this chapter I survey allusions to the Orphic cosmology in the works of Plato and of subsequent Platonizing authors. My theme in this chapter is to look once more at a group of symbols accorded particular status among Neoplatonic authors. As in the previous chapter, I start from the text of Plato and work forward in history. In all likelihood, the central Orphic myth implied the ritual death, dismemberment, and reconstitution of the initiate. Plato makes use of this ritual motif to underscore his analysis of selfhood and self-transcendence. Later in the tradition, the initiatory associations with Orphic symbolism are appropriated to authorize supposedly esoteric interpretations of Plato's dialogues. Orpheus, from the enchanted visionary of the earlier tradition, becomes a metaphysically astute theologian for the later Neoplatonists.

Throughout its transmigrations over the centuries, one particular episode in this myth, the rending of Dionysus, enjoys perhaps the greatest celebrity or notoriety.[1] This episode has clear ritual associations, as the initiated candidate and the suffering god undergo parallel experiences in different zones, so to speak. The mythohistory of the cosmos revealed in the Orphic theology contains as its final episode an etiology for specifically human consciousness, in the rending of Dionysus at the hands of the Titans. The physical details of the myth, with its elements of androgynous self-impregnation, solipsistic world swallowing, transgression, rebellion, and finally sexual sparagmos – collapse of the androgynous self into a gendered being – provide all the necessary elements for a psychoanalytic read-

[1] The classic article on this episode remains Pépin, "Plotin et le mirroir de Dionysius."

ing.[2] While I will not be subjecting versions of this narrative to a psychoanalytic reading per se, it is nevertheless my contention that these versions offer models or perhaps more accurately, explanations, for the specifically human form of consciousness. At times (as, for example, in the *Phaedo* commentary of the sixth-century exegete, Olympiodorus) we find this myth invoked to explain such phenomena as egotism or envy. In this sense, there are psychoanalytic applications for the myth within the tradition itself. In this chapter, I look at the Orphic theology within the Neoplatonic exegetical tradition, paying particular attention to the Dionysus episode. This narrative motif is used by Plato and the subsequent tradition to develop the theme of philosophical initiation.

Nevertheless, the Neoplatonists exude a kind of enthusiasm for Orphic detective work that perhaps exceeds their roles as exegetes; we find them playing fast and loose with the narrative structure of the myth, hypostasizing or reifying some of the most unlikely elements, and importing their almost baroque metaphysical schemas into the most unlikely parts of the text. Although here I can only briefly sketch some of the forms this narrative takes in Late Neoplatonism, in chapters 8 and 9, I will take up, respectively, Proclus' and Damascius' overall theory of philosophical exegesis. Only then will their treatments of the Orphic material become fully intelligible.

In the last chapter, we looked at the geometric tradition as offering a textual emblem representing the space of consciousness and signifying the reflexive stance within which a singular dialectical position was formulated. By contrast, the Orphic myth leads the reader in a confusing search for the identity that it conveys, in a number of competing directions, throughout the history of its textual deployment. Its first significant appearance, in Plato's *Symposium*, tells the story of a fragmented consciousness or absence of a unified subject. In subsequent metempsychoses, for example, in the writings of Proclus, it conveys the stages of a visionary journey and,

---

[2] In fact, one might trace the Lacanian ungendered "hommelette" ultimately to the androgynous Phanes who gives birth to the world egg. After all, Lacan offers this metaphor in his remarks on Aristophanes' speech in the *Symposium*. In a similar vein, we might consider the Nietzschean utilization of Dionysus' sparagmos as emblem of the pluralistic nature of self-identity as yet another appropriation of this Orphic narrative. See Gillespie, pp. 203–54, and Lacan, pp. 196–7.

in the work of Damascius, even an abyssal, negatively signifiying semiotics.

Throughout the tradition, the Orphic myth is used to describe a moment of vision in which the soul comes to understand the world in which it is situated and the origins of that world, as well as the unique world that the soul itself projects, the private world of the imagination that is never glimpsed by another. In Late Athenian Neoplatonism we find the Orphic myth drawn into a more elaborate angelology, or catalogue of deities. The myth's protagonist, known alternatively as Phanes, or Protogonos, or Eros, finds his place in Platonic theologies of Syrianus, Proclus, and Damascius, at the center of the intellectual world, at the juxtaposition between the intellectual and intelligible regions. The myth recounts the moment in which the individual soul wakes up and discovers its connection to a structure that is repeated ad infinitum throughout the multiple planes of existence. This moment of recollection is peculiarly captured in the Dionysus episode, which both tells the story of the fall into human consciousness and also functions as the source for a new orientation. In the tradition of the mysteries, this vision enables the soul to return to its origin, to the One, to the intelligible mundus, and so forth. The Neoplatonists recur to Orphism in an attempt to communicate their conception of the pedagogy of the soul or mystagogy leading to self-realization.

Recent work has done much to uncover Plato's own appropriation of Orphic and Pythagorean teachings, and Peter Kingsley has now devoted an important book to establishing this connection through a close reading of the mythic passages in Plato's *Phaedo* and *Gorgias*.[3] The discovery of the Derveni papyrus, a work that will be discussed in more detail later, has confirmed scholarly conjecture about the Orphic setting or tone of the myths in both of these dialogues, since this papyrus "consists of the allegorical interpretation of a poem ascribed to Orpheus."[4] In particular, the subterranean geography in the *Phaedo* myth, together with its underground rivers and unhappy residents, those moral failures condemned eternally to "lying in the

---

[3] Kingsley, pp. 115, ff. One of the most important scholars to work on the connections between Orpheus and Plato was Dietrich, in his *Nekyia.*
[4] Kingsley, p. 116.

mud," are explicitly attributed to Orphic texts in the later commentaries of Damascius and Olympiodorus.[5] Again, as Kingsley shows in his book, the importance of the evidence supplied by both the Derveni papyrus and the testimony of Damascius concerning the underground bodies of water in the *Phaedo* lies in the fact that we must now attribute the allegorizing use of Orphic material to Plato himself, and not only to the Late Neoplatonists.[6]

Versions of the Orphic Cosmogony

The central Orphic myth narrates a cosmogony in which the androgynous being, Phanes (whose name means "The Revealer"), springs from a cosmic egg and gives birth to the world through a miraculous act of auto-procreation, whereupon Zeus promptly swallows the creation. It also includes a sequence in which the Titans consume the infant Dionysus (later repaired by Apollo) and then pay dearly for their crime with a blast of Zeus' thunderbolt. Their blood falls to the earth and spawns the human race. In all likelihood, this myth implied the ritual death, dismemberment, and reconstitution of the initiate; hence its association with initiatory ritual.

Before the discovery of the Derveni papyrus, three versions of the Orphic myth were distinguished: first, the Rhapsodic Theogony, preserved by Damascius and Christian apologists, in which Chronos produces a cosmic egg, which then hatches into Phanes, the bisexual being who creates the world. Phanes is eventually swallowed and regurgitated by Zeus, who recreates the world through this act of digestion. Second, the Eudemian and the most ancient version, mainly attested in Aristophanes' *Birds*, 414 B.C.E., lines 693–703, but also supposedly known by the Peripatetic Eudemus, in which Night creates the cosmic egg. A third version, that of the enigmatic Hieronymus or Hellanikus, was attested to solely in the writings of Damascius.

Damascius summarizes three different versions of the Orphic theogony toward the end of his monumental work *Doubts and Solutions Concerning First Principles*. His account of the different versions i

---

[5] See Kingsley, chapter 10, "Plato and Orpheus." On Damascius and Orphic mythology, see below and especially Brisson 1990.

[6] On this controversy, again see Kingsley, p. 126, and Brisson 1995b.

obscured by his overarching schema, which consists in forcing the various narrative episodes to fit into his triadic model of what he calls the "noetic diacosm." He begins his summary by referring to the "Theology [narrated] in these currently circulating Orphic Rhapsodies." West has concluded that this so-called Rhapsodic Theogony "was a composite work, created in the late Hellenistic period as a conflation of earlier Orphic poems. Under the Empire it was *the* Orphic theogony, and it was frequently quoted and alluded to, especially by the Neoplatonists" (West 1983, p. 69).

Damascius gives only the barest outline of this Rhapsodic version and goes on to discuss in considerable detail the

Theology propounded by Hieronymus and Hellanikus (unless he is the same person) [that] goes like this: Originally there was water he (Orpheus) says, and mud, from which the earth solidified: he posits these two as first principles, water and earth ... The one before the two, however he leaves unexpressed, his very silence being an intimation of its ineffable nature. The third principle after the two was engendered by these – earth and water, that is – and was a serpent with extra heads growing upon it of a bull and a lion, and a god's countenance in the middle; it had wings upon its shoulders, and its name was Unaging Time and also Heracles. (R 317–19, translation of West 1983, p. 178)

These versions of the theology were formulated at various times throughout the centuries that preceded Damascius' writings: on the basis of the reference to Herakles, for example, West conjectures that the version of Hieronymus was a Hellenistic, Stoicizing version. What is poignant about their inclusion at the end of the *Doubts and Solutions* is their historical placement. This treatise represents, as we shall see in chapter 9, the last word, so to say, of Neoplatonist metaphysics and the closure, therefore, of pagan philosophy. Damascius prefers to seal this compendium of Neoplatonic teachings with the "purification of our own pronouncements" (R. 316) about the nature of the divine, and so turns to a revealed tradition.

The importance of Damascius' *Peri Archon* for our knowledge of Orphism consists in its being a source for many of the Orphic fragments. In fact, it possesses a double interest from a textual point of view. To quote from Luc Brisson:

1) Damascius is the only Neoplatonist to have mentioned three different versions of the Orphic Theogony: The *Sacred Discourse* [or the *Rhapsodic Theogony*], certainly, since that was the current version, but also that of

Eudemus (which was an earlier version) and that of Hieronymus. 2) With regard to the *Rhapsodic [Theogony]* the testimony of Damascius permits a comparison between the testimony of Proclus and the testimony of Olympiodorus.

Brisson draws four conclusions from his study of Damascius' attestations in the *Peri Archon*:

1. During the time of Damascius, the most current version of Orphic doctrine was the *Sacred Discourse*, containing a theogony and a cosmogony, both of which formed the basis of Orphic ethical praxis as well as Orphic initiation rites.
2. In order to interpret the *Sacred Discourse*, Damascius must have made use of a lost work of Syrianus entitled *The Agreement Between Orpheus, Pythagoras, Plato, and the Chaldean Oracles*.
3. In order to justify his own name for the first principle, "the Ineffable," Damascius cites a version of the theogony attributed to a mysterious personage named either Hieronymus or Hellanikus. This version gives a prominent place to the deity Chronus, and the presence of this deity shows the influence both of Stoic cosmogony and of Mithraicism.
4. The quotation that Damascius makes from the version of Eudemus gives us information about the Orphic poems circulating during the classical period, which can be used together with Aristophanes' *Birds*, Plato's *Symposium* and the Derveni papyrus to comprehend which episodes belonged in the earliest version of the Orphic drama.

Let us glance quickly at the question of how extensively Orphic lore was known and transmitted within the classical period.[7] We have almost certainly advanced, with the discovery of what seems to have been an Orphic cult at Olbia dating from the fifth century B.C.E., beyond the pessimism of Linforth's denial that there was indeed an Orphic modus vivendi in the classical period. But the reconstruction of stemmata for the Orphic theogonies is complicated by the very late date of its major testimonia. The efforts of the last of the Platonic successors to present a rival cosmogony to the Christian version, complete with a doctrine of original sin and eventual redemption, reversed pagan reticence on this subject but has left later

[7] West; Linforth.

centuries in somewhat of a quandary concerning its provenance and antiquity.[8] With the discovery of the Derveni papyrus, containing as it does a commentary on some version of the Orphic poem, and dating from the fourth century, we have corroborating evidence that the classical period was immersed in Orphic lore.[9] The Derveni version corresponds in certain details to the Eudemian version, but according to the reconstruction of Claude Calame, in place of the cosmic egg, we have a kinky hybrid entity, part Hesiodic primophallacism, part Orphic oviparous cosmology. In this version, the *aidoion*, the originary genitals perform the part of Phanes/Eros, for from them are said to proceed all of the immortal gods, as well as the elements. In any event, Plato was almost certainly familiar with a version known to the author of the Derveni papyrus, since he quotes, in *Laws* 716a, lines that correspond to line 26 of the Derveni papyrus (o.f. 21a): "the god holding the beginning, middle, and end of all beings."

The Orphic Cosmology in Plato's *Symposium*

We are all familiar with the Aristophanic parody at *Symposium*, 189 ff. Originally, the human race consisted of three sexes, male (descended from the sun), female (descended from the earth), and the *androgune* (descended from the moon). These originary beings conspired to inveigh against heaven with their might, and Zeus, in punishment, divided them like eggs. After Apollo healed the scars of these half-people, they were condemned to a lonely search for their other half. The myth is an etiology for the human passion, eros, recounted by the comic poet Aristophanes. In Plato's version, the ancestors of the human race must represent all the players of the original Orphic cycle: the egg itself (note the comparison to eggs at 190c), the god Phanes (at least, the *androgune* resembles the bisexual Phanes), the Titans (they scale heaven and are punished for it), Dionysus (like Dionysus in the theology, they are dismembered and then healed by Apollo), and finally, the living members of the human race.

[8] For a detailed and compelling critique of West's admirable attempts to reconstruct a stemma for the transmission of the Orphic theologies, see Casadio 1986.
[9] On the Derveni Papyrus, see Rusten and Obbink.

Phaedrus refers to the tale of Orpheus and Eurydice in the middle of his speech (179d2), casting Orpheus in a rather negative light, as someone who failed in his mission because he was unwilling to die on behalf of his beloved. Without going too deeply into the narrative structure of the *Symposium*, it is worth pointing out that Alcibiades refers to his painful wound as more fierce than a snakebite (218a5) and that under the influence of this bite he has partaken in the Bacchic celebrations of mania (218b4). We will return to the figure of Alcibiades shortly, but for now, it seems plausible to suggest that in this tale Socrates functions as an Orpheus figure (note the references to Socrates' enchanting music at 215c5), who enters in to a kind of underworld for the purpose of rescuing his beloved (Alcibiades) but notably fails in his mission. At any rate, this possible narrative motif only underscores the centrality of Orphic symbolism in the *Symposium* as a whole.

Another name for Phanes/Protogonos, the Demiurgic source of the universe, was Eros. Note that the name "Aristophanes" contains the word "Phanes" and that *Birds* contains an etiology for Eros that depicts the originary cosmic egg. The roles assigned to Zeus as divine nemesis for the hubris of an original race, to Apollo as restorer of the human species, and to a kindlier, gentler, post-lapsarian humanity in Plato's myth, seem closely modeled on the Protogonos narrative. The circle beings in Aristophanes' speech, then, are emblems of Protogonos/Eros, and so Plato's Aristophanic parody alludes to or invokes the Orphic cosmogony. Plato was aware of an Orphic cosmogony circulating rather freely in the classical period, and he alludes to it in this Aristophanic tale of the circle-beings. But what difference does it make to our reading of the *Symposium*? One answer would be, "very little." Plato borrows some themes from the Orphic myth in an effort to polish his Aristophanic parody. In it, we are supposed to recognize Aristophanes' own riposte to the Sophistic mythographers and their utopian theorizing, and Plato's take on this material would be an instance of the intellectuals getting a bit of their own back. That is one answer, but left unanswered are the questions, what function does the initiatory motif have in the *Symposium* as a whole, and what role specifically does the allusion to Orphic cosmogony play?

Obviously, the whole ladder of love is metaphorized in terms of mystery language. Diotima speaks of lesser and greater mysteries, and the vision of the beautiful is presented as *epopteia.* In fact, Plato very often uses the language of mysteries as a purely metaphorical device, especially when concerned with the theme of eros. A good example is *Republic* 8, the genealogy of the democratic man. This person is said to be the son of an aristocratic father fallen on hard times. The son, confused and shamed by the daily abuse to which his father is subjected, falls in with a group of accomplices who awaken the stirrings of Eros, slumbering within his soul: "And they possess and initiate his soul with magnificent and costly rites, then proceed to lead home from exile insolence and anarchy and prodigality and shamelessness, resplendent in a great attendant choir, and crowned with garlands . . ." Here Plato speaks about the decadence of the mystery rites, in keeping with what we find elsewhere in philosophical writers, including the author of the Derveni papyrus, who complains that the initiated depart from mysteries still unenlightened.

If we look carefully at the metaphor from the *Republic,* we can see that Plato is talking about the evolution of the erotic subject. That is, he is talking about the shaping of desire and how Eros is configured both within the internal psychic economy of the subject and within the larger external economy of the community in which the subject lives. The language of initiation is associated in Greek literature with the erotic tradition; this initiatory Eros, functioning on a social level, is the subject of Pausanias' speech in the *Symposium.* It harkens back to the lyrical tradition, to Theognis and to Sappho, but it is also reflected in the vase paintings designed for Sympotic occasions. A cosmogonic Eros, of which there are two central traditions in Greek poetry, the Hesiodic and the Orphic, is the subject of Erixymachus' speech but is also alluded to in the Hesiodic lines of Phaedrus.[10]

In one tradition, a Demiurgic Eros is the mediating principle between chaos and an organized, differentiated world of multiplicity; in the other tradition, Eros is an initiatory guide into the social world of the polis and its institutions. Demiurgic Eros produces the exterior, spatial world; Sympotic Eros produces the interior, psychic world, carried out within the temporal demarcations of a life span.

---

[10] On initiatory Eros, see Claude Calame, "Eros initiatique et la cosmogonie Orphique," to which I am extremely indebted in this section.

Both forms converge in the speech of Aristophanes: cosmogony and psychology collapse in the synchronic presentation of the myth. Demiurgic Eros is present as cosmic Phanes, the bisexual being who spawns the universe at the dawn of time. The myth also narrates the emergence of the socially constructed erotic subject who is born into a fixed set of sexual mores.

The cosmological and social functions of Eros are intricately interwoven throughout the text, as Hesiodic Eros is juxtaposed with the Orphic tradition in the opening speech of Phaedrus. The Orphic myth promises a return to the undifferentiated state before sexual identity arises, promising to deliver us back inside the egg to become, in the Lacanian sense, hommelettes. But of course, this is a delusional aspiration, as the myth makes clear, and it is in fact a self-destructive delusion. This myth, just as the *androgune* is divided into two, suffers severance from within. The myth of the circle-beings is just the outer covering for a later, Socratic revelation.

Enter Diotima, who in her dissection of self-identity at 208 accomplishes her first task as mystagogue, namely, to destroy the initiand's old self. No ideology could survive Diotima's scrutiny: mind and body arise together as mutually conditioned constructions. Self-identity ebbs away in the flow of memory while consciousness disappears without a trace of its previous contents. Disclosing this radical dissociation from a stable selfhood is what Diotima aims at in her dialectical antidote to the delusions generated in conventional discourse. Here is yet another reason for the Orphic myth. The Orphic mystery purports to be an esoteric tradition, one that liberates people from the petrifying conventions of the mass sex-gender machine. Its purpose is to re-create the subject, to wrench him away from the public fiction in which he has hitherto been schooled.

Alcibiades is the initiatory candidate in our dialogue, and he complains bitterly of the voice of the demos that, sirenlike, calls him away from the vocation of philosophy. Conspicuously wearing an initiand's crown, he recounts his spiritual death at the hands of Socrates, using language borrowed from the mysteries (*mania, bak xeias*, 218b4). By quoting the Orphic proem just before he describes the cloaking scene, Alcibiades intimates that an initiation took place. Here for the first and evidently last time, he experienced a loss of self. At that moment, Alcibiades tells us, Socrates' persona was cleft and the brilliance of his virtue shone forth. This moment was also perhaps Socrates' epiphany as a Phanes avatar; Plato applies the adverb, *dixa*, to the halving of Silenic status and to the halving of our spherical ancestors.

Notwithstanding the external, historical reasons for linking Alcibiades to initiation rites, I think it important to emphasize the ritual associations of the *stephanos*, which marks Alcibiades as the candidate for initiation. One passage that illustrates this convention is *Clouds* 256, the initiation of Strepsiades into the worship of the *Nephelai*:

So: Now sit on the sacred couch
ST: I'm sitting.
So: Now take this garland here
ST: What's the garland for? Oh no, Socrates. Please don't turn me into an Athamas.
So: Don't worry; but we go through all of this for the initiates.

The symbolic role of the *stephanos* is complicated by its diverse usage outside of the mainstream celebratory occasions of victory festivals, which is of course the obvious explanation for Alcibiades' crown in the *Symposium.*

On the gold leaves of Thurii, we read the distich:

κύκλου δ'ἐξέπταν βαρυπενθέος ἀργαλέοιο
ἱμερτοῦ δ'ἐπέβαν στεφάνου ποσὶ καρπαλίμοισι

They have flown the grievous circle of heavy sorrow
and stepped on the much sought crown, with swift feet.

As Richard Seaford explains, "it seems that the *stephanos*, worn by initiand and corpse, expresses here that release of the dead initiate which had been celebrated with these deliberately enigmatic formulae in his initiation into the mysteries. Whatever the primary reference of circle, I detect a riddling contrast between two kinds of circle, the undesirable imprisoning circle, and the desirable circle of the crown."[11]

The myth of the circle people tells us about this cycle of self-perpetuation and of self-perpetuating misery, although the ancestors of humanity must eventually submit to a ritual dismemberment, a service that Diotima nobly replicates as the high priestess of this rite in her disassembly of selfhood. In this respect, I would emphasize

[11] Seaford, *HSCP* 90.

that Diotima meets certain ritualistic expectations. One of these expectations might be more fully comprehended if we recognize in the Diotima figure a rather standard mystic motif, in which a spirit guide, in the form of a consort of the opposite sex, reveals to a disciple the presence of a ladder that carries him into the upper worlds.[12]

Socrates becomes the shamanistic counterpart to Diotima. In his eerie trance (*Symposium* 220c7) and superhuman *enkrateia*, he seems fully in control of his elemental world. Untouched by the heat of Eros or the frozen depths of winter, his world cannot harm him since it is his own projection, and he knows it. He cannot become intoxicated by it, and he is never afraid of it. If the world that we inhabit is a construction of desire, then this world lacks a final reality. But to live in a fictional world is madness, while not to recognize its nature as a fictional construct is both dangerous and stupid. If Socrates has any wisdom, perhaps it is just this awareness of his own fictionality, with which he holds a unique iconic relationship: likened to a Silenic statue, Socrates embodies the very form of the *eikon*, the idol. Stony outside, his divine power is not visible.[13]

The myth also incorporates its own rupture, and the self-enclosure of the solipsistic self who refuses to admit the autonomy of the erotic object is severed when the terms of inner and outer are reversed. The circle-beings are replaced with the new, enlightened version of humankind, the subject who recognizing a lack of self thus becomes subsumed in the erotic drive to transcend this fictionality. But how different could the reconstructed self be from the old self? Not that different, as we gather from observing Alcibiades.

---

[12] Whatever we make of Diotima's femininity, it is no more or less real than is any of the other characters' masculinities. We are clearly shown the fictionalization of masculine erotic subjects every bit as constructed as the woman in the text: mere figments of Hesiodic mythology, or tragic poetry, or medical texts. In fact, each of the characters appears not in the guise of a real, raw masculinity, but as a fabricator of discourse, a self-fabricator imbricated with the layers of social conditioning that dispenses only pseudo-identities.

[13] On shamanism and Orphism, see Casaro, p. 312, and extensive references there. He quotes A. Hultkrantz, "A Definition of Shamanism," Temenos, 1973, pp. 25-37, defining the shaman as: "A social functionary who, with the help of guardian spirits, attains ecstacy in order to create a rapport with the supernatural world on behalf of his group members." On shamanism and its association with Orphism see Guthrie, Dodds, and West. Also, Eliade.

In my reading of the Orphic cosmology in Plato's *Symposium*, I have emphasized its function as an etiology for human consciousness, prior to its regeneration by philosophy. This is the exoteric mind that desperately requires enlightenment but because of its conditioning, all too rarely seeks it. Because the initiatory sequence intimated within the narrative structure invokes a moment of self-awakening, or self-transcendence, and because Plato allegorizes this initiation as involving an insight into the transient, centrifugal aspect of the socially constructed self, it reads as a complex meditation on the meaning of selfhood. One aspect of selfhood lies in its social construction, its location within a specific cultural matrix, and its inscription by various foundational discourses. Plato's understanding of the relationship between cosmogonic Eros and socially operative sex-gender systems evinces his sensitivity to the pragmatics of such discourses. Thus each of the Symposiasts calls upon a different elemental, cosmic configuration as part of his or her own persuasive arsenal.

This is not to say that Plato leaves us with an absolutized notion of the pluralistic self. Instead, the text itself is a puzzle, offering both a mirror for self-reflection and a mask for self-deception. It is this aporetic textuality that is finally signified in the persona of Socrates: in the end, despite the prolific gossip about Agathon's dinner party, there remains a secret. Socrates, although he does take a ritual bath for the occasion, denies that he initiates anyone. He ends and begins the whole affair in *euphemia*, silence.[14]

Although this discussion of the Orphic myth alluded to in Plato's *Symposium* has been brief, nevertheless the ability to detect the presence of the theology in the dialogue helps us to accomplish several tasks. First, the allusions to the Orphic myth tie together the narrative structure of the *Symposium* and help us to explain the dramatic sequences and gestures that allude to initiatory ritual, such as the crowing of Alcibiades, his death by snakebite, the epiph-

---

[14] This silence hints that there is some sort of antidote to the poison that Alcibiades has digested, some *pharmakon*. We are supposed, within the dialogue, to recognize this antidote as philosophy itself and to recognize, in Diotima's philosophical *askesis*, a form of self-transcendence that also allows one to leave behind the socially constructed self. Nevertheless, the process of seeing into the nature of social conditioning in terms of how selfhood is configured within this complex, is an important element in Plato's narrative.

any of Socrates, and shamanistic associations of both Diotima and Socrates.

Second, these allusions to initiatory ritual are important because they strengthen our understanding of the initiatory aspects of the Dionysus episode as reconstructed in the Eudemean version of the Orphic theology. As West points out, the sequence involving the Titan's devouring of the young Dionysus is the narrative equivalent of a shamanistic psychodrama, in which a candidate literally experiences his complete dissolution on the physical order, and becomes reconstituted and reborn on the order governed by the initiation:

> The story of Dionysus seems to show elements of both the types of initiatory death that I have mentioned. The fact that he is cut in pieces by evil gods who proceed to boil him and eat his flesh corresponds to the typical shaman's ordeal, which is a subjective religious experience, not a concrete ritual. But the references to the coating of the Titans' faces with gypsum and to a collection of objects with which they deceived Dionysus strongly suggest that the myth reflects a ritual in which the death-dealing ancestral spirits were impersonated by men, that is to say an initiation of the tribal or secret-society type.[15]

Not only does the camouflaged appearance of the rending of Dionysus in the *Symposium* confirm West's conclusions, that the Dionysus episode was already present in the Eudemean version of the theology, but it also importantly confirms the conclusions of Kingsley's research into the Orphic origination of certain of Plato's myths. I quote Kingsley:

> Habit dies hard and in spite of the evidence of the Derveni papyrus it is still normal to find the allegorizing of Orphic poetry and mythology presented as a primarily Neoplatonic phenomenon. Here [sc. in the *Phaedo's* allusions to mythical landscape that corresponds in part to regions of Sicily], however, we have the allegorizing interpretation of Orphic literature not only attested before Plato's time, but actually feeding into and creating the Platonic myths themselves.[16]

Finally and most importantly, the rending of Dionysus is the mythic equivalent of Diotima's philosophical dissolution of self-identity and Plato's linguistic analysis of the origins of the empirical self and its erotic structure. This psychological detective work into

---

[15] West 1983, p. 145.
[16] Kingsley 1995, p. 126.

the origins of the empirical self as a public fiction that must be vociferously and painfully renounced before the contemplative life can flower, shows that the Orphic myth functions in Platonic contexts as a meditation on the limitations of discursive awareness, as I hope to show when we turn to examine its appearance in Neoplatonic texts.

Proclus Reads Orpheus

As we have seen, a great deal of our information concerning the Orphic theology comes from the attestations of Late Athenian Neoplatonists. Proclus is by far the richest source in terms of sheer numbers of fragments, even though his Orphic references are by comparison far fewer than allusions to the Chaldean Oracles. From the comment of Damascius in the *Doubts and Solutions Concerning First Principles* cited earlier concerning the "current" form of the Orphic theology, we know that the Neoplatonists generally used the *Hieroi Logoi in 24 Rhapsodies*, which is listed in the *Suda* under the heading Orpheus. An anecdote from Marinus' *Life of Proclus* also confirms the origin of many of Proclus' Orphic citations:

Once when I was reading the works of Orpheus with him [Proclus], and hearing his exegeses not only on what is in Iamblichus and Syrianus but further material, apter to theology, I asked the philosopher not to leave such an inspired poem unexplained but to write a fuller commentary on this too. He said he had often felt an urge to write one, but had been prevented by dreams in which he had seen his tutor himself [Syrianus] deterring him with threats. I thought of a way round, and proposed that he should mark the passages in his tutor's volumes which he approved. He acquiesced (image of goodness that he was), and marked the commentaries in the margins. We collected the passages together, and thus obtained his notes and comments on quite a number of verses of Orpheus, even if he did not manage to mark up the whole of the divine mythology or all of the Rhapsodies.[17]

These works of Syrianus were *On the Theology of Orpheus* and the *Concordance of Orpheus, Pythagoras, and Plato Regarding the Oracles*. It is this latter work that both Proclus and Damascius draw upon in their explications of Platonic theology, Proclus, extensively thoughout his works but most frequently in his *Commentary on Plato's Timaeus*, and

---

[17] Marinus, *Life of Proclus* 27, translated by West 1983, p. 228.

Damascius, in his *Doubts and Solutions Concerning First Principles*, and his *Commentary on Plato's Parmenides*.

Primarily, Proclus refers to the "Rhapsodic Theogony," a poem composed toward either the end of the first or the beginning of the second century B.C.E. The date of this version is a matter of contention, with Luc Brisson pointing to aspects of the fragments akin to techniques of Stoic allegorizing, to argue for a later date than that proposed by West. I refer now to Proclus' summary of this "Rhapsodic Theogony" found in the *Commentary on the Timaeus*, vol. III, chapter 168:

"Let us now inquire," Proclus says, "which Orphic doctrines one ought reconcile with the teaching of Timaeus concerning the Gods. Orpheus taught that there were Divine regents presiding over everything, equal in number to the perfect number, that is, six: Phanes, Night, Ouranos, Kronos, Zeus, and Dionysus."

These six reigns encompass a theogony, telling the birth of the gods from the primordial egg; a cosmology, recounting the origins of the present world order, brought to unity in the bowels of Zeus; and an anthropology. Before going into the details of Proclus' theological adaptation of this cosmogony, let us step back and ask, what is going on here? What motivates the Neoplatonic appropriation at this particular phase of the tradition? To focus this question, it would be well to remember that Porphyry's references to the Orphics are by and large confined to his tract, "On the Cave of the Nymphs," while Plotinus himself never mentions Orpheus at all. His only allusions to the Orphic myth are found in the discussion of Dionysus' mirror, in *Enneads* IV.3.

The method followed by Proclus in his *Platonic Theology* and elsewhere, is to research the correspondences between Plato, Orpheus, and Pythagoras. This method was the unique province of the Athenian school, founded by Plutarch of Athens. Syrianus and Hierocles of Alexandria were both students. The research program carried on by them bears out this thesis: Hierocles authored a work on Providence, whose fourth chapter was devoted to showing the correspondences between Plato, the Chaldean Oracles, and theurgy. Hierocles' *Commentary on the Golden Verses of Pythagoras* also evinces this strategy. In all of this, Hierocles and Syrianus and their successors, were following in the footsteps of Iamblichus. Late Athenian Neopla tonism was a peculiar mixture of scholasticism and pagan religious cults, all blended into a syncretic system by the third-century Syrian philosopher, Iamblichus. Pressed by the example of Christianity to become a tradition associated with a revealed theology, Neoplatonists accorded a scriptural status to the writings of Plato, Homer, Orpheus, and the Chaldean Oracles, even while embracing non-Greek theologies as expressions of a larger, universal revelation. The researches of the Athenian school were designed as a return to the original wisdom that gave birth to their tradition. Proclus in the *Platonic Theology* can say: "All of Greek theology is the child of Orphic mystagogy: Pythagoras was the first to receive initiation from Aglaophamos, Plato in turn received from the Pythagorean and Orphic doctrines perfect knowledge concerning the gods" (1.5.25–26).

Proclus divided the writings of Plato into four groups, according to their manner of expression; inspired, dialectical, symbolic, imaginative. Likewise, the great theologians fall into four distinct types: Orpheus uses images, Pythagoras employs symbols, the Chaldeans are inspired, and Plato is scientific.[18] Proclus too is interested in the initiatory aspects of Orphism, so that he equates Orphic doctrine with an esoteric interpretation of Plato's dialogues:

Mythology comprises two branches: one is concerned with the correct education of youth, the other with the hieratic and symbolic evocation of the gods . . . The second method, which hints at the nature of the gods through secret formulae, belongs to those who initiate in the most profound mystery, by which Plato himself thinks it right to support his own teachings. (*IR* 85.1)

This esoteric interpretation is made quite explicit by Proclus in *Commentary on the Parmenides* and in *Platonic Theology*. Although it is a highly original composition and a remarkable departure from the tradition of Commentary writing that dominated the Neoplatonic school after the death of Plotinus, in fact the *Platonic Theology* rests upon two central discoveries, or, as we might prefer to think of them, two assumptions by Proclus' teacher, Syrianus, who worked in the Commentary tradition. In studying Plato's *Parmenides*, Syrianus found that every aspect denied of the One in the First Parmenidean Hypothesis was affirmed of the One in the Second Parmenidean

---

[18] *Platonic Theology* I 4, 19–20.

Hypothesis and that the fourteen conclusions of the second hypothesis corresponded to the complete hierarchy of all gods.

Proclus simply takes the Orphic myth and distributes its members along the axis of ontological levels Syrianus had already discovered in the second hypothesis of Plato's *Parmenides*. Thus Chronus represents the One, and Ether and Chaos represent the two monadic principles of limit and the unlimited that succeed the One in Proclus' ontology. Toward the end of the chain of being, we see the typical Proclan profusion of entities, with the multiplication of deities to fill in the missing gaps in the burgeoning theology. The theology is replete with repetitions, such as the androgynous pairing of Phanes with his feminine self repeated in the incestuous mating of Zeus with his feminine self, either his mother, Rhea, or his sister, Hera. Moreover, Zeus is identified with the feminine deity, Metis. The "Rhapsodic Theogony" ends with a famous hymn to Zeus, in which his identity as the *coincidentia oppositorum* is revealed:

Zeus was born first, Zeus was born last into the brilliant light. Zeus is the head, Zeus is the middle, and Zeus flows though all things. Zeus is male and Zeus is an immortal virgin.

This vision of the world of Zeus gives us a kind of mirror of the Proclan universe, in which each being is in all, and all beings are in each. The mirroring of the triadic structure of reality that is everywhere pervasive in Proclus, constantly mediated by the opposing categories that represent the initial dyad, is here developed in the liturgical language of a hymn. These repetitions exactly capture the Proclan vision of reality: all things are in all things, each according to its nature. The multiple states of being, each level mutually reflecting all of the others, proliferate as a hall of mirrors. It is this great world of mutual interpenetration endlessly expanding as a single drama, that the Orphic theogony captures. And not surprisingly, this vision is exactly the mythic equivalent of Proclus' central metaphysical views.

Particular details, such as the hierarchic distribution of elements within the myth, are interesting in that they coincide closely with the metaphysical structures adumbrated discursively. Thus the Proclan One is signified by the Orphic Chronos, a move that Proclus justifies on etymological grounds: causation is identified with temporality (*PT* I.28). Here we see a metaphysical tenet, that is, Proclus' acceptance of the causal aspect of the One, under dispute at the time, buoyed up by a theological reference.

By contrast, when we turn to the sixth-century Neoplatonist Damascius, we find that his unique contribution to the exegesis of the Orphic myth involves a rather suspect presentation of an otherwise unknown version.[19] To justify his own name for the first principle, "the Ineffable," Damascius cites a version of the theogony attributed to a mysterious personage named either Hieronymus or Hellanikus. This version gives a prominent place to the deity Chronos, and the presence of this deity shows the influence both of Stoic cosmogony and of Mithraicism.

Damascius ends his *Doubts and Solutions* with a theological testimony to the truth of his unorthodoxy, that is, his position that before the One there is the Ineffable. (C-W, III, p. 161). Damascius reports that the theology of Hellanikus or of Hieronymus begins with two principles, water and *hyle*, existing before Chronos. Moreover, there was a single principle, the cause or source of both water and *hyle*, that goes, according to Damascius, unnamed in the theology of Hellanikus. Now Damascius interrupts this narrative to remark that since the more commonly cited theology, the *Sacred Discourse in 24 Rhapsodies*, or *Rhapsodic Theogony*, lacks any mention of these three elemental principles, they transmit, by their very silence, the fact that the originary principle is, as Damascius understands it, the Ineffable.

We will return in chapter 9 to Damascius' ineffable discourse and to the theological complexities Damascius embraces as part of his critique of earlier Neoplatonic metaphysics. For now, I note that Damascius not only authorizes his own metaphysical innovations by alluding to a primordial tradition, but he also verifies his understanding of metaphysical discourse as presenting a lack of adequate signifiers. In short, the only absolute signifier is the unsignified. This abyssal semiotics is his most authoritative statement. It marks the end of his history of Neoplatonic metaphysics with an almost breathtaking theology of absence. If that which cannot signify authorizes all forms of discourse, and if this ineffable principle finalizes Damascius' presentation of his own metaphysical tradition, it only demonstrates that such textual extremes could be sanctioned by a traditional critique of discursive thinking.

---

[19] For the history, place, and philosophy of Damascius, see below chapter 9.

Before turning in more detail to the function of the Dionysus episode, it is worth asking about the overall purpose of the Orphic elaboration of Neoplatonic metaphysics as it appears in the Commentary works of Proclus.[20] The correspondences begin with the Orphic "first principle," Chronus, and range all the way through Proclus' sublunary deities, to which correspond the Orphic duplicate and even triplicate Zeus, Ouranos, Hera, and a number of the Titans who also make an encore appearance at this level. Interspersed between these extremes are some surprising forms of hypostatization, such as the Proclan "Separative Monad," represented in the Orphic myth by the castration of Kronos, or the reified "Size-of-the-Orphic-egg" (!), which equates with one of the intelligible gods.

Here, I think most interpreters would agree, one must return to some sort of historical context for interpretation. Granted that the versions of the Orphic theogony discovered within the annals of Neoplatonism, in the words of Brisson,[21]

can only be understood within the framework of a constant and very close relation to allegoresis having as its objects the Homeric and Hesiodic poems for the older version of the Orphic theogony and the previous versions of the Orphic theogony for the more recent versions.

But lest we fall into the labyrinth of a hermeneutic *mise en abyme*, it is important to realize that exegesis is actually fundamental to revelation, in the sense that prophetic texts are often bound together with an argument that purports to break the secret code. Thus the author of the Derveni papyrus refers to certain rituals that he connects with a theory of reincarnation and a religion of salvation through Dionysus. M. L. West argues that these elements, the ritualistic and the theogonic, belong together, perhaps as forming the basis of an initiatory religion, concerning which the author of the Derveni papyrus then theorizes.[22]

What I am suggesting here (and will continue to show in the chapter on Proclus' *Platonic Theology*) is that it is difficult to separate

---

[20] Luc Brisson, H. D. Saffrey, and Hans Lewy have shown in meticulous detail the distribution of the Orphic narrative by reconstructing it from Proclus' *Platonic Theology, Commentary on the Parmenides*, and *Commentary on the Timaeus*.

[21] Brisson 1997, "Chronos in Column XII of the Derveni Papyrus."

[22] West 1997, "Hocus-Pocus in East and West," in Laks and Most 1997.

exegesis from symbol.[23] In particular, the initiatory goals of Orphic religion are to some extent met through the kind of philosophical exegesis Proclus is performing. The recent reconstruction and translation of the Derveni papyrus allows us to glimpse, however tentatively, a possible analog text, in which the goal of initiation is mirrored in the developments of the text itself. Column XXI of the Derveni papyrus is translated as follows:

And when he says "by jumping" he makes clear that divided up into small pieces they were moving in the air and were jumping, and by jumping they were set in relation to one another. And they went on jumping until each one came to its fellow. Heavenly Aphrodite and Zeus (and to aphrodise and to jump) and Persuasion and Harmony are established as name for the same god. A man mingling with a woman is said by common usage to aphrodise. For when the things that are now were mixed with one another, it was called Aphrodite.

This fragment allows us to see sexual union as a metaphor for the great cosmic harmony set in place through the reign of Zeus. This divine state, here referred to as Heavenly Aphrodite, is the result of the mixing of all things, the gathering of separated and dispersed elements, and so represents the reign of love, or unity.[24] Unity, a gathering of dispersed elements, a sense of wholeness, peace, and union, all of these words could well describe the goal of the initiatory process. This sense of the whole can be seen in terms of social unity, certainly, since initiatory rites often precede one's entrance into a group identity. But this wholeness is also of course related to the equally powerful force of union with the deity whose presence is invoked by means of the rite.

With this historical digression in mind, we turn once more to Proclus' use of the Orphic theology. As already mentioned, Proclus ends his discussion of Zeus' role in the developing cosmos with Orphic fragment 167, the hymn to Zeus:

The shining lights of Aether and of immense sky, the depths of the ocean and of the deadly sea and the glorious earth, and the vast ocean and Tartartus the foundation of the earth, and the rivers, the oceans without limits, all the rest and all the blessed immortals, gods and goddesses, and all that has

---

[23] Along these lines, see further, Obbink, "Cosmology as Initiation."
[24] Claude Calame, "Figures of Sexuality and Initiatory Transition in the Derveni Theogony and Its Commentary," in Laks and Most 1997.

already come to be and all that will come to be, all that was born and found itself together in the belly of Zeus.

For Proclus, the Orphic theology, in offering a vision of the great world encompassed in the pleroma of the human intellect and embodied within the perfect person, Phanes, shows forth the soul as an *imago dei*.[25] It is this recognition that in itself constitutes a form of initiation, making possible the soul's access to the fullness of reality that the *Platonic Theology* describes.

I would go further and suggest that within the Neoplatonic tradition, at least since the time of Syrianus,[26] Orphism attaches itself to metaphysics in order to transform the latter into ritual. Or rather, the language of metaphysics is grafted on to a traditional narrative whose goal converges with the metaphysical conception. The entire process of metaphysical expansion and contraction becomes a theophany as the reader constructs an image of unity or perfection that rests entirely within the mind. We might think that this recitation or mnemonics is the narrative equivalent of the spherical image. Both the sphere and the theology provide the reader with images that involve an intense concentration, the ability to unify disparate elements, and the sustained vision of these elements as revealed by means of a powerful theurgic symbol.

Once more, this creative, divine energy that pours itself through the various stations of being as stages within the theology is initiatory in function. It ends with an explicitly initiatory sequence that implies the transformation of the initiate. The world of Zeus and the strange *coincidentia oppositorum* this world contains are to be seen in a vision that takes place after initiation.

The Dionysus sequence forms the crux for interpreting the entire theology. But in the terms of the myth, the rending of Dionysus reveals both the preinitiated state of the celebrant and the collapse or loss of the god's presence. For example, Proclus quotes an Orphic fragment (25 Kern) describing the rending of Dionysus in his *Commentary on the Parmenides*:

---

[25] As he tells us in the *Platonic Theology*, bk. 1.

[26] We have evidence of his Orphic interpretations from the scholia to Hermias' *Commentary on the Phaedrus*, which seems to be more or less a transcription of Syrianus' own commentary. We also have evidence about Syrianus' Orphic exegesis from remarks that Proclus makes in the *Commentary on the Parmenides* and especially in the *Platonic Theology*, bk. 4.

This is why the theologians say that at the dismemberment of Dionysus his intellect was preserved undivided through the foresight of Athena and that his soul was the first to be divided, and certainly the division into seven is proper primarily to Soul. (*IP* 808)

According to Proclus, the divided soul of Dionysus explains why the human soul operates as it does, in a divided way, or discursively:

> It is therefore appropriate that soul should have the function of division and of seeing things discursively. It is no wonder, then, that whereas the divine Forms exist primordially together and unified in the demiurgic intellect, our soul attacks them separately. (*IP* 809)

What follows is one of Proclus' most explicit descriptions of the conceptual nature of discursive thinking. The reign of Dionysus represents the human condition and, in particular, the scattered or distracted state of the mind before the unifying effects of the symbolic narrative.

For most Late Neoplatonists, the dismemberment of Dionysus signifies both a stage in the history of the cosmos, when the soul is divided or distributed into the world of space, and an anthropology, setting the stage for the soul's ultimate liberation from matter. The later tradition reads back into the text of Plato this same anthropology: for Olympiodorus, the prohibition of suicide in the *Phaedo* is related to the episode. Human beings arise from the soot of the Titans' ashes after they have consumed the god; the human body belongs to Dionysus, originating from his flesh (Olymp. *In Ph.* 1.3). According to Olympiodorus, this is the eosteric reason behind Socrates' strictures against suicide.

Again, the "reign of Dionysus" is also a symbol for the human soul in its embodied condition. This is the life of division, signified by the "chewing" of the Titans: "Dionysus is the patron of this world, where extreme division prevails because of 'mine' and 'thine.' " (Olym. *In Ph.* 1.5) In these examples, and most famously in *Enneads* IV.3, the Dionysus episode reveals the fragmentation of human consciousness.[27] The uninitiated, ordinary human being is characterized by a distracted, dispersed form of attention that is egoistic, self-centered, and desperately in need of enlightenment.

---

[27] Cf. also Proclus *In Cratylum* 133 (p. 77): The intellect in us is Dionysian and thus truly a shrine to Dionysus. Whoever wrongs it and scatters its undivided nature through much divided falsehood sins against Dionysus.

The Neoplatonists do not investigate the social or psychological aspects of this consciousness in the way that Plato does; admittedly, it is Plato who proves the better psychoanalyst. Instead, the Neoplatonists concentrate more on the spiritual suffering of the individual and offer a psychotherapy that aims at awakening the individual from his perpetual distractions (so they read the mirror of Dionysus). The theurgic aspects of the Orphic theology are an instance of this therapy.

8

Language and Theurgy in Proclus' *Platonic Theology*

Introduction: Exegetical Methods in the *Platonic Theology*

Proclus' *Platonic Theology* is an exegetical text that bears the unmistakable imprint of the Late Athenian school. Not only does it present the works of Plato in constant dialogue with competing theological systems to which the Neoplatonists accorded scriptural status, such as the Chaldean Oracles and Rhapsodic theology, but the *Platonic Theology* offers itself as a theurgic text in its own right. For Proclus, Plato's discourse on the nature of the divine constitutes a mystagogy, an initiation into theurgy.

Proclus sets out the plan of his work in chapter 2 of the *Platonic Theology*. There he outlines the book according to three central divisions: Plato's teachings concerning the nature of the gods, the structure of the divine hierarchy, and a miscellany of Platonic gods, *hypercosmic* and *encosmic*, that appear less systematically in the writings of Plato. Thus the *Platonic Theology* treats Plato's dialogues according to a scheme in which various aspects or attributes of deity are dispersed triadically within the *Laws, Republic, Phaedrus, and Phaedo.* The second part of the work describes, as Proclus promises, the central constituents of the divine world, although some of the plan is missing from the work as we have it. Beginning with the One (bk. II), the *Platonic Theology* continues down the grades of reality, to the Henads, the intelligible gods, the intelligible-intellective gods, the intellective gods, and the hypercosmic gods. This level is as far as our text reaches.

We have already seen that Proclus relied on Syrianus for the enumeration of this divine hierarchy, inasmuch as the latter discovered that the second half of Plato's dialogue, the *Parmenides*, mapped onto the levels of existence detailed in the rather baroque schemes of the Athenian school. Consequently, in the *Platonic Theology* Proclus sets out to enumerate the successive orders of gods along the axis of the Parmenidean ontology, elaborating six levels after the One: the intelligible, the intelligible-intellectual, the intellectual, the participated intellect, the psychic and individual souls, and nature.[1] Within the six books of the *Platonic Theology*, Proclus completes this schema only as far as the level of the participated intellect, or in the Iamblichean scheme, to the level of the supermundane gods. Formally, the work is closely aligned to the tradition of Parmenidean exegesis, although in Book One, Proclus works from a list of several dialogues, including the *Laws, Republic, Phaedrus, Phaedo*, and *Cratylus*, as the basis for his enumeration of the principal divine attributes.

Proclus actually employs two distinct principles of theological exegesis in his approach to the Platonic dialogues. The first rule will be discussed further in connection with Damascius: the Neoplatonists believed that the *Parmenides* both charted the emergence of every possible state of being after the One and indicated the transcendence of the first hypostasis over the posterior realities. According to the Neoplatonists, the first One never shows up in the Platonic *Parmenides*, which instead starts at the second hypostasis, when Zeno begins with the *protasis*, "If the One is . . ." In the *Platonic Theology*, Proclus also shows that the remaining Platonic dialogues affirm the ontological structure adumbrated in the *Parmenides* so that they too must be read in terms of their location on the Parmenidean axis. Thus Proclus will try to locate the mythological narrative of the *Phaedrus*, for example, within the Athenian system of the intellectual-intelligible gods. Employing the second exegetical rule,[2] Proclus reads the dialogues of Plato as though they were mapped onto the Parmenidean structure. But Proclus in turn elucidates this Parmenidean structure by referring to non-Platonic traditions.

Hence we come to the second basis of Proclus' exegetical activity

---

[1] This basic scheme is altered to take in account certain of Iamblichus' theological innovations, as, for example, the Iamblichean distinction between encosmic and supermundane gods.

[2] For this second exegetical principle, see *PT* I and Saffrey 1965, vol. I, Introduction.

in the *Platonic Theology*, that is, his assimilation of Orphic, theurgic, and Chaldean traditions to Plato. For Proclus, the authenticity of Plato's philosophy is vouchsafed by his place in an ancient lineage in which wisdom was transmitted orally from master to disciple in an unbroken succession. As quoted in the previous chapter, Proclus, in the *Platonic Theology*, affirms:

All of Greek theology is the child of Orphic mystagogy: Pythagoras was the first to receive initiation from Aglaophamos, Plato in turn received from the Pythagorean and Orphic doctrines perfect knowledge concerning the gods. (I.5.25–26)

O'Meara has recently shown that Iamblichus' elevation of Pythagorean philosophy was part of a concerted effort to uncover the authentic inspiration behind Plato's works. In his life of Pythagoras, Iamblichus shows that Pythagoras himself was initiated by none other than Orpheus. According to Iamblichus, there is a direct line of transmission from Orpheus to Pythagoras to Plato. The theory behind Proclus' synthesis of various philosophical dialects into a single theological language is the unity of primordial tradition.

By reading Plato in Pythagorean terms and Pythagoras in Platonic terms, by insisting upon the equivalence of *muthos* and *logos*, by substituting mythic names for metaphysical terms, and by authorizing his interpretations through reference to the Chaldean Oracles, Proclus creates a totalizing speech that sweeps up the entire history of philosophy. Paradoxically, to have motivated the *Platonic Theology* along such quasi-historical lines is to have de-historicized the text of Plato. Thus in Proclus' view, Plato is yet another exponent of the *philosophia perennis*. Therefore, although Plato does teach in a unique manner because he alone uses scientific discourse, he is not teaching a unique philosophy. If Proclus belongs to an exegetical tradition, this tradition exists only because of the primordial wisdom that it seeks to expound. For this reason, the *Platonic Theology* is more than an exegetical text; Proclus tells us that it is an initiatory text. Consequently, its reader is not debarred from belonging to this same perennial tradition. But the fact that initiation can take place by means of a text suggests that the concept of the text itself has a highly unusual significance in the *Platonic Theology*.

Ritual Aspects of the Text

Proclus' programmatic statement on the nature of theological language is found at *Platonic Theology*, I 4, p. 20, 1–25:

> Those who attempt to reveal the divine speak [in different ways] sometimes [speaking] in a symbolic or mythic mode, making use of images, and among those who expose their own thoughts without veils, some compose their discourses in a scientific manner and others under the inspiration of the gods.

At the very outset of the work, Proclus is quite open about the difficulties of his project. He even exhibits some self-consciousness about the methodology he intends to employ:

> We will now distinguish the manner according to which Plato teaches the mystic doctines concerning the gods. He very obviously does not pursue the same method everywhere, but sometimes, he teaches in an enthusiastic mode, sometimes, he employs dialectic, and sometimes he employs the symbolic method to communicate their secret attributes, and finally sometimes departing from the icons he ascends to the level [of the gods].

Here we observe Proclus' caveat: he is not going to pursue a consistent line of interpretation. Having introduced his text as belonging to a non-traditional genre, that of scientific discourse, he infuses a ritualism into the text and assimilates Platonism to a more pervasive Late Antique religiosity. That is, the *Platonic Theology* will come to resemble the kinds of texts it seeks to explain. For this reason, *Platonic Theology* also shares in the typology of many ritually inspired or informed texts, such as heavenly ascent narratives, divine invocations, theurgic rites, and letter mysticism.[3] I hope to show, in the remainder of this chapter, that the *Platonic Theology* is meant to be a support, not for argument, but for vision. The text can be seen as iconic, and the system that it supposedly conveys is more like a ritual invocation or theurgic rite than a handbook of metaphysics. In the terms of Iamblichus or the *Hermetica*, one could say that the *Platonic Theology* conveys an "intellectual theurgy"[4] or "speech offer

---

[3] For a recent survey of these texts, see Janowtiz 1996. On ritual language, see Tambiah 1979. On heavenly ascent, see Himmelfarb 1993 and Scholem 1964.

[4] See Shaw 1995 on Iamblichus' principle of theurgy, which assigns appropriate sacrifices to agents based on their intellectual qualifications.

ing";[5] it is a textual object that is meant to fill out the reader's consciousness, to be held in vision, and to replace the usual objects of consciousness.[6] Like the statues of the theurgists, this text is meant to become enlivened through the invocations of the gods that form its itinerary. As we shall see, it presents itself as an initiatory text, or even as a textual *symbolon,* a ritual token of the divine reality it purports to describe.

Perhaps the most striking feature of Late Antique religious texts in general is the almost magical power or divinely guaranteed efficacy of certain kinds of language. In the Jewish, Christian, and Chaldean traditions, for example, the invocation of a divine name or recitation of a formula can have very important consequences in the world beyond the text.[7] Because of this efficacy, and because of the formulaic qualities of many religious texts, it has seemed increasingly important to some scholars to emphasize the mutual affiliations of text and ritual.[8] Given that ritual is always a performance,[9] and that a performance assumes both a context and an audience, the ritual elements of religious and philosophical discourses require an exegetical pragmatics.[10] To the extent that a text instantiates a performance, its pragmatic markers must delimit the interpretive universe in which the text belongs.

The question before us is, how are we to read the *Platonic Theology?* Do the text or the traditions to which it belongs provide such a pragmatics of interpretation? The history of the exegetical tradition helps to provide an answer. Iamblichus revolutionized Neoplatonic methods of exegesis through his assimilation of Plato to the Orphic/Chaldean traditions, as we have seen. Not only did he create a new form of exegetical practice by means of a pervasive intertexuality, he also changed the concept of text itself. Obviously, the idea of a text made sacred through its association with divinely revealed wisdom is

---

[5] Cf. *Corpus Hermeticum* 11 for a nearly contemporaneous text that employs the notion of speech offering, a ritual use of language that has a highly signficant initiatic function.

[6] On the idea that this text substitutes a Platonic universe for the more usual publicly available word, see the introductory remarks of Saffrey 1965, vol. I, Introduction.

[7] For a thorough discussion of this topic, see Janowitz 1996, Introduction.

[8] Tambiah, Janowitz, Scholem, Fossum, Shaw.

[9] On the performativity of ritual, see Tambiah 1979.

[10] As defined previously, "pragmatics" here consists in the contextual implications of a given utterance. For an introduction to this concept see Levinson.

different in kind from that of a dialectically generated text, such as a theological exegesis of Plato. No doubt the intellectualism of the tradition pulled in another direction entirely, demanding an almost exclusive reliance on texts whose relationship to a more authentic strain of wisdom remained continually dubious and under suspicion. Perhaps this tension is most manifest in a contest between theurgy and *theoria*, a context that forever changed the status of the philosophical text.[11]

For it is not thought which joins the theurgists to the gods, since (if that were the case) what would prevent those who philosophize theoretically from having theurgic union with the gods? For when we are not engaged in intellection, the *sunthemata* themselves perform by themselves the proper work, and the ineffable power of the gods, to whom these *synthemata* belong, knows by itself its own images. (*DM* 96.13)

Looking ahead to Damascius, we can see the direction the tradition followed. Far from relying on the dialectical methods of his predecessors, Damascius insisted upon an abrupt departure from philosophical discourse, as we saw. At the end of his *Doubts and Solutions Concerning First Principles* he retains only revealed wisdom as the foundation for what is unabashedly acknowledged as Neoplatonic faith.[12] This repudiation of Neoplatonic metaphysics verges on unorthodoxy and would be even more surprising were it not for the fact that it was anticipated by Proclus' own sympathies toward theurgy. The *Platonic Theology* is nothing less than a textual emblem of the marriage that took place between ritual and dialectic in the Neoplatonism of this period.

To say that the *Platonic Theology* relies both on Neoplatonic metaphysics and on Neoplatonic religious ritual is still not to comprehend the kind of text it is. To understand this fusion of philosophy and ritualism we must turn to the text for assistance. Its purpose as an initiatory text is to effect a metamorphosis within the reader thereby bringing him or her into the primordial tradition. Absorbed in the world of the text, one is to leave behind the world of natural objects and ordinary thoughts. What takes their place is no less than an entire tradition, one purporting to redescribe the universe, locat

[11] See Janowitz 1996, chapter 7, "Theurgy."
[12] It is quite interesting to note the theurgic emphasis on the virtue of faith in the *Platonic Theology* itself, which is a topic that we will come back to.

ing the soul in the center of an unfolding cosmology that is enacted precisely through the soul's ascent, or recitation, we might say, of its cosmic liturgy.[13] As a recipient of the text, the reader is located both historically as a link in the chain of transmission and ahistorically as a part of the world evoked through this transmission.

To read the text as an ideal reader is to take part in a theurgic ritual. For both Iamblichus and Proclus, theurgic ritual operates primarily through the structure and place of the human soul in the intelligible world. While Iamblichus emphasizes the Demiurgic function of the embodied soul, Proclus sees the soul primarily as a cosmic pleroma. In the *Platonic Theology*, Proclus attempts to awaken the soul to its inner world by providing it with an icon of its own reality.

Each soul is the pleroma of reality: καὶ ἡ ψυχὴ πάντων πλήρομά ἐστί τῶν εἰδῶν (*IP* 896.4). Far from being a tabula rasa, the soul is more like a theater or a screen that projects images within a kind of psychic space, the imagination. Proclus has much to say about the function of words as images of reality, and appreciates the place of the imagination in the world of the soul:

The soul therefore was never a writing-tablet bare of inscriptions; she is a tablet that has always been inscribed and is always writing itself and being written on by Nous. (*IE* 16)

We know that this passage is almost a quotation of *Enneads* V.3, but in its context, the quote helps define what Proclus means by the imagination.[14] As the borderland between the material world and the purely immaterial world of the intellect, this space of the imagination offers a transitional domain that the mind can come to inhabit. This visionary space does not contain external objects nor illusions nor hallucinations. Rather, it is above all a realm of self-illumination, as Proclus says:

Every god is without figure, even though it is viewed with a figure. For the figure is not in it, but it is part of it, since the seer is incapable of seeing without figure that which is with figure, but that which is seen in a figured way corresponds to the nature of the seer. (*In Rem.* I 40, 1–4)

But when the soul or mind thinks, the thoughts that it entertains can reflect two very distinctive kinds of reality:

---

[13] For a discussion of this sort of text, see Corbin.
[14] See Charles 1971 and Moutsopoulos 1985.

When we give the title of "thoughts" to the projections of the essential reason-principles, by virtue of which we understand how the soul is in a way the totality of all the forms, we must be understood to use the term "thoughts" in a very different sense from that which we use to describe what is produced in the soul as a result of projections from individual sense-objects. (*IP* 896)

Proclus constantly stresses that language can be a very powerful image of higher reality, one that is connected by its very nature to the highest elements of the cosmos. What is known outwardly through the imagination can be assimilated and traced back to its root. As Proclus goes on to say, "all things are in us in a psychic mode and that is why we are capable of knowing all beings, by awakening the powers that we have, *which is to say, the icons of the universal reality (IP* 1076).[15]

Since we reflect reality in ourselves, it is necessary to retrieve or to distract the outwardly directed attention of the mind away from its habitual gaze. By using images of the inner world, Proclus hopes to draw the attention of the soul back in to its original seat. This image of what the world looks like or can look like from the inside out, is exactly the function of the *symbolon*. By constructing such an image in the text of the *Platonic Theology*, Proclus hopes to bring about a response within the soul – a change of mind. He adumbrates this strategy in *PT* I 3.21:

> For Socrates correctly says in the *First Alcibiades* that the soul will see all things and even god by entering into itself. For by inclining itself toward its own unity, which is to say to enter into all likeness and by getting rid of multiplicity and the variety of its multifarious faculties, the soul will attain to the watchtower of all beings.

In this linguistic theurgy, the text can be considered an icon of a reality that is gradually brought into view. This iconic function of the text must now be considered. Two considerations will occupy us here: on the one hand, the textual tradition within which Proclus works had been fixed, so that exegesis is the primary vehicle of philosophical doctrine. On the other hand, this very canonization of

---

[15] On the monadology of the soul, see Trouillard 1982, chapter 7, and Trouillard 1972b. As Trouillard has shown, the concept of the soul as the pleroma of the ideas is a constant theme in the Proclan corpus. See, e.g., *IP* 9.1072, 18; 1080, 31;1081, 10.

texts meant for Proclus a "givenness," that had to be accommodated by a theory of language. Thus the persistence detected by Proclus in the use of signs and symbols within his tradition was itself a mark of their sanctity. The fixity of his texts meant that Proclus had at hand a system of signs that could be read as a complete language, a sacred discourse that revealed itself beyond the text, in the fabric of universe and in the history of its discursive representation.

Language and Ritual

Before discussing in more detail the ritual aspects of the *Platonic Theology*, it is important to consider whether or not Proclus thinks that language can have ritual associations and whether or not he thinks that correct interpretation depends on correctly identifying ritual aspects of the language. In his *Commentary on the Republic* Proclus establishes a theory of poetic expression by analogy to the practice of theurgy. It is because poetry is analogous to the hieratic art that poetry is at once uplifting and misleading. Since reality itself contains multiple states or levels of being, the divine series necessarily includes both the highest and lowest members. Likewise, since poetry mirrors this process, there must be both high and low poetry. That poetry reflects all the multiple states of being is what gives it its special veracity: "The authors of myths have a regard to the procession of the gods and are anxious to lead the myths upwards for each sensible particular into the entire series" (I 78.25).[16]

Myths, Proclus tells us, clothe themselves in superficial attire, covering up their secret truths. The final explanation for the fact that "the poets attempt to conceal their vision by means of false surfaces"[17] lies in a more technical understanding of the nature of symbolism. Poetry works after the manner of the hieratic art: each order (*taxis*) of being contains members who are farther up or lower down on the ontological totem pole.[18] A word expressed at the literal level can have associations with the higher members of the series.

---

[16] Lamberton 1985 discusses this passage. Those familiar with Lamberton's work will recognize how much this section owes to his wonderful book.

[17] ὧν ἀποκρύπτειν τοῖς φαινομέναις παραπετάσμασιν τὴν θεωρίαν ἐπιχειροῦσιν.

[18] For the most concise expresson of this idea, see the fragmentary "On the Hieratic Art," published in vol. I, pp. 134–6, of Festugière 1951.

Proclus elaborates on the poetic masking of truth insofar as it is rooted in the sympathy or correspondences between words and their references:

In each order, stretching from the gods to the lowest members and pervading all the classes of beings, the last members of the series can be seen having attributes that the myths assign to the gods, attributes that instantiate and refer to events by means of which the poets clothe their secret vision of the first principles. (*In Rem.* I 78, 1-10)

Finally, poetry is like a mystery religion; poetry and initiation function in precisely the same way. Proclus advances the same parallels in his theological writing:

In the most sacred rites of initiation they say that the initiates at first meet with various classes of god but entering further without turning back, and guarded by the rites they are engulfed by the divine illumination and, stripped of everything, as the Oracles say, they share the divine nature. In the same way also in the practice of the contemplation of the [whole] the mind, looking beyond itself sees only the shadow of reality, but turning inwards it sees itself and begins to unravel its own wisdom. And at first it is as if it only sees itself but deeper knowledge reveals the intellect within the soul and the orders of reality, and with intellect the soul can contemplate the class of gods and even the henads of reality. For all things are in us in a psychic manner, and because of this we are naturally capable of knowing all things by awakening our divine energy and the icons of the whole. (I.3.16.1)

Particularly noteworthy is line 8: τόν αὐτόν οἶμαι τρόπον καὶ ἐν τῇ θεωρίᾳ, where Proclus draws an explicit comparison between theurgic initiation and contemplation. This passage invites the participation of the reader as the icon by means of which the initiation is to take place.[19] More precisely, as we will see, the soul itself is the *sunthema* – the ritual token involved in the rite. Proclus often depicts the soul as such a ritual emblem, at times comparing the soul to statues or to icons:

The soul is composed of the intellectual words and from the divine *symbola* some of which are from the intellectual ideas, while others are from the divine henads. And we are in fact icons of the intellectual realities, and we are statues of the unknowable *sunthemata*. (*Phil. Chal.* 5, 8-11, Jahn)

---

[19] Cf. Plotinus, "Make oneself the vision" (VI.7.15.30).

We know from his other writings on the concept of divine *sunthemata*, and especially on the "flower of the soul"[20] or "One in us,"[21] that in our passage Proclus alludes to the individual soul's eventual union or identification with the One.[22] This notion of the soul as the token of the One was also important in Iamblichus' *De Mysteriis*.[23] As Gregory Shaw explains, "Iamblichus used the terms sunthema [or] sumbolon to describe the theurgic 'token' that divinized the soul."[24] For Iamblichus, this concept of *sunthema* was related to the participation of souls in the divine theophany. As Shaw states, in the Chaldean system the *sunthemata* or *symbola* are "sown . . . throughout the Cosmos" by the Demiurge.[25] As the divine powers informing the cosmos, the *symbola* have both cosmogonic and anagogic functions. The process of descent and return by means of *symbola* was part of a providential trajectory that souls traverse. The Iamblichean theurgic vision is based upon the reciprocal relationship that exists between the human soul and the divine order. Not only does the human soul, through its realization of unity with the divine, thereby sacralize its own world and thus "save" the world of matter, but the process of self-realization alters the very meaning and direction of what is otherwise described as a divine descent: "For this reason the gods have sent the souls down to this realm, in order to call them back. Therefore there is no change arising from such an ascent nor are

---

[20] Cf. Sheppard 1982, who discusses this term in some detail. For the term, ἄνθος νοῦ, see also *PT* 6, 35; *In Crat.* 47.15; *In Alc.* 519, 136–8.

[21] For the "One of the Soul" in Iamblichus, see Shaw 1995, chapter 11.

[22] ἀνεγείρουσα δὲ τὸ ἄρρητον σύνθεμα τῆς τῶν θεῶν ἑνιαίας ὑποστάσεως (*In. Rem.* I 177).

[23] On this text, see Shaw 1995. For those unfamiliar with the *De Mysteriis*, a brief word of introduction. The text purports to be a response by the Egyptian priest, Anebo, to a sustained attack on theurgic rituals promulgated by Porphyry. Prophyry's criticisms appear in the beginning of the work, and the exposition of theurgy in the second half of the text is organized around Porphyry's questions. Iamblichus, the author of this work, is considered to be the "forerunner of Julian" (Witt 1975) and authored a lost Commentary on the Chaldean Oracles that ran to 28 books (Witt 1975, p. 46). Like the rituals adumbrated in the surviving fragments of the Chaldean Oracles, the theme of the *De Mysteriis* is "the solar descent and ascent of the soul" (Witt p. 46). Iamblichus taught that Plato's teachings were "integrally related to the sacred traditions of the Egyptians, Chaldeans, Assyrians" (Shaw 1995, p. 6). The *De Mysteriis* is the text in which ritual is pitted against speculation, "theurgia" instead of "theologia" in Iamblichus' effort to defend the sanctity of the world and the efficacy of pagan soteriology (Shaw 1995, Introduction).

[24] Shaw 1995.

[25] Shaw quoting Chaldean Oracle 108 on p. 138.

descents and ascents of souls opposed to each other" (*DM* VIII.8; 272, 8–12).[26]

In the *IT* Proclus alludes to the "ineffable symbols of the gods which the father of souls has sown in them" (24). For Proclus, these *symbola* are related to the chains or orders of being, which occasion "the bringing about of fitness for participation in the gods, those things that have come to be in the divided realm, by means of symbola" (III 155.18). In this sense, the divine *sunthemata* are related directly to the perfection of the cosmos, just as in Iamblichus, the *symbola* complete the cosmos by allowing souls to return to the divine.[27]

Thus the worshipper in a sense reproduces the cosmos, thereby re-creating the world in a consecrated manner. He now invokes and summons a spiritualized world. An important aspect of this theurgic rite is its attention to completion. By incorporating *sunthemata* from every divine *taxis*, the theurgist unifies all the powers of the gods, creating a whole cosmos. It is this creation of the whole that finally brings about the divine sympathy, or *philia*, that enables the soul to ascend.

In the theurgic rites involving statues and material *symbola*, this universe of power was a material construction, but this re-created world could also be modeled in language. Support for this idea can be seen in both Iamblichus and Porphyry, who differentiate between different levels of sacrifice or ritual. Iamblichus mentions a kind of offering that is wholly immaterial (V.15). Offerings can be made to higher or lower gods; the higher gods can be worshipped only by "intellectual" gifts. For this kind of worship, wisdom is the true sacrifice or offering: σοφία δωρεῖται.[28] Again, in the *De abst.* II, 34 Porphyry distinguishes different levels of sacrifice. At the highest order, Porphyry says, "the sacred sacrifice," consisting of wisdom, is made.[29]

---

[26] Quoted by Pearson 1992, p. 264, and Shaw 1995.

[27] As Smith says, the *sunthemata* "are present in the world to remind us of the gods" (*IT*. I, 213, 17: πρὸς ἀνάμνησιν).

[28] On different levels of materialism in offerings and on the concept of the immaterial offering, see Smith 1974. See also Shaw, chapter 14, p. 151, on the fitness of sacrifices, which had to be "connatural" (*sungenia*) both with the soul who offered it and with the god who received it.

[29] Cited by Smith 1974.

Proclus compares words to sacred statues: "[nous] contains images and substantive words that emanate, which are like statues of the forms, as if the names imitated the intellectual forms" (*In Crat.* 6, 13). On page 19 of the *In Crat.*, Proclus compares the theurgic investment of statues to the act of naming, and in the *PT* I 29, p. 125, he again compares the use of divine names to the theurgists' statues: "[*episteme*] produces each name as if it were a statue of the gods."[30]

If language can be compared to the theurgists' statues, then a text can be understood as a *symbolon*. By pressing this analogy, it becomes possible to conceive of the *Platonic Theology* as a kind of textual *symbolon*. The *Platonic Theology* presents itself as a catalogue of divine attributes as well as a full disclosure of the various names used for the gods. Proclus claims to be offering a complete enumeration of the names and orders of deity, for him evinced above all in the dialogues of Plato. At the same time, this enumerative concern is complemented by the cosmogonic nature of this text.

As if it were a theurgic rite, combining all the divine series in order to re-create a sacralized cosmos, the *Platonic Theology* divulges a kind of cosmic prehistory in which the psychic landscape, the geography of ascent and descent, is traversed in detail. The notion of a textual *symbolon* is both familiar in Late Antique religiosity and fundamental for an appreciation of ritualistic language. Cosmic ascent takes place through the disclosure of divine names. In the second chapter of book 1, Proclus employs another comparison to the mysteries and so indicates that this text carries with it certain pragmatic expectations that must be met by the reader.

It is requisite that the shape of the discourse as well as the preparations of the audience be adequate, just as in initiations, the specialists prepare the appropriate vessels, and they don't always employ lifeless media for the same gods, nor non-human creatures, nor human beings for the invocation of the deities, but employ a corresponding medium in each case for the particular rite. (I.2.3.1–5)

What becomes clear is that the text itself has the status of a ritual invocation. This sacred invocation is a very important feature of the Proclan concept of theurgy. Proclus often compares theurgic ascent

---

[30] Saffrey 1979 discusses these texts in connection with Pseudo-Dionysius' appropriation of this image.

to the process of divine invocation, as in this fragment from the *Chaldean Philosophy:* "the soul offers the secret *sunthemata* to the Father which the Father has placed inside the soul in the primary procession of reality. For these are the intellectual and invisible hymns of the soul on its way up" (*Phil. Chal.* 1 16–19, Jahn).

Divine Names

When Proclus turns to a discussion of divine names, as distinct from the human language of poetry or myth, he reveals the deeper roots of language:[31] "There are names appropriate for each level of reality, divine names for the divine, discursive names for the discursive reality, and opinionated names for the level that requires the use of opinion" (*IT* I, p. 273, 25–27). For Proclus, as we shall see, language is analogous to world making; the Demiurge is the first speaker whose words imply the process of cosmic manifestation. In his *Commentary on the Timaeus*, Proclus elaborates on this theurgic view of language. Proclus first explains that at the level of intellect, creation and the act of naming are one and the same:

> The positing of a name is in fact creation since intellect there is not cut off from creation, but rather the gods create by means of intellection. Thus it is that they bring about things by means of their activity of naming. (*IT* I)

At this point in the text, Proclus breaks into a digression on the theurgic power of language.[32]

> If I must give my own opinion, it is possible to observe in this discussion the secret doctrines of Plato concerning contemplation, namely that he did not only posit the Demiurge as the first name giver, insofar as the Demiurge named the two parts of the soul [sc. the circle of the same and the circle of the other] but that the Demiurge even before these names revealed the essential character (magical sign) of the soul by showing the two separate sides and the *Chi* that results and the two circles that result from the *Chi.* (*IT* II 255)

Somewhat obscured in this passage is how the chiastic system described by the letter *chi* fits into Proclus' general views on the

---

[31] On this passage, see Trouillard 1972.

[32] For this whole discussion, see Festugiere vol. III, p. 29, and the references there. See also Troulliard.

speech of the Demiurge in Plato's *Timaeus*.[33] The Demiurge is of course responsible for cosmic manifestation; in terms of Proclus' divine hierarchy, the Demiurge represents the lower limit of the intellectual gods. The two circles described in the soul are related to the two essential moments of this manifestation, that is, procession and return, as we can deduce by comparing this passage with the *Commentary on the Cratylus*:

> The name has two powers, one that teaches and communicates thoughts, the other that discerns the reality, since the Demiurge also has two sorts of powers, one that produces identity and another that produces alterity. (*In Crat.* 51.20.18–21)[34]

The soul, as the channel of cosmic manifestation, reads the world under one of two signs: the world is "other" than or outside the soul when it is engaged in the process of descent, whereas it is "the same" as and within the ascending or returning soul. Both of these great names are thus pronounced and understood by the soul, while in the moment of its pronouncement, the world itself is expressed. In fact, the world as a whole is just such a system of signs, due again to the activity of the Demiurge:

> The name "cosmos" is appropriate as applied to a creation of the Demiurge. And if it is possible to call the world by both [names], [it is] "Ouranos" as looking up and seeing the intelligible and as participating in the intelligible being, and "cosmos" . . . as that which proceeds . . . Heaven and Earth are therefore signifiers, the one signifies the procession from there and other the return. (*IT* I 273)

Thus the tradition of divine names reveals that the world as a whole is a system of signs and can be read according to a series of interpretive choices.

The first names that Proclus mentions in his *Platonic Theology* are "The One" and "The Good." The divine names are not just names that human beings have for the One; they are also the elements of divine speech, because by means of these names, the One communicates with all things. At the same time, these divine names also represent the way that human beings are capable of approaching

---

[33] For an overview of Proclus' views about the Demiurge in Plato's *Timaeus*, see Festugière vol. IV, appendix two.

[34] On this passage, see Trouillard p. 243.

the One; they are modes of revelation that at once manifest and veil the One.

Therefore, as we have said, the manner of indicating the One is twofold: for the names that Plato hands down to us for this secret principle are also two. In the *Republic* he calls [the One] "The Good," and he uses the term to indicate the source of the truth that unifies the knower and the known. But in the *Parmenides* he uses the term, "One," designating this principle by means of this term and reveals it as the cause of existence for the Henads. (II.6.40.1–5)

Once more, then, of these names, the one is the name for the procession of the universe, and the other is the symbol of [its] reversion. On this account it brings all things into existence and all things proceed from this first principle. (II.6.40.5–10)

But do not for this reason assume that the Ineffable is capable of receiving a name nor that the cause of all unity is dual. In this case as well, such names as we apply refer to what is after the [One], either to the procession that comes from it or to the reversion that returns to it. (II.6.41.1–5)

For Proclus these names of the One are actually modes of discourse: the name "One" is the root idea for the mode of negation, and the name "Good" is the root idea for the mode of affirmation. Proclus likens these names to "divine images" that are technically theurgic because they are designed to capture the first principle by means of its effects.

Consequently, it is not always easy to "read" the cosmos, since its legibility depends, paradoxically, on a deferment of meaning:

But just as certain symbols connected with statues and made by initiates are obvious, certain other symbols have an esoteric meaning and refer to the divine presence, and these are known only to the initiates, in the same way the world itself is an image of the intelligible and it has been fashioned by its father containing certain obvious signs of its divinity, while others are secret symbols.

Here we are warned that misunderstanding is likely, since the world not only is a symbol of the two great names of divinity but also hides within its disclosure another name that is not likewise revealed. If procession and return are the great names of the divinity, then everything finally is a sign of the ultimate sign, and this leaves the whole series unexplained in an endless deferment of meaning.

This cosmic language is a totalizing system that encompasses everything in reality, proceeding from the Ineffable and pervading into the very fabric of the world, including all within the domain of signs. But cosmic manifestation is just one root of the divine, just as procession is only one term within the fundamental Proclan triad. In fact, because Proclus talks about the divine names in terms of remaining, procession, and return, he is concerned to demonstrate that reality as it exists in itself also has a name, even if this name is unknowable.

> Therefore a divine name must exist for the power of remaining . . . just as there exists a name for the power of procession. Yet this name is ineffable and unutterable and is made known to the gods alone. For there are names appropriate to each level of reality: divine names for the gods, discursive names for the discursive intellect, and names rooted in appearances for the sensible faculty. (*PT* II.6.92)

For Proclus, any name applied to the One is already a limitation and presents the One according to a certain power or aspect. Because activities manifest their causes, they at once delimit the nature of their causes and, at the same time, distort or compromise them. Therefore the names "the One" and "the Good" veil the first god under two different aspects, that of unity and that of creation. As Trouillard says, there is a fundamental contrast in Proclus' thinking about language: on the one hand, language in the strict sense has its appearance only among rational and discursive souls, and on the other hand, language is rooted in the unifying and generative power of divinity.[35]

If the cosmos is a sign for God, however, and signifies God insofar as God communicates, then we are presented with a system that allows no translation and no referentiality. Ultimately, the circle of the Same and the circle of the Other can enclose the soul within a discourse whose terms must remain unexplained. Either excluded from this totalizing system, (in the circle of the other) we find it impenetrable and meaningless, or comprehended by it, (in the circle of the same) we at once find it meaningful. And yet this meaning cannot be disclosed to another since it only becomes apparent to the soul once it sees behind the veil of cosmic manifestation and return. This enigmatic circularity is just the great name of the divine.

---

[35] Trouillard, p. 239.

It cannot be grasped by human reason or made to signify within a conventional system of discourse. As Proclus says, "To summarize, then, the foremost and most authoritative names one must suppose are seated in the divine itself" (*PT* I 29).

Symbol and Imagination

So far we have seen that the *Platonic Theology* does not employ language in any ordinary sense. That the divine names are the subject matter of this work has implications for the ritual status of the text; moreover, the theoretical considerations concerning the reality of language also have implications for its interpretation. It is time now to take stock of these implications.

What does it mean for an interpretation to say that language is rooted in the nature of the One and that all language is a ramification of the two great names for the One, that is, the One and the Good? An astonishingly radical view of language is at work in this theory. Proclus here reveals nothing short of a pathway to God, based upon the way of invocation. If the deepest roots of language can be traced back to the One (again, to recur to the text just cited, "foremost and most authoritative names one must suppose are seated in the divine itself"), language cannot fail to have theurgic value. The names of the gods that Proclus recites in the *Platonic Theology* have no conceptual equivalents, even though they are stationed, as we have seen, along the Parmenidean axis. Therefore, to interpret the text is to invoke these names. But what follows from this invocation? The language of the *Platonic Theology* is a language of vision.

The text deliberately uses a gradation of names, language, and dialect that mirrors the veiling power of the lower realities that we saw operative in the case of poetry. This hierarchical deployment of language represents the devolution of reality by exploiting both different modes of speech (visionary, mythic, or theological) and a geometric schema, in which the expansion of the One is mirrored by a geometric proliferation of principles at subsequently lower stages of reality. The effect is the creation of a textual symbol, a circle of expanding parts emanating from a single center. The geometric scheme imposed upon the whole is effected through its mul tiplication by triads, that is, through an exponential increase in the number of elements farther down in the cosmic decline. The basic structure that Proclus describes in his *Platonic Theology* involves the production of a series of monads, each one replicating itself so that its individual members reflect the contents of the entire structure. The effect is that of a hall of mirrors. The progression of the *Platonic Theology* follows the triadic structure of Being, Life (or Power), and Mind, that together comprise the Proclan version of the second hypostasis.[36] These levels proliferate exponentially in their infrastructure, with the triads exploding into nine, twenty-seven, seventy-two, over one hundred, and, finally, indefinitely many members. Within each successive level, the prior levels repeat themselves by mirroring the basic structure of definite, indefinite, and mixed. This triad reappears in subsequent levels of reality as the paternal, generative, and perfective orders. Since lower orders are not capable of receiving or reflecting the entire content of prior orders, each order distinguishes itself as a partial revelation of its cause. At the same time, this rule ensures that there are indefinitely many reflections of every member of the intelligible order and that each one reflects the contents of all the other members.

Although the *Platonic Theology* is an ontological map of the Proclan universe, it also implies the participation of the reader for whom the ontology is conceived as a subjective transformation. Its greatest achievement is to have created an initiatory language that at once purports to reveal the hidden codes within the textual tradition as well as to situate the subject within the interpretive universe. We return to the discussion of Proclan subjectivity. It is because the *Platonic Theology* purports to be an image of theurgic ascent that it functions as an icon of the subject.

Proclus reads Platonic and Orphic mythology for their associations with theurgy. The text is Proclus' attempt to reveal a sacred space that the soul is supposed to fill out with its vision. In Proclus' exegesis of this mythic material, he emphasizes the sudden moment of psychic transformation when the mind's vision opens up beyond

---

[36] Rosan is still the best description of Proclus' noetic world. Rosan relies heavily on Proclus' descriptions in the *Platonic Theology*. For another good description or overview of Proclus' nous, see Lloyd 1982.

its accustomed limits. Thus the *Platonic Theology* is concerned with the psychology of contemplation and here Proclus employs an almost visual approach to theurgy. Finally, it is the psychic space of the imagination that becomes the most important vehicle for theurgy in the *Platonic Theology*.

> Therefore just as the nature stands creatively above the visible figures, so the soul, exercising her capacity to know, projects on the imagination, as on a mirror, the ideas of the figures; and the imagination, receiving in pictorial form these impressions of the ideas within the soul, by their means afford the soul an opportunity to turn inward from the pictures and attend to herself. It is as if a man looking at himself in a mirror and marveling at the powers of nature and at his own appearance should wish to look upon himself directly and possess such a power as would enable him to become at the same time the seer and the object seen. In the same way, when the soul is looking outside herself at the imagination, seeing the figures depicted there and being struck by their beauty, she is admiring her own ideas from which they are derived.

Although this quotation is from Proclus' *Commentary on the First Book of Euclid's Elements*, it provides us with an understanding of the relationship between icon and imagination in Proclus' thought. As the mind's attention is redirected into this imaginal space, the space of consciousness, it learns to take up more room, so to speak. Proclus has transformed the Platonic dialogues into a book of divine visions. The dialogues reveal the true art of the soul; the beauty of the intellectual world consists in the art of seeing, as Proclus tells us in his interpretation of the Phaedrean myth: "Socrates says, explaining the method of ascent to the intelligible beauty, how following the gods that exist prior to the body and prior to birth, we attained that blessed vision" (IV.9).

The Language of Vision

How to attain this vision? And what is the vision about? As indicated earlier, the vision developed in the *Platonic Theology* consists primarily in the expansion of consciousness within an interior world. Proclus attempts to convey this interior world, with its ever-widening center, by interpreting the language of myth as its representation.

In books IV and V of the *Platonic Theology*, Proclus turns to the extra-Platonic narrative tradition, to Orphism and to the Chaldean

Oracles, as source material for his exegesis of central Platonic myths. Thus in book V, by drawing on the Orphic succession myth to explicate the *Timaeus*, Proclus discusses the Demiurge's projection of the Platonic Forms into *chora* or the receptacle. Again, in book IV Proclus explicates the *Phaedrus'* myth of the soul's hyperouranian flight by alluding to the stations of psychic ascent evinced in the Chaldean Oracles.

Turing now to his exegesis of the Timaean Demiurge, we see Proclus recasting the Demiurge as the Orphic Zeus and citing Orphic fragment 68 to motivate this interpretation. For Proclus, the Platonic account of the Demiurge causing the world of space and time had to be rewritten. Proclus does not accept the Platonic account in which the intellect is directly related to the world of particulars. Instead, Zeus gives birth to an intelligible world, a world in which exteriority and multiplicity are only foreshadowed.[37]

In *Platonic Theology*, Proclus uses the metaphor of "binding" to emphasize interiority of the intellectual world:

Zeus therefore, being at the same time intellectual and intelligible, intellectually perceives and comprehends himself, and binds the intelligible in himself. But binding this in himself, he is said to bind the intelligibles prior to himself, and to comprehend it on all sides. For entering into himself, he proceeds into the intelligible prior to himself, and by the intelligible which is in himself, intellectually perceives that which is prior to himself. And thus the intelligible is not external to intellect. For every intellect possesses that which is in itself without any difference with respect to itself. But again, intellect perceives in itself that which is prior to itself. For every thing which is external to intellect is foreign and adventitious, and pertains to an inferior nature. (V.5.22:3–10)

Nowhere does Proclus admit that the Demiurge reflects ideas in matter. For Proclus, the dualism inherent in the Platonic account of creation is inconceivable:[38] "Matter, therefore, and the whole of that which is the subject of bodies, proceed from the first principles,

---

[37] In the *Platonic Theology*, Proclus underscores the difference between his own and the Platonic accounts. He stresses the Demiurge's creation of souls and emphasizes the correspondences between the hebdomadic divisions of the intellectual gods and the *Timaeus'* account of the creation of the soul: "After this also, the Demiurge divides the [soul] into one circle and seven circles. Whence therefore are this monad and hebdomad derived, except from the intellectual gods?"

[38] On Proclus' lack of the usual Neoplatonist matter-form dualism, see Lloyd 1990.

which on account of their exuberance of power, are able to generate even the last of beings.''

In the Orphic theogony, the squalls of the infant Zeus are disguised by the dancing of the Curetes' armor. In terms of Chaldean theology the Curetes represent the Guardian class, whose function it is to purify the intellect of its associations with the material order. Proclus etymologizes the name of the Curetes from the word for maiden and from the word for purity (τὸ κόρον). In book V, Proclus delineates the structure of the intellectual cosmos: it is hebdomadic, rather than triadic. The aspect of Being is represented by the triad of the parents (Kronos, Rhea, and Zeus) and the aspect of Power is represented by the triad of the immaculate gods, called in the *Platonic Theology*, the Curetes; there is also a monad that divides three classes of gods: the transcendent gods, the lesser gods, and the encosmic gods. This monad is represented by Proclus as the act of castration of Kronos! The parental triad is also associated with the five *megiste gene* of the Sophist, so that Kronos is equated with Being; Rhea with Rest and Motion, and Zeus with Sameness and Difference.

Despite his switching in and out of various mystical dialects, there can be no doubt that Proclus conceives of the Chaldean tradition as primary throughout his exegetical efforts. The second part of Proclus' exegetical program relates, as we have already seen, to the unity of the primordial tradition, or the accord between Plato, the Oracles, and Orpheus. The fourth book of the *Platonic Theology* furnishes us with the blueprint for this Chaldean interpretation of Plato: "Here it is right to admire the divinely inspired science of Plato because he has explained the method of ascent to the intelligible domain according to the chief initiators.''

The Oracles and their interpretation by the theurgists is a chief source for the doctrine of the noetic-noeric gods that Proclus elaborates in book IV of the *Platonic Theology*. It is clear that Proclus has created a visionary exegesis of the Platonic dialogue, at the same time trying to communicate an initiatory form of language that relies heavily on the notion of language as *symbolon*. In this book, we see Proclus engaging in a dialogue with his own exegetical tradition by synthesizing the language of theurgy with the language of Platonism.

Particularly noteworthy is the reification of the Phaedrean myth through the invention of a visionary topos that is situated both inside and outside of the text. Proclus starts with the Cratylus' definition of "Ouranos" as "sight seeing what is above"; the hyperouranion topos, heaven itself, and the vault below heaven (*Phaedrus* 247b) constitute, respectively, the three triads that belong to this realm. In the next paragraph, Proclus neatly explicates Plato's myth in terms of three classes of Chaldean gods: the Leaders, the Leaders of perfection or Teletarchs, and the Connectors.[39] Proclus closely correlates the Phaedrean myth with these Chaldean ranks by discussing the topology of the myth in terms of the theurgic rites of ascent. In the next ten chapters, Proclus expands upon the Chaldean-Platonic synthesis, subdividing the ouranian topography into more elaborate triads. Thus the hyperouranion topos consists of the three subtriads: the plain of truth, the meadow, and the nutriment of the gods; truth, justice, and temperance; and the uncolored, the unfigured, and the intangible. Proclus closes this section by reiterating the Chaldean interpretation of the myth as degrees of initiation: *telete, muesis,* and *epopteia.*

Throughout book IV, Proclus reifies Platonic language to impose his scheme of proliferating triads on the Phaedrean myth. The result is a series of competing narratives, in which the original story of the heavenly charioteer and the tripartite soul is redescribed in terms of a mythic journey.

Stepping back from the narrative, it may not seem that Proclus' exegesis is terribly effective. After all, he has merely substituted one myth for another, and Plato's language itself borrows from an earlier initiatory tradition. And yet it is here that Proclus not only reveals that his exegetical practice rests upon his belief in a primordial tradition and in the unity of all religions but also suggests that this hypothesis can be tested because both Plato and the Chaldeans transmit a wisdom that exists outside of discursive thought, outside of writing. In our passage, Proclus more than once refers to the limitations of thinking:

For it is not by means of intellection nor in general discrimination, that initiation takes place, but by means of the silence that surpasses Gnostic energy, which gives faith and faith seats us in the ineffable class of gods. (IV.9.193.10–15)

---

[39] On the classes of Chaldean gods, see Majercik.

Again, the soul, in its final degree of initiation, encounters in the supercelestial realm the divine *sunthemata* and magical signs of the intelligible world. These signs are only symbols of a more authentic silence:

> initiation (*muesis*) and revelation (*epopteia*) are themselves symbols (*symbolon*) of the ineffable silence and of the unity with the intelligible by the method of mystic revelations. (IV.9.193.15–16)

Here we see Proclus deliberately reshaping the Platonic material, working out the correspondences between the myth and theurgic rites. As a result, the language becomes infused with the theurgic symbolism and thus operates within the realm of non-discursive thinking. *Muesis*, initiation, is literally interpreted as silence. In Proclus' hands, the myth shifts directions and seemingly indicates a non-discursive space. That is, the mythic landscape, already subsumed into a triadic scheme by Proclus (the hyperouranion topos, heaven itself, and the subcelestial arch)[40] is now redescribed not only as a visionary world but also as a world peopled by deities who reflect the soul's own visionary status:

> Plato elevates the souls and the gods themselves through the fountains by means of the detached leaders for the visions and the journeys both blessed and entirely full are especially in those, in which the theurgists place their entire hope of salvation. They are therefore blessed through the unmixed monad, full through the cause of divine otherness, and visions and journeys from the fountains and through the fountains to the leaders of perfection (for after the many and divided intellections the good of the perfective gods appears, and descending from the intelligible and intellectual gods they fill us up and enlighten us, and before our own souls, the class of whole soul and before these, the gods themselves). But from the perfective class they journey to the connective of the entire noeric order. (IV.9.192.5)

Although compressed, the details of this paragraph describe a rather dramatic encounter between soul and deity, between inner and outer worlds, as the soul meets its guides and prepares to leave its abode in the cosmos and thus to discover its true identity.[41]

---

[40] Of course, Proclus denies that this triadic structure of the Phaedrean landscape is original with him and provides evidence that other exegetes had also recognized his divisions. (*PT* IV.23).

[41] See Corbin, *Avicenna and the Visionary Recital*, for a discussion of this kind of mystical genre, in which the soul meets a divine guide during the course of a mythical journey.

Proclus interprets the myth of the *Phaedrus* as a journey upon which the soul will encounter its divine guide and so be led to its original home. The text is now punctuated by an exegetical awkwardness. If Plato's myth is about the soul's union with the intelligible world, why doesn't the narrative accommodate this interpretation? Here Proclus must employ a kind of reverse *argumentum ex silentio*: mystical union is a difficult moment to describe. From the point of view of ascent, the soul has now overcome the discursive realm: of course, it is impossible to communicate the nature of this transformation. What is of interest is the extent to which theurgic language become prevalent within this discussion:

And how the souls accomplish their union with the first rank of the intelligibles is no longer indicated through the texts of Plato; for it is a mystery also that occurs by unspeakable means, just as it seemed to them [the theurgists] as well, and it is through this station that the mystic unity occurs with the intelligibles and the first causes. Therefore the same method of ascent is also found among us and on this account the method of theurgic ascent is more credible. (IV.9.192.24–193–5.)

The exegetical complexity becomes acute at this point: discussing a mythical passage of the *Phaedrus*, Proclus interprets it in terms of the *Parmenides*. But the exegesis of the *Parmenides* depends on a Chaldean tradition of the noetic-noeric gods. And finally, the whole passage is said to refer to a theurgic ritual involving the soul's union with intellect. After such an elaborate exegesis, Proclus almost incredibly claims that the text is describing a ritual. Its true meaning is extra-textual and outside of language altogether.

The Space of the Text

It is not difficult to imagine that Proclus views this theurgic ascent as exploration of the limits of the subjective. Proclan metaphysical realism demands that for every level of reality within the subject there is a corresponding objective level that informs it. But since subjectivity itself is reified or formalized within this text, metaphysical realism becomes to say the least obscured. Its ornate elaboration of the various triads seems at times to arrest the mind with an impenetrable discursive landscape, as if to give a sense of the overflowing fullness and vastness of the intelligible world. And yet, this text does not openly reflect upon the central ontological fact of the entire description; namely, that in all of this, reality devolves by means of more and more limited forms of being, that is to say, more and more individualized modes of consciousness. By contrast, not only is Plotinus very concerned to discuss the structure of consciousness on its own terms, but he actually views contemplation as a kind of objectless or pure consciousness. Proclus never discusses the idea of objectless awareness. The text presents us with a proliferation of objects, as if to leave no room at all for the subject of awareness.

At any rate, we are left with the question of just how this textual theurgy is supposed to operate. Superficially, the book is simply about texts; it presents us with an intertexual reading of Plato that creates a kind of false genealogy for the texts it sets out to explain, positing a historical reversal that makes the earlier Platonic text an anticipation of the later theurgic texts. Proclus nevertheless insists that the true reference point of the text is extra-textual. We are left to consider this paradox.

At this point, it will be helpful to recall the formal explanation for this paradox, the fact that the text itself has theurgic associations, as we have seen. For Proclus, language is inherently theurgical, both because all forms of discourse are an extension of the divine names and because language reiterates the hierarchical nature of reality. Moreover theurgical ritual is graded according to the intellectual development of the person practicing, and speech offering is a sublime form of the ritual. Theurgic rite involves the creation of a ritual cosmos, which is then sacralized through its capacity to draw down the power of the gods. In the case of our text, the text itself becomes such a ritual cosmos and hence possesses talismanic properties.

If Proclus presents the *Platonic Theology* as an initiatory text, it then appears to create an anti-discursive space, replacing the textuality of Plato with a ritual that is supposed to operate in non-discursive terms. In fact, Proclus achieves just the opposite effect. Far from presenting the subject with an alternate to discursive forms, he translates the subject in terms of a textual space. Thus the very purpose of this text seems to be an inscribing of the reader within the textual tradition, into the linguistic landscape of the text. At last we must conclude that the ritual affiliations of the *Platonic Theology* do not succeed in overcoming its textuality. Rather, the reader is expected to enter into the world of the text. The result is the immersion of the subject within a highly textualized discursive practice.

Conclusion: Visions of Language – An Overview of Proclus' *Platonic Theology*

Proclus works within a framework of language that reaches across a number of different categories: prayer, talisman, revelation, myth, divine names, initiation, and even silence. Amidst this barrage of linguistic categories, it does not escape our attention that what he is primarily doing is a form of exegesis. His work presents Plato's dialogues as a sacred scripture that supports an exegetical universe comprised by tradition, revelation, and interpretation.

The hermeneutic circle constructed by this procedure is almost impenetrable while its argument is almost disingenuous: Proclus begins the book by promising a scientific discussion and exposition of the Parmenidean levels of being. What he delivers is a universe of language that exists on so many different levels that it at once over-determines the possibilities of interpretation and exegesis. If the truth in language is more fiction than truth and if this fiction is perpetrated by all the seers of truth, this leaves human beings in a terrible predicament.

Even though some writings can claim an impressive set of credentials because of either their prestige or their origin, this fact alone cannot reassure us that the narrative strands Proclus manages to weave together are coherent. The problem remains that traditions, as Proclus presents them, are either too syncretic to be authentic or too fragmentary and fractured to have any force. Exchanging metaphors and narrative styles, translating myth into metaphysics and metaphysics into myth – all of this is an attempt to force the issue of language into an uncompromising dilemma.

Either language does not refer to anything outside of its own fictionality, and truth merely translates into fragmentary truths, or reality itself must finally give way to the weight of traditional narrative. This assault upon the psyche – its overwhelming with language and the displacement of its orientation – is calculated to forever change the mind.

Finally, one enters into this interpretive universe from which the only escape is to take another direction. Perhaps this trap of language hides some hidden doorway. The categories of traditional language overlap and intersect each other with no apparent order. While distinguishing types of traditional discourse, Proclus assimilates them in practice, so that interpretation becomes primary despite the prestige of these texts. The interpretive universe that Proclus constructs loses its contours in the web of narratives that constantly displace each other. If prayer, revelation, theology, and mythology all originate in the same interpretive world that permits the equation of forms of discourse that normally compete with each other, then this is because they are all elements in Proclus' own vision of language.

Proclus' program, his attempt to recover a primordial tradition by crossing the boundaries between traditional genres and creating an intertexuality among texts that originally do not refer to each other, shows his sophistication as an exegete. He realizes that no text can be isolated and willingly reads texts through the traditions that have come to displace the original texts. But Proclus has left the traditional categories of language intact. They are not mere tropes or metaphors for ordinary descriptive language. Exegesis itself is only a pretext for the creation of something vastly more important than a commentary, albeit Proclus writes in the commentary tradition.

This subordination to tradition and the refusal to claim originality in his work suggests that exegesis is the key to the tradition. No matter what the text says, it is read through an exegetical framework that can translate the original text into an equally authentic voice. Thus nowhere does philosophy as a system of analyzing texts appear as a contribution to the enterprise. In fact, translation into a language that pretends to be intelligible is mere deception. By translating the theology of Plato into the language of myth and magic, Proclus does what he has to as an apologist for the Neoplatonic tradition. Ultimately, Proclus is not interested in conveying a strictly linear reading of the *Parmenides* or the Platonic corpus. Instead, he is after an effect that can be achieved through only an oversaturation in the discursive realm.

Traditional narrative is always disclosed within the context of ritual – it is at once a performance as well as a recital. Prayer, *voce mysticae*, divine names, oracles, and mystical numbers are all forms of ritual speech that appear in the text of Proclus. Moreover, the overall pattern of the text resembles traditional ritual genres, such as heavenly ascents or descents, hymns, mystical cosmologies, and initiatory myths. Thus although Proclus writes in a prestigious and elite philosophical institution that historically invoked the mythic while simultaneously diffusing its ritualism, we see a reversal in his case.

For Proclus, the constraints of tradition presented him with a discursivity that had to be interrupted through the superimposition of a different kind of language. That this strategy at once violates the genre of exegesis and threatens to avoid the task of interpretation by the displacement of meaning onto a ritual language lacking any discursive counterpart is the inevitable consequence of his membership in a tradition in which discursivity was the final obstacle overshadowing the text. Proclus' text, then, fights with itself and with its tradition in an effort to articulate the limits of linguistic interpretation.

If in the midst of this theological exegesis we find the remnants of a linguistic mysticism that defies the philosophical tradition in which he operates, this does not mean that Proclus reads naively or perversely. Rather, Proclus realizes the power and responsibility implied by the act of interpretation and by the authorized or institutional dissemination of a text. Proclus and other members of his tradition are committed to a form of exegesis that leaves the doorway to vision open, precisely because for them these texts are the best and even sole guarantee that this doorway can and will remain open.

Were it not for the textual artifacts that constrain the mind of the reader to search in a realm that seemingly does not yield its meaning readily or apparently, and one that operates, moreover, in defiance of the text, this whole process of interpretation would come to an abrupt end. The distinction between speculative texts, exegetical texts, and magical or ritual texts is deliberately obscured. This is Proclus' final pronouncement upon the status of the text in a tradition that uncompromisingly repudiates the discursive, despite that its most appropriate *symbolon* can only be the text.

If this strategy appears arbitrary or even contradictory, this is only because Proclus finds the very concept of interpretation dangerously seductive and highly charged with possibility. Proclus is fully aware of the interpretive choices that govern his own construction of the visionary universe. But that universe does not and cannot emerge independently of that choice. This means finally that the interpretation will not yield its meaning to someone not willing to embrace the vision that the text presents. Only after this has been accomplished, when the universe of interpretation is embraced as one's own world, can the reader be said to have fulfilled the pragmatic expectations of the text. This is not to deny the reader his or her own interpretive choices nor to suggest that the meaning of text is outside of its own deliverances. In fact, the last token required for the completion of the ritual cosmos instantiated by the text can be contributed only by the reader.

9

Damascius' Ineffable Discourse

Introduction to Damascius and the *Aporiai kai Luseis Peri Proton Archon (Doubts and Solutions Concerning First Principles)*

Damascius (ca. 462–538) was scholarch when the Christian emperor Justinian shut down the Platonic Academy in 529, issuing a decree that banned all pagans from teaching in Athens. Damascius' title, Diadochus, marked him as last in the ancient lineage of Platonic Successors.[1] His attempts to revitalize the foundering school no doubt made it a target of anti-pagan persecution, a persecution that followed in the wake of violent attacks directed against Neoplatonists active in the city of Alexandria.[2] Upon the closing of the Academy, Damascius led a band of pagan philosophers out of their patron city and into exile.[3] We learn from the historian Agathias that

> Damascius the Syrian, Simplicius the Silician, Eulamius the Phrygian, Priscian the Lydian, Hermeias and Diogenes from Phoenicia and Isidorus of Gaza, all the finest flower, as the poem says, of those who did philosophy in our time, since they did not like the prevailing opinion among the Greeks, and thought the Persian constitution to be far better . . . went away to a different and pure place with the intention of spending the rest of their lives there.[4]

There is some disagreement about the fate of the exiled philosophers after their disappointment over conditions in Persia. It is now

---

[1] *Vita Isidore.* Saffrey and Westerink, tome 1, Introduction; Cameron 1969.
[2] Athanassiadi 1993
[3] See Blumenthal's account of Damascius' perigrinations in *Aristotle and Neoplatonism in Late Antiquity*, pp. 41–4.
[4] Agathias, 2.30-3-4, quoted and translated by Blumenthal, p. 42.

disputed that they settled at Haran and thereby transplanted a branch of the school into Near Eastern soil.[5] At any rate, Damascius' work, *Doubts and Solutions Concerning First Principles*, is significant because it is one of the few original metaphysical treatises to have survived from Late Athenian Neoplatonism and because it presents a compendium of pagan philosophical and religious traditions as they existed at the close of an epoch.

Doubts and Solutions Concerning First Principles (hereafter referred to as the *Peri Archon*) is thus a philosophical and historical monument, the work of a man charged with both defending pagan faith and bolstering the intellectual morale of his own colleagues. Faced with increasing hostility and competition from Christianity, the Neoplatonists found it was time to break the silence maintained for centuries concerning their mystery religions and to publish their own, alternative salvation narratives as part of a concerted effort at a pagan revival.[6] Because it is a celebration of pagan mysteries as well as a critical overhaul of Platonic school doctrine, the *Peri Archon* is of inestimable value for the study of the histories of Western metaphysics and Western religions. Specifically, it shows the Neoplatonists engaged in an intense debate over the issue of metaphysical dualism throughout their centuries of dogmatizing. The *Peri Archon* offers a brilliant internal critique of Neoplatonic metaphysics, shedding much light on questions of method and dialectic within the last phase of the Academy.

Earlier we looked at Proclus' *Platonic Theology* and saw that Neoplatonists held that Plato's *Parmenides* was a theological disquisition that charted not only the fundamental principles of reality but also the emergence of any possible form of being from one transcendent source.[7] It is in this tradition of exegesis of Plato's *Parmenides* that the *Peri Archon* finds its place.

Plotinus launched the tradition. In *Enneads* V.1 he interprets the

---

[5] Cameron 1969; Combès, 1986–91, tome 1, Introduction, p. xxi. For the dispute, see Blumenthal, pp. 44–6, and M. Tardieu, "Les Calendriers en usage à Harran d'àpres des sources arabes et le commentaire de Simplicus à la Physique d'Aristote," in *Simplicius, sa vie, son oeuvre, sa survie*, Actes du colloque international de Paris, Peripatoi 15 (Berlin and New York).

[6] Athanassiadi 1993; Saffrey 1992.

[7] Saffrey 1987.

three initial hypotheses of Plato's *Parmenides* as adumbrating his own metaphysical doctrine, according to which reality has different levels; some things are, quite simply, more real than other things. The three major divisions of reality in Plotinus' schema are the One, Intellect, and Soul. If the One is beyond Being (a premise that Plotinus took directly from Plato's *Republic*) then Being emerges only as a subsequent stage of reality, at the level of Intellect, while transitory Being originates in the third hypostasis, or Soul. Plotinus left it for his followers to iron out the details of precisely how the entire dialogue mapped onto the universe as a whole. Proclus, the fifth-century Athenian Neoplatonist, left a catalogue of these attempts in book VI of his *Commentary on the Parmenides* (col. 1052.31 ff.). There he set forth in astonishing detail the evolution of this exegetical tradition, beginning with Plotinus' disciples, Amelius and Porphyry, and ending with the interpretation of his own teacher, Syrianus.[8]

On all of the surviving manuscripts, *Doubts and Solutions Concerning First Principles* is found in continuation with another work of Damascius, his *Commentary on the Parmenides*. As we have just seen, the *Peri Archon* forms part of the exegetical tradition on Plato's *Parmenides*, yet it is not formally a commentary and should perhaps be seen as an independent work apart from the *Parmenides* commentary. The *Peri Archon* concerns itself with the first hypostasis, the Ineffable, the One, and the noetic triad, whereas Damascius' *Commentary on the Parmenides* proceeds by discussing the theological implications of all nine of the hypotheses recognized in the Neoplatonist's reading of the dialogue, beginning with the intelligible diacosm. *Marianus Gr.* 246, the unique manuscript witness to Damascius' major writings, contains one small clue about the overall nature of his project in the *Doubts and Solutions Concerning First Principles*. In F. 435ʳ we read the following colophon: "The Doubts and Solutions of Damascius the Platonic Successor on the Parmenides of Plato, matching and disputing the Commentary of the Philosopher [sc. Proclus]."[9] This title fits well with the work's structure. Damascius often proceeds by using Proclus' *Commentary on the Parmenides* as the basis for the lemmas in

---

[8] Dillon and Morrow 1987, Introduction, section B. Saffrey 1965.
[9] Δαμασκίου διαδόχου εἰς τὸν Πλάτωνος Παρμενίδην ἀπορίαι καὶ ἐπιλύσεις ἀντιπαρατεινόμεναι τοῖς εἰς αὐτὸν ὑπομνήμασιν τοῦ φιλοσόφου.

his own commentary; in the *Peri Archon*, Damascius seems more interested in scrutinizing the fundamental doctrines of Proclan metaphysics.

The handbook of metaphysical puzzles that appears under the title, *Doubts and Solutions Concerning First Principles*, then, relates to the first two Neoplatonic hypostases, the One, and Being/Intellect. By far the most difficult issue involves the causal status of the first principle, or One. Tensions between a transcendent One, utterly unrelated to any form of Being, and an originary One, source and support of all reality, broke out in the doctrinal disputes of Plotinus' successors, with Porphyry elevating the causal aspect of the One at the risk of collapsing the second hypostasis into the first. Responding to this solution, Iamblichus proposed that there were two first principles before the level of Being: the first One, not associated with causality, and a second One, which was.[10] We learn of this debate in the *Peri Archon*, where Damascius' historical narrative punctuates his own metaphysical queries. Damascius uses this issue as an introduction to his handbook. At the heart of the Neoplatonists' metaphysical enterprise is a fundamental contradiction, according to Damascius: If all things come from the absolute, then the absolute is a principle or a cause of other things. But if the absolute is a cause, it is no longer the absolute, since it then exists in relation to others.

In the *Peri Archon*, central Platonic dogmas are analyzed and often swept away. What is left in their place? Damascius characterizes the results of his inquiry as "a reversal of discourse." To motivate this reversal, there are a number of methodological resources at his disposal, including certain techniques that recall Skeptical strategies, a tendency to argue *in utramque partem*, and a heavy emphasis on the *via apophatica*. The "reversal of discourse" that Damascius so often alludes to refers to an emphasis upon method, to an investigation of the process of inquiry. This methodological self-awareness is one of the most innovative features of the *Peri Archon*.

Moreover, the *Peri Archon* discusses theoretical issues underlying the Neoplatonic theories of causation and emanation, according to which successively lower orders of reality proceed from the first principle, or One, in a process of undiminished and indefinite self

---

[10] Dillon, *Iamblichi Chalcidensis in Platonis dialogos commentariorum fragmenta.*

extension on the part of this first principle. Damascius affirms the principle previously enunciated by Proclus, that this entire devolution of reality is based on a series of negations. If we negate the Ineffable, the result is the One. Failing to grasp the Ineffable, the mind projects the idea of the One in the form of a series of Henads, and so forth. This failure and subsequent projection continue to occur all the way down the long chain of being. Yet unlike the extreme realism of Proclus, for whom the ontological categories of traditional metaphysics were all reified as components of reality's fullness, Damascius hints that the devolution of reality is itself only partially real. We will return to this observation shortly.

Compared to prior Commentators in this tradition, Damascius' innovations are the replacement of the One by the Ineffable, a move whose methodological and doctrinal consequences will be surveyed, as well as a continuation of the concept of procession through the four negative hypotheses of Plato's *Parmenides*. Previously, Neoplatonists had worked only with the positive hypotheses of Plato's *Parmenides*, that is, with all the theses couched in such terms as "if the One exists." In the exegetical tradition beginning with Plotinus, Neoplatonists argued that the Parmenidean hypotheses described the process of emanation from the One; Plato's "consequences" represent the various stations of Being that derive from the One, in Proclus' words, "the genesis and procession of the gods."[11] Damascius, by contrast, also discussed the levels of reality associated with the negative hypotheses, or with those theses expressed in such terms as "if the One does *not* exist." This last innovation has become the basis of a somewhat controversial interpretation of Damascius' philosophy as a whole, developed systematically by Joseph Combès in a number of articles as well as in the introductions to his translations.[12]

---

[11] Proclus, *Platonic Theology*, III, p. 162. On this passage, see Steel, chapter 4. See also the survey of Saffrey-Westerink in the Introduction to volume I of Proclus' *Platonic Theology*, pp. lxxv–lxxxiv.

[12] All the relevant articles are cited by Combès on pp. xxxii–xxxiii, n. 5, of his Introduction to tome I of the *Traité des premiers principes*. See especially Combès 1977, "Damascius et les hypothèses négatives du Parménides" According to Combès' interpretation, Damascius turns to the the negative hypotheses of the *Parmenides* (if the One is not) to seek the principles that allow the sensible to manifest. Damascius thus continues the exegesis of Plato by concentrating on Plato's interest in the origins of illusion, of the phenomenal world. Combès discusses the *Parmenides* and

Overview of Damascius' Philosophy: Non-dualism

Already I have adumbrated several differences between Damascius and Proclus in the realm of ontology. The first five principles alluded to in the *Peri Archon* refer to a structure or system consisting of the Ineffable, the One, and the noetic triad,[13] which are roughly the equivalent of the first two Proclan hypostases, the One and Being/Intellect, also called the dyad.[14] As we will see more clearly by the end of this chapter, Damascius also criticizes Proclus' views on the Henads, causation, emanation, and intellect. However, it is not just doctrinal disagreement that occasions Damascius' objections to Proclus. In his methodology, Damascius is aporetic rather than dogmatic, is more appreciative of the provisional nature of certain metaphysical solutions, and places a great deal of emphasis on a non-dual perspective. By "non-dual" in this context, I mean that for Damascius' philosophy, a certain perspective remains operative and conditions any statement made about the nature of reality. This perspective is perhaps best expressed by Damascius when he writes:

As many things as constitute the multiplicity in a divided mode, the One is all of these things before its division ... The One dissolves all things by means of its own simplicity and it is All things before [they are] all things. (C-W I, 24.11)

In Damascius' debate with the tradition, what is at stake is the status of the One. The dialectical examination of transcendence itself stems from a certain commitment to carrying out implications of non-dualism within his philosophical methods. Damascius intends

Sophist in terms of their reification of non-being and believes that Damascius treats non-Being not just as a linguistic phenomenon, but as integral to his own ontology as well as to Plato's. Damascius, according to Combès, sees the soul as the principle of non-Being and is interested, accordingly, in a "discourse of appearance" that takes as its rightful subject the soul. Since this chapter concerns itself only with the *Doubts and Solutions Concerning First Principles*, I will not be studying the implications of Damascius' innovations with regard to the Parmenidean hypotheses. Damascius' concern with the psychology of illusion is, I believe, an interesting topic because it complements his theory of the completely descended soul.

[13] This enumeration of five principles is somewhat tendentious because of the provisional or contested nature of Damascius' solutions to the earlier dispute concerning the status of the first principle.

[14] On the relationship between Damascius' noetic triad and Proclus' dyad, see Linguiti, chapter 3.

not to inculcate an ontology of the One, but rather to inculcate a philosophy that is situated within the first principle. As a consequence, all statements about lower hypostases or about an ontology situated outside of the first principle are subject to the caveat that "the One dissolves all things by means of its own simplicity." All things, including Being itself, fall short of the One; their reality is merely provisional. Sometimes we see Damascius questioning fundamental Neoplatonist principles, such as the identity of knower and known in the act of intellectual knowing, or the complete transcendence of the One with respect to its effects. This non-dual approach to metaphysics can often look like Skeptical *epoche*. Although Damascius was no doubt acquainted with the writings of Sextus Empiricus and other Skeptics, the destructive side of his metaphysics represents his own attempts to bolster the tradition from within.[15] In this chapter I will be arguing that the *Peri Archon* is of great importance for the history of Neoplatonism because it shows how deeply felt was the critique of discursivity within this tradition, despite its seemingly positivistic conceptions. The aporetic method of Damascius subverts the metaphysical ambitions of his tradition insofar as they threaten to abandon the search for wisdom in favor of a complacent dogmatism.

In his general introduction to Proclus' *Commentary on the Parmenides*, John Dillon attempts to sketch some of the fundamental principles of Procline metaphysics. He starts with Proposition 11 of the *Elements of Theology*, "All that exists proceeds from a single first cause." As we will shortly discover, Damascius explicitly criticizes this proposition in the opening paragraphs of the *Peri Archon*. For now, we turn to Dillon's discussion of *ET* 11:

> The basic problem with which all Neoplatonic speculation is concerned, from Plotinus on, is how a multiplicity, and worse, a multiplicity of levels of being, can derive from a totally transcendent and simple One. Plotinus had propounded the theory of undiminished giving by the One, the image of the inexhaustible spring, which creates without being affected by its creation (e.g. *Enn.* V,3.12). The universe thus produced from the One is a plenum, in which no gap can be tolerated (e.g. *Enn.* II,9.3). From Iamblichus on, as I have said, this principle leads to a progressive multiplication of entities . . . of moments within each hypostasis. The principle which Dodds calls the

---

[15] On Damascius' appropriation of Skeptical techniques, see Rappe 1998a and 1998b.

"law of continuity" is well stated by Proclus at *De Prov.* IV, 20: "the processions of real being, far more even than the positions of physical bodies in space, leave no vacuum, but everywhere there are mean terms between extremities, which provide for them a mutual linkage."[16]

Damascius begins his critique of Procline metaphysics by raising an aporia concerning the status of the first principle:

Is the one principle of all things beyond all things or is it one among all things, the summit of everything that proceeds from it? And are we to say that all are things with the [first principle], or after it and [that they proceed] from it? (C-W I.1 = R I.1.1-3)

To understand this puzzle, the reader must remember the debate, already mentioned, between Iamblichus and Porphyry concerning the status and number of principles before the first noetic triad:

Next let us turn to the question of whether there are two first principles before the first noetic triad, especially that [principle] which is completely Ineffable and which has no relationship to the triad (just as the great Iamblichus has it in his Twenty-eighth Book of his most perfect *Chaldean Theology*), or as the majority of those who came after him have supposed, after the Ineffable cause (which is also the One) comes the first intelligible triad, or should one go beneath this principle and agree with Porphyry in saying that the one cause of all things is itself the Father that belongs to the noetic triad? (C-W II.1.1–14)[17]

Damascius examines the issue fully in II 1–15 and tends to approve the position of Iamblichus as against Porphyry, without committing himself entirely to the Iamblichean solution. The name for the first One in the *Peri Archon* is the *arreton*, the Ineffable. Damascius surveys four arguments in support of the Iamblichean position and then goes on to refute these arguments from the viewpoint of the Ineffable. For example, Damascius considers the argument that posits a Pythagorean system according to which Remaining, Procession, and Return are hypostasized as the monad, dyad, and triad, respectively. This system would leave the Ineffable as that with which the monad remains, etymologizing from the name "monad" (μόνας) to the word μονή (C-W II 3–4). But as Damascius says in his critique of this

---

[16] Dillon 1987, pp. xvi–xvii, with a few omissions.
[17] For the details of this debate, see Dillon, Introduction to *Iamblichi Chalcidensis in Platonis dialogos commentariorum fragmenta.*

argument, it would then be difficult to distinguish this monad, or One, from the Ineffable:

> Now if the One is after the Ineffable, the departure from the One could not take the form of a Procession, since there would no longer be such a departure. The One would unify all things with each other and also with their native causes, to the extent that all things are One with the One, so that it would not even be able to distinguish itself from the Ineffable. Therefore, in positing this One, it nevertheless is shown to exist in the manner of the Ineffable. (C-W II 14.1–6)

Against the argument that attempts to distinguish a One unrelated to the noetic triad from the monad that is related, Damascius reminds the reader:

> In reality, concerning the argument based on the difference between the One and the Monad, we must recall that neither the Monad nor the One exists there in truth, so neither can we set up a difference between the One and the Monad. Rather the same hypothesis and the same figurative language covers both terms. (C-W II 13.1–5)

The point here is that the Ineffable cannot be the subject of a metaphysical argument or the basis of a metaphysical system at all. It cannot be either incorporated within or accounted for outside of the causal system that forms the structure of Neoplatonic metaphysics. From the point of view of the Ineffable, no such system exists. From the point of view of metaphysical discourse, the Ineffable is a term that can occupy no fixed place within the system:

> It is not above or below; it belongs neither to the category of first or ultimate, for there is no procession [from it]. It is not replete with all things nor yet does it contain all things; it is not within the realm of that which can be spoken, nor is it the One itself. (C-W I 24.7–10)

Consequently, all arguments for the Ineffable are ineffectual, if not self-refuting. In these sections, we can see the provisional nature of Damascius' solutions to the enigmas of Neoplatonic ontology. He does by all accounts found his own discourse on the Ineffable, but he is also careful to show that this principle is not a hypothetical construct, a logical consequence of a prior philosophical system, or a part of an explanatory apparatus.

As already mentioned, this historical debate forms the background for Damascius' introduction to the *Peri Archon*, to which we now return:

Is that which is designated as the one principle of all things beyond all things or is it one among all things, the summit of everything that proceeds from it? And are we to say that all things are with the [first principle], or after it and [that they proceed] from it? (CW I1.1–5) [18]

Damascius begins his treatise by asking, "Is the one principle of all things beyond all things, or is it one of all things?" Characteristically, he denies both sides of the dilemma: since "all things" designates that from which nothing is lacking, "all things" must include the cause of all things:

The term "all things" [refers] in the strict sense to that from which nothing is absent. But [now we are supposing that] the principle itself is missing. Therefore that which comes after the first principle is not in the strict sense all things, but rather all things except the first principle.

From its inception, the *Peri Archon* seemingly violates the fundamental assumption of Neoplatonic metaphysics, canonized in Proclus' *Elements of Theology*, that multiplicity derives from unity. For our purposes, number 75, that "every cause properly so-called transcends its effect," is breached at the outset in Damascius' *Peri Archon*, when he suggests that the "cause must be ranked among the effects." After dismissing the first half of the dilemma, Damascius goes on to reject the second. If all things include their cause, there is no cause for all things, since the cause will be included among its effects. But without the cause, the effect cannot exist.

Now if all things are together with the first principle, there cannot be a principle for all things, since on the supposition that the principle can be subsumed by all things, there would be no principle [i.e. no beginning, no cause] for all things. Therefore [let us say that] the single coordinate disposition of all things (which we designate by the term, 'all things') is without a first principle and uncaused, lest we [continue the search] *ad infinitum*. (C-W I 2.9–12)

Therefore, he concludes, all is neither from a cause, nor a cause: τὸ ἄρα πάντα οὔτε ἀρχὴ οὔτε ἀπ' ἀρχῆς.

---

[18] With this opening sentence of the *Peri Archon*, one can compare *ET* 5, "Every manifold is posterior to the One." To demonstrate this proposition, Proclus assumes the contrary, that the many are coexistent with the One, and that the One and the many are of the same order, σύστοιχα, by nature. He concedes that there is no objection to the One and the many being temporally coordinate. This admission will be important when we compare the Skeptics on the temporal aspect of causal relation.

In fact, Damascius denies the basic Neoplatonic theory of causation, the thesis that a cause is greater than its effects. In keeping with this theory of causation, Neoplatonists assume that the proliferation of effects from their causes means that reality constantly dispatches itself into inferior states of being. In a section of *Peri Archon* entitled "On the Unified," Damascius investigates the question of what would motivate this procession or descent, responding directly to the views of his predecessors, Syrianus and Proclus.

Now it is worth considering what brings about the distinction between the unified and that which comes after the unified. For the unified itself could not be the cause of this distinction. That would be like the case of an opposite generating [its] opposite. Should we agree with the philosophers and answer that *the effect must be inferior to the cause?*

Here Damascius answers Proposition 7 of the *Elements*, "Every productive cause is superior to that which it produces,"[19] with the objection that derivation from a cause does not in itself account for the differences between cause and effect. Plotinus argued that the full nature of the cause was available for transmission to the effect.[20] It was only the inferior capacity of the effect to express the qualities of the cause that introduced the difference between cause and effect.[21] But why is it necessary that an effect prove inferior to its cause? Damascius applies his more general critique of causation to the specific case of procession:

Now [let's look] in another way at a puzzle that is both ancient and modern. Either procession is from that which exists, in which case, how could what already exists previously [be able to] proceed? Or else procession comes from something that doesn't exist, yet what kind of being could come from something that doesn't exist? Something actual cannot come from something potential, since the former is superior to the latter, while the effect is always inferior to the cause. (R.I 226)

Having studied Damascius' reflections (C-W II.115) on this issue in the preceding quotation, we are in a better position to appreciate the import of his rather striking formulation, "therefore [let us say that] the single coordinated disposition of all things (which we designate by the term, 'all things') is without a first principle and un-

---

[19] Dodds 1963 translation.
[20] Lloyd 1990, pp. 106–107.
[21] Lloyd 1990, p. 107.

caused" (C-W I 2.9–12). On the surface, it looks as if Damascius here is simply denying Proclus' *ET* 11, "All that exists proceeds from a single cause." Although this is not literally false, it would be more true to say that here and throughout his discussion of causation, Damascius cautions us about the provisional nature of metaphysical tenets as such. Damascius does not specify a cause for all things or set up a unique cause that can be designated as the "first principle," but he does not thereby negate causation or posit a self-causing principle, since both of these alternatives would also be metaphysical tenets subject to the cautions established at the outset of the treatise:

> But if it is necessary to [assert something] by way of demonstration, then let us make use of the apophatic provisions, and say that It is neither One nor Many, neither Generative nor without issue, neither Cause nor without causal properties, and yet, [let us be aware that] these very provisions overturn themselves, I imagine, indefinitely. (C-W I 22.15–20)

At the beginning of this section, I quoted from John Dillon's introduction to *Proclus' Commentary on the Parmenides*. Dillon rightly points out that Proclus shapes the *Elements of Theology* as a speculative metaphysics, positing, in a sense, unity or the One as the exotic or extopic explanans for plurality, conceived as immediate, present to hand, and therefore requiring explanation. We can see that Damascius shifts the perspective of his metaphysics; he struggles to create a metaphysical discourse that accommodates, insofar as language can, the ultimate principle of reality. After all, how coherent is a metaphysical system that bases itself on the Ineffable as a first principle? Instead of creating an objective ontology, Damascius writes ever mindful of the limitations of dialectic, of the pitfalls and snares inherent in the very structure of metaphysical discourse.

The Status of Metaphysical Discourse

Damascius recognizes that the language of metaphysics functions to signify something beyond itself. It is best thought of as a mnemonic device; its purpose is to deliver human beings from their own ignorant determinations about the nature of reality, without thereby imprisoning them in a metaphysical system that displaces reality itself. Hence apophasis, denial or negation, is a method that not only negates all lesser realities, leaving only the Ineffable, it also applies to the language of metaphysics itself. A certain denial or demotion, one might say, of the metaphysical enterprise as such, must be programmed into the very structure of such discourse.[22] As we saw, it had become already a standard topos for Plotinus that his designation for the absolute principle, "the One," was not semantically significant, did not pick out any object, but simply indicated the refusal to designate. But for Damascius, the ineffability of the One engulfs the metaphysical enterprise, infecting it with nonsense, with in-significance. Because of it, we are forced to confront the question, how does the experience of ineffability ground the prospects for truth seeking? Here we turn to Damascius' own definition of "apophasis," in book I, chapter 42, of the *Peri Archon:*

In one way, [the term] "The Ineffable" is apophatic. By this I do not mean that the term designates anything positive at all, but that this term is not even a negation: it is complete removal. It is not merely not-a-thing (since what is not-a-thing is still something) but it absolutely has no reality. So we define this term, "ineffable," in such a way that it is not even a term.

The "Ineffable" is a term that does not possess a meaning in the ordinary sense, since it has no semantic function. It is not a term so that its deployment in language conveys nothing at all to the reader or listener. That this word nevertheless forms the basis of Damascius' philosophical activity inevitably leads to a self-conscious meditation on the status of his own language, which Damascius often refers to as a radical reversal, or *peritrope*, of language. This admonition concerning the misdirection built into metaphysical language is related to a technical term, *endeixis*, a word that appears over one hundred times in the text of the *Peri Archon*. In our treatise, the word *endeixis* typically conveys the idea of hinting at or of suggesting a reality that is then left indeterminate. For Damascius and his school, the language of metaphysics is even at its best allusive; although metaphysical discourse provides us with an image of truth it cannot be conflated with truth and so is more symbolic or iconic than discur-

---

[22] Here I would like to invoke the concept of "performative intensity," that Michael Sells uses in his book, *The Mystical Languages of Unsaying*, to explain the otherwise mystifying *epoche*, or suspension of belief, that drives the structure of Damascius' exposition. Sells delineates an apophatic linguistic style characterized by a "continuing series of retractions, a propositionally unstable and dynamic discourse in which no single statement can rest on its own as true or false, or even as meaningful." Sells 1994.

sive. Thus Proclus and Simplicius both allow that any teaching about realities such as intellect and soul must take place by means of *endeixis*, by means of coded language.[23] Throughout the treatise, Damascius is at pains to remind the reader that he is speaking as a whole only provisionally, *kata endeixin*. In Neoplatonic texts, the word *endeixis* is linked to Pythagorean symbolism and conveys the sense of allusive or enigmatic language, though the history of its meaning must be recovered through aversion to Hellenistic scientific discourse.[24]

This word became prevalent in later Hellenistic epistemology as a means of distinguishing different kinds of signs.[25] Sextus Empiricus discusses primarily two sorts of signs: the mnemonic and the indicative.[26] Unlike the mnemonic sign, which simply formalizes the expected associations between any two events, where expectations follow directly from experience, the indicative sign designates a logical condition obtaining between two events or states of affairs.[27] To paraphrase Michael Frede, an indicative sign is one from which one can rationally infer the presence of an otherwise unmanifest object, as, for example, an atomist might infer the existence of the void from the existence of atoms. When used by ancient medical writers, the indicative sign stood for a method of diagnosing and treating illnesses.[28] The assumption governing the rationalist practitioner's

---

[23] Cf. Simplicius, *On Aristotle's On the Soul* 1.1–2.4, sections 26, 11–19; 28, 19; 30, 5, etc. Cf. also Proclus *In Parm.* 1027, 27–30; *In Rem.* I.5, 8;56, 3, 61, 9, etc. For these passages and a wealth of other references, see Peter Lautner's Introduction to the English translation of Simplicius' commentary on *De anima*, pp. 8–10: Simplicius, *On Aristotle's On the Soul 1.1–2.4*, translated by J. Urmson with Notes by Peter Lautner. Cornell 1995. I wish to thank Dr. Lautner for providing me with the reference to his work and for discussion about the subject of *endeixis* in Late Athenian Neoplatonism.

[24] Frede 1987b, pp. 263 ff., 276, 289, 293.

[25] This evidence is important in evaluating the Skeptical affiliations of Damascius, not least because it demonstrates his familiarity with a word that proved to be central in the epistemological debates between Skeptics (who discussed it in conjunction with denial of the possibility of logical inference) and dogmatists. The frequent appearance of this word in the *Peri Archon* increases the evidence that Damascius read the actual writings of the Skeptics and also suggests that his thought was colored by Skeptical modes of analysis. Sextus Empiricus *PH* II, sections 104–33; Mates, pp. 274–9.

[26] Sextus Empiricus *PH* II, sections 97–103.

[27] Frede 1987b, pp. 264–5.

[28] Frede 1987b, p. 265, quotes Galen *De sect. ing.* 2, 3; 5, 17; 10, 22.

approach to disease was that an indicative sign could lead to knowledge beyond the scope of personal experience. Thus, for the rationalist, "indication" signified the relation obtaining between the manifest state of the body (that is, the patient's symptoms) and the underlying hidden abnormal state, the disease.[29] As used by Damascius, the word *endeixis* suggests that the language of metaphysics must be acknowledged to be at most a prompting toward inquiry into something that exceeds its own domain as descriptive.[30] The result of this inquiry tells us more about our own states of ignorance than about the goal of the search:

> If, in speaking about the One, we attempt the following collocations, viz. that it is ineffable, that it does not belong to the category of all things, and that it is not apprehensible by means of intellectual knowledge, then we ought to recognize that these constitute the language of our own labors. This language is a form of hyperactivity that stops on the threshold of the mystery without conveying anything about it at all. Rather, such language announces the subjective experiences of aporia and misapprehension that arise in connection with the One, and that not even clearly, but by means of hints . . .
> (C-W I 6.5–10)

Endeixis, hinting at reality, becomes a technique that captures features of the psychology of inquiry without successfully transcending the subjective. To describe philosophical discourse as *endeixis* is to limit its ambitions.[31] *Endeixis* in this sense is not a descriptive use of language, but encompasses a number of different linguistic devices. Thus, for example, the language of negation is not referential; negative adjectives when applied to the Ineffable do not attribute anything to it nor determine its nature. Instead, by using negative language we succeed only in delimiting our own discursive practices:

> Nor do we affirm that [the Ineffable] is unknowable in the sense that the unknowable has a determinate nature, being something other, nor do we call it "being," nor "one," nor "all," nor "principle of the all" nor "beyond all things." We deny that it is possible to make any statement about it at all. But this again is not its nature, viz., the expressions "not a thing," "beyond all," "causeless cause," and "unrelated to anything," nor do these attributes

---

[29] Frede 1987b, pp. 269–75.
[30] For the word *endeixis* in the *Peri Archon*, see Galperine 1987, Introduction, p. 34, n. 108.
[31] On this topic, see Galperine 1987, Introduction, pp. 34–5.

constitute its nature. Rather, they serve simply to remove anything that arises after the Ineffable. (R.I 11, 15–25)

Again, Damascius does not reify the conventions of apophatic discourse, nor does he claim that such negative language succeeds in referring:

No name will be able to convey the meaning of the transcendent, since a name belongs to a system of reference. One must finally deny the [name of the transcendent] as well. But even denial is a form of discourse, and that makes what is denied an object of discourse, but the transcendent is nothing, not even something to be denied, in no way expressible, not knowable at all, so that one can not even negate its negation. Rather the only way of revealing that of which we speak is simply the deferral of language and of conceptions about it. (C-W I.21.12–18)

A discourse on the Ineffable is not a metaphysical treatise in the usual sense of the word. Its purpose is to remove confidence in established doctrine and to reverse, as Damascius puts it, the more usual direction of language. Language turns back upon itself because its purpose is to negate its own function. Damascius' chosen name for his style of metaphysics is *peritrope*, and this word too has a history in the annals of Skepticism.[32] Although it can be literally translated as "reversal," its sense in the context of dialectic refers to arguments overturned by means of premises internal to them. Sextus Empiricus, for example, refers to a whole class of such overturning arguments, or arguments whose very assertion undermines the dialectical stance of the person who asserts them.[33] Damascius' appropriation of this Skeptical term relates primarily to any statement made about the Ineffable, since the Ineffable is by designation and definition outside the reach of any linguistic system: "our language is self-refuting when we attach such predicates to the Ineffable a 'Outside of Language,' 'Nothing at all,' 'Ungraspable by the Intellect' " (C-W I.10).

In the history of their debates with the dogmatists, Skeptics were often accused of hoisting themselves on their own petard, particularly with regard to their stance of *akatalepsia*, their assertion that

---

[32] For the history of the word *peritrope* in Skeptical debates, see Burnyeat 1976.

[33] See Burnyeat 1976. For example, someone who asserts that causes do not exist undermined if he or she attempts to demonstrate this assertion by invoking reasons for this assertion.

nothing is apprehensible. The Skeptics reply that *akatalepsia* is not a descriptive or indicative term; it does not purport to describe a state of affairs in the world, but rather signifies the the Skeptical *epoche*, the refusal to make any statement about the nature of things.[34] If the Skeptics embrace *epoche*, suspension of belief, as their solution to the impending dangers of *peritrope*, one could argue that, in a parallel way, Damascius embraces silence or ineffability. As he says concerning the first principle, "we define this term, 'ineffable,' in such a way that it is not even a term" (C-W I.62.10). The "limit of philosophical discourse" (πέρας τοῦ λόγου) refers to the complete removal of any proposition or any statement about reality. This limit is "silence without recourse" (C-W I.22), or "silence that frees us from [our own] productions" (C-W I.22).

Doctrinal Consequences

The Henads

So far we have seen that Damascius' approach to the first principle has methodological implications. Nevertheless, as Damascius himself says concerning the Ineffable, this method does not leave one with much to say about reality, especially given that the name, "Ineffable," does not name any kind of reality. As long as there remains something to name, one has not yet taken away all that is added to reality from outside, from the productions of the mind.

In a certain way the Ineffable amounts to a negation, and in using this kind of language, I do not intend to predicate anything of it or to posit anything about it. Rather, what I intend by this name or by what it names is neither a denial nor an affirmation, but the complete removal of everything. (C-W I, 62.4–7)

Still, it is legitimate to ask, and Damascius does ask, "Can one posit any intermediary between the Ineffable and what can be expressed in language?" (C-W I, 62.3) In other words, does Damascius have

---

[34] "A story of the painter Apelles applies to the Sceptics. They say that he was painting a horse and wanted to represent in his picture the lather on the horse's mouth; but he was so unsuccessful that he gave up, took the sponge on which he had been wiping off the colours from his brush, and flung it at the picture. And when it hit the picture, it produced a representation of the horse's lather" (I 27, Annas and Barnes translation).

anything at all to say about the nature of reality apart from the Ineffable? To look at this question, we must consider once more the thought of Proclus. In asking this question about what is intermediary, Damascius no doubt alludes to the Procline tendency to multiply levels of reality in general, as we saw earlier "the processions of real being, far more even than the positions of physical bodies in space, leave no vacuum, but everywhere there are mean terms between extremities, which provide for them a mutual linkage" (*De Prov.* IV, 20). Damascius especially has in mind Proclus' doctrine of the Henads, which function as intermediaries between the One and particular beings, and between Being/Intellect and that which exists before Being.[35] Although they find their place within the cosmos as causal principles, coming first in the *seirai* or *taxeis*, the orders of Being, that together constitute the vast diversity of all possible forms of existence, they are also *theoi*, gods, and perhaps no less than names or aspects of the divine principle whose fullness is thus expressed. Although these brief remarks do not provide an adequate account of the Procline doctrine, it is perhaps enough to contrast the realism of Proclus with the somewhat hesitant nature of Damascius' own discussion of the Henads.

Ideally, to apprehend reality, the mind should be able to strip itself of all of its determinate notions, all of its concepts or preconceptions. According to Damascius, however, such a feat is impossible, since the mind by its very nature invents things. Mind operates by projecting its own determinate notions onto a reality that surpasses binary oppositions. In trying to apprehend the One, the mind inevitably fails and instead grasps the One under the aspect of the Henads, namely, the One-Many, the Many-One, and the Unified. That is, the mind must contemplate the One as all things, or else it must contemplate all things as dependent upon the One, or else it must contemplate the expansion of the One into all things. Each of these ways of looking at the One is a kind of projection that the mind conjures up as it grapples with intractable metaphysical problems. It would be better to admit that when the mind unifies itself, it tends to apprehend unity, whereas when the mind pays attention to a number of objects, then it tends to apprehend multiplicity:

[35] Cf. *ET*, 113–65 and *Platonic Theology* III, 1–6.

Neither "the one" nor "all things" accords with [the One]. These are a pair of binary oppositions that divide our consciousness [of the One]. If we focus on the One as simple, we lose sight of the complete perfection of that principle. But if we conceive it as all things simultaneously, we destroy its unity and simplicity. The cause of this is that we ourselves are divided and we distractedly consider its characteristics as if they were separate. (C-W I, 80.19–81.2)

Damascius does not say that the Henads are unreal, but he does caution that the basis of any attempt to know reality must be the Ineffable; anything that falls outside of this principle is, in a certain respect, illusory. Throughout his discussion of the Henads, he suggests that these are really methods of contemplating the first principle, necessary, perhaps, as stages of approach, but ultimately not to be reified as absolutes: "What I was just now attempting to explain, is that the division of these multiple acts of gnosis must be contracted into a complete gnosis of the complete one that is the simple unity of plural henads" (C-W I.66). Damascius elaborates this method of first using the Henads as a way of approaching the unity of the first principle and then detaching from them as a greater, more expansive form of contemplation liberates the mind from its own activity of grasping:

That is how we arrive at being, first by means of each form which we experience as a separate entity, we meditate on that form as not only without parts but also as unified, trying to see all of them in each, if one can put it this way. And then we take them all together, discriminated as they are, but remove their circumferences, just as if we were making many streams into one pond that has no boundaries, except that we do not meditate on it as unified from all forms as we do the one body of water, but rather as before them all, as one the form of the water before the actually divided bodies of water. That is how we concentrate ourselves in the One, first by gathering together [multiplicity] and then by detaching ourselves from that which is gathered, into that One, which transcends their multiplicity. (C-W I, 82.19–82.6)

This habit of grasping aspects of reality and absolutizing them is the greatest obstacle to the student: "This is the cause of all of our problems, that our thoughts run off into complete separation if we hear the name 'other,' and muddle things together if we hear the name, 'identity.'" From Proclus' solemn enumeration of reality's various stations, Damascius turns his attention to the knower, looking at how the knower's own conditioning intrudes and insinuates itself into the total occasion, so to speak, of what is being known.[36] There is a subtle difficulty in assessing the extent to which Damascius can be said to uphold the reality of the Henads. Often his language suggests that outside of the Ineffable, illusion reigns; all that is below the One is somehow superimposed on the One.

In this sense, the Ineffable designates that which, even within human beings, remains unbounded by the projections that constitute our ordinary notion of reality. Damascius asks: "Is it the case that nothing of the ineffable encroaches upon the things here?" He answers, "As many things as constitute the multiplicity in a divided mode, the One is all of these things before its division . . . The One dissolves all things by means of its own simplicity and it is All things before [they are] all things" (C-W I, 24.11). At the level of ordinary objects, Damascius transmutes the ineffability of the absolute into a puzzle about the status of individuation: picking out an object in the world as a particular entity involves absolutizing some one determinate property, creating a kind of synecdoche that falsely views any given individual as isolable from all other individuals, by virtue of this characterization.

In fact, to use a species name as, for example, "human being," or to use a generic term such as "living being," amounts to a virtual catachresis: "The earthly human being is [designated in accordance with] a particular property from which [the Form] human being also gets its name; one could say the same about any other human attribute, as well as the property of being [the Form] Human Being." In using language, we seize upon differences in such a way as to absolutize the bearer of a different predicate, or we are tricked by a common name into assuming an ontological unity. Perhaps nowhere is this cautionary attitude or wariness of illusion more pro-

---

[36] Damascius' apparent dismantling of the fundamental structures of Neoplatonic metaphysics through sustained criticism of such tenets as causation, emanation, intellection, and reversion is matched by his equally critical stance toward the ontological orientation of Neoplatonism as a whole. Hence although Damascius is not a subjectivist or strong anti-realist (he does not think that the ontology of such principles as the Henads, the intellect, and so forth is the result of psychic projection), he does at times distance himself from an ontological approach. This distance results from his concern to reorient the philosophy of Neoplatonism away from the baroque scholasticism that begins to preponderate in the Athenian school.

nounced than in Damascius' critique of Neoplatonic theories of intellect.

Intellect

In what follows, I will be investigating Damascius' critique of the Neoplatonic theory of intellect, as well as his own views on the limitations of intellect. In this material most of all, Damascius' familiarity with Skeptical techniques is pronounced. Quite obviously, the critique of knowledge forms the basis of Academic Skepticism and later Pyrrhonism; the undermining of all dogmas is in fact subsidiary to this project, in the sense that *akatalepsia*, non-apprehension, is both a foundational premise of Skepticism as well as a method for achieving its goals. Just as the Skeptics need not provide their own criterion of truth to successfully demolish the dogmatists' *katalepic phantasia*,[37] Damascius works by showing difficulties inherent in Neoplatonic conceptions of intellect.

Damascius' strategy is most interesting; he subverts the identity thesis, according to which intellect is its objects (the Neoplatonists appropriated the Aristotelian doctrine of isomorphism)[38] and instead insinuates a correspondence theory of truth into the Neoplatonist theory: "we can say, therefore, that knowledge completely accords with its object, *but it is not its object*." From a standard Neoplatonic perspective, the position at which Damascius arrives is one of extreme unorthodoxy. One way of framing Damascius' strategy in terms of the history of philosophy, is to say that he takes an anti-Aristotelian line against Plotinus and Proclus, though of course his language is influenced by the epistemological vocabulary of the Stoics.[39] The Aristotelian doctrine of isomorphism is enunciated at

---

[37] Some scholars do accept that Carneades' *pithanon* functions as such an alternative criterion, but see Bett 1989 for an opposite viewpoint.

[38] Cf. *Enneads* V.3.5.45.

[39] Here even the standard Neoplatonist account will differ from that of Aristotle. For Plotinus explicitly *denies* that the object of thought can act upon the mind or that the mind *receives* the form in the act of intellection. Instead, such receptivity occurs only at the level of *doxa*, or opinion. Plotinus etymologizes the word δόχα (opinion), from the verb δέχομαι (to receive), in keeping with Aristotelian isomorphism: opinion receives, indeed, that is why it is opinion, because it receives something from an object that is substantially different from that which receives it.

De anima III.8; in thinking, the mind becomes identical with the form of the intelligible object. Aristotle employs a strong analogy between sense-perception and mental perception, describing ordinary thought as a kind of mental receptivity to form.[40] Here is the relevant passage from the *De anima*:[41]

> But if thought is like perception, then the mind must be acted upon by the thought object or something else must [happen] which is analogous to this. Therefore, the mind must be impassive, but must be capable of receiving the form.

In the following passage we see that Damascius preserves the strong perception/intellection analogy that Aristotle relies on, but nevertheless inserts a modified Stoicizing account, in which the object of knowledge becomes analogous to the impression, the *phantasia*, which presumably carries representational features of the world. Damascius is careful to disassociate his theory from standard Neoplatonic accounts of intellection by coining a new term, *gnosma*, which is formed by analogy to the word, *noema*, but presents none of the associated epistemology of noesis.

> For sense perception corresponds to the object of sense perception, the faculty of representation corresponds to the impression, and the same is true of the faculty of opinion and of discursive reason: the one corresponds to the object of opinion and the other corresponds to the object of thought. In general, then, knowledge corresponds to the object of knowledge, to coin a new term for this, and the object of knowledge is that which is capable of being known when it has come to be an object of knowledge for a knower. We can say, therefore, that knowledge completely accords with its object, *but it is not its object.*

Most Neoplatonists agreed with Plotinus that in the case of intellectual knowledge, "it is necessary for the knower to be *identical* with the known and for the intellect to be *identical* with its object" (V.3.5.22).[42] Earlier we found Damascius exceptionally denying the

---

[40] For a more detailed discussion of the differences between Plotinus' understanding of the identity theory (the doctrine of isomorphism) and Aristotle's notion of the identity that obtains between the form actualized in the act of perception and the form inherent in the hylopmorphic compound that becomes the object of perception, see chapters 4 and 5. See also Emilsson 1988.

[41] *De anima*, III.4.13–16; 429a3.

[42] For the continuation of this doctrine in Proclus *IT* II 287, 3–5: "Truth is assimilation of the knower to the known." Cf. further II 287, 9–11.

identity thesis: "we can say, therefore, that knowledge completely accords with its object, *but it is not its object.*" Even when Damascius' arguments apparently recall a Skeptical position, however, they are not always motivated by Skeptical ends, as will become apparent when we compare Damascius with Sextus.

In the following text, Sextus Empiricus argues against the possibility of intellectual knowledge by demonstrating the weaknesses inherent in a correspondence theory of truth. There is no way to guarantee the representational accuracy of one's impressions, since the mind is always conditioned by its own experiences.[43]

The intellect does not of itself get in contact with external objects and receive impressions from them, but it does so by means of the senses; and the senses do not apprehend the external objects but only their own *pathe,* if anything. And so the phantasia will be of a sensory pathos, which is not the same thing as the external object.

Nor again can one say that the soul apprehends the external objects by means of the sensory experiences because the experiences of the senses are similar to the external objects. "For from which will the intellect know whether the *pathe* of the senses are similar to the objects of sense, when it has not itself met with these external objects . . . Therefore not even on the basis of similarity will the intellect be able to judge these objects in accord with the phantasia."[44]

Read alongside of this passage from Sextus Empiricus, Damascius hardly seems to be a Skeptic. After all, Sextus insists that the soul *does not* apprehend any external object, but only its own representation of a putative object. Again, the Skeptics will deny that objects correspond to our representations of them,[45] whereas Damascius asserts that because intellect conforms to its objects, it is capable of revealing those objects. Therefore the mind does truly know, per-

---

[43] It is important to keep in mind that Sextus here assimilates all forms of thinking to intellectual knowledge and maintains no distinction between intellectual and other kinds of mental activity.

[44] Sextus Empiricus, *PH* bk. 2, sections 70–72.

[45] On the Skeptics' distinction between appearances and what appears to us, cf. Annas and Barnes 1985, p. 23: "To say how things appear is to say how they impress us or how they strike us, whether or not it is via our perceptual apparatus that the impression is made. In this sense we regularly contrast how things appear or seem with how they really are. This contrast lies at the heart of Pyrrhonism and its Ten Modes."

ceive, and opine about objects: "knowledge corresponds to the object of knowledge."

Nevertheless Damascius criticizes the Neoplatonist theory of intellection and specifically the identity thesis that underlies it, in the same way that the Skeptics criticize Stoic epistemology and the correspondence theory that underlies it. Since the Skeptics must show only that the representational account of perception given by the Stoics itself entails that the mind immediately grasps merely *phantasiai* and not objects, they can at once insist on the representational gap that this account leaves open.[46] Similarly, Damascius emphasizes the substantive distinction between the knower and the known to show that the intellect never encounters its object, being, as it is in itself. Moreover, he uses premises supplied by Neoplatonic metaphysics to demonstrate this non-identity of subject and object.

In his own words, Damascius wants to show that knowledge is a relationship that must maintain "the actual distinction between the knower and the known, with no crossing of boundaries" (R.I.181) The context for his attack on the identity thesis is Proclan metaphysics. Specifically, he exploits Proclus' exposition of the triadic rule of causation (*ET* 30;31) according to which every effect remains in and returns to its cause.[47] Since every immaterial entity (for example, soul or intellect) has the capacity for self-reversion as well knowledge is the exemplary instance of epistrophe;[48] knowledge equates with the reversion or return of intellect to its own hypostasis being. It remains for Damascius to overturn this theory from within a task most easily accomplished by accepting Proclus' account o knowledge as reversion: Because it returns to Being and to the affir mation of Being, knowledge could correctly be called "a return" (C W II.148).

Here at last the identity thesis becomes the target. Althoug knowledge entails the reversion of intellect to being, reversion itsel entails the fundamental distinction between that which reverts an that to which the knower reverts:[49]

---

[46] On the nature of Stoic representations in terms of theories of truth, see Anna 1991, *Hellenistic Philosophy of Mind* (Berkeley).

[47] Dodds 1963, pp. 217–18. On this topic, see Gersh 1973.

[48] For this doctrine, see Lloyd 1990, pp. 126–33.

[49] Although the argument Damascius uses to defeat the identity thesis seems heuristi and even ad hoc (what reason does Damascius offer for his denial that the separa

Now it is the nature of intellect to return to being and of knowledge to be directed toward being. Furthermore, every return is of something that has proceeded and is already separate and therefore in need of return, although return does not eradicate the separation. Rather that which is separate returns to that from which it has become distinct just insofar as it remains distinct and in exactly the way that it remains distinct. All of this is evident from the name, *gnosis*. (C-W II.149)

There seem to be three steps in Damascius' refutation of the Neoplatonic identity thesis. In step one, Damascius accepts Proclus' theory of intellectual reversion, but, in step two, he concludes that reversion entails the non-identity of the knower (intellect) and the object known (or being). Finally, in step three, Damascius applies this denial of the identity thesis to Neoplatonic epistemology and concludes that the intellect never knows being as it is in itself because the intellect can never be strictly identical with being. It is this last application that raises the most interesting questions about Dasmascius' own theory of knowledge.

As a consequence of his denial of the Neoplatonic identity thesis, Damascius concludes that knowing and being known is a relationship that consists in alterity:

[Question:] what does it mean to say, "capable of being known," and how does this differ from Being? [Answer:] Something is an object of knowledge insofar as it exists in relation to another, whereas it is Being by virtue of what it is in itself. (C-W II.149)

But if the intellect never knows being as it is in itself, must one then conclude that intellect fails to know being at all, that being is unknowable? Being is not exactly unknowable, but it is available to the knower only *qua* object of knowledge:

[Objection:] But it is Being that intellect desires. [Answer:] It may desire Being, but it attains Being as an object of knowledge. Perhaps we should say that its desire is also of Being insofar as it is known since desires naturally correspond to the capacity to attain the objects of desire, and it follows that, for the knower, to attain Being is to attain it insofar as it is known. (C-W II.150)

tion of knower and known can be eradicated?), it rests upon a refinement of Proclus' theory of reversion, according to which there are three different modes or degrees of return: vital, substantial, and cognitive. Damascius wants to rank the different kinds according to the degree of unity achieved by means of the reversion; cognitive reversion, or knowledge, is the least unitive form.

Again by analogy to the Skeptics who assert that the intellect knows only its own *pathe*, and never reaches the object itself, Damascius concludes that the intellect knows its object *qua* object known. In other words, as he puts it, "intellect knows Being as the appearance (τὸ φανόν) of Being" (C-W II.150). After a lengthy and somewhat tendentious argument, Damascius offers his version of the Skeptical thesis we saw operating before in Sextus Empiricus. While the Skeptics maintain that the mind can know only the *phantasia*, or impression, Damascius renders this doctrine with the Neoplatonizing counterpart, that intellect can grasp only the *phanon*, or appearance.

Obviously, there is a divergence as well as a similarity when we compare the results of Damascius' critique of knowledge with that of the Skeptics, especially at the linguistic level of comparison. Few if any direct linguistic echoes connect Damascius' critique of Neoplatonist theories of intellect to the Skeptics, though one could argue that he deliberately modifies the Skeptical endorsement of "appearances only" by speaking of "manifestation." Like the Skeptics, Damascius takes premises from within the dogmatic system he criticizes to undermine a theory of knowledge that is foundational to that system. The position at which he arrives – the unknowability of being as it is in itself, the separation of intellect and its object, Being, and the denial of the identity thesis – has, it seems to me, recognizable analogs in the Skeptics' maintenance of *akatalepsia*.

A further question remains concerning the meaning and results of this stance with regard to the intellect, though constraints of space permit merely a survey and not a resolution of the issues involved. Some scholars have suggested that one observes an emergent antirealism or even a subjectivism operating in the philosophy of Damascius.[50] While this view has been harshly criticized,[51] one is still left with the need to interpret the often striking formulations encountered in the *Peri Archon*:

Being, insofar as it is in itself alone, is also undifferentiated. But when intellect, separated off, stands apart from Being and Being becomes no longer undifferentiated, but rather something differentiated from that which

---

[50] Cf. Combès's Introduction to Volume I of C-W. Cf. also Combès 1976.

[51] Beierwaltes, for example, criticizes in a rather sweeping way the "Bergsonian" flavor of certain strands of scholarship concerned with Late Athenian Neoplatonism in his monograph, *Denken des Einen* (Frankfurt, 1985).

has been differentiated, to this extent the object of knowledge is revealed in it. (*C-W* II.152. 5–8)

One could say several things in light of this passage without invoking idealism. For example, it is easy to point out that Plotinus had already insisted on the differentiated nature of intellectual knowledge and on the multiplicity inherent in intellectual apprehension. Again, it becomes increasingly common in the later tradition for Neoplatonists gradually to assimilate non-discursive thinking to discursive thinking, by offering more subtle distinctions in the intelligible world (for example, Proclus distinguishes between noetic and noeric), and by relying on the doctrine of the Henads to theorize about the possibilities of a truly unified consciousness. Finally, however, Damascius' criticisms of the Neoplatonic identity theory must be seen within the context of dialectic within the Late Academy. This critique of knowledge initiates a strategy that goes against the grain of Neoplatonic orthodoxy by undermining the dualism fundamental to the entire metaphysical construction. Platonic metaphysics traditionally relies upon the distinction between appearance and reality, or between being and phenomena. Damascius subverts the central ambition of Neoplatonism: the attainment of knowledge that unites the knower with reality.[52] He readily concedes that this ambition, which ties the ontological affirmation of the subject into a theory of knowledge, is the basis for the traditional Neoplatonic conception of gnosis, going so far as to etymologize this word in accordance with it: "Another meaning of the word knowledge (*gnosis*) might be, a production (*genesis*) of Being (*ontos*) and of essence (*ousias*), since it is by means of a return to Being that the knower comes to possess Being or essence."

In the Neoplatonic tradition, this doctrine motivates the search for wisdom, which becomes a rescue mission for the recovery of reality on the part of an alienated subject whose very status as a subject drives a wedge between himself and being. Finally, this drive toward unity itself must be the last reliable assurance that our loss can be made up. What is singular about this appetite, according to Plato, is that of all appetites, it cannot be deceived: we can never be satisfied with the appearance of a good, we want what is actually

---

[52] On the soteriological conception of the spiritual circuit, see Lloyd 1992, the chapter entitled "The Spiritual Circuit."

good for us.[53] So with the loss of being: we do not want to appear to be, we want to be. Reality and its appearance are not interchangeable.

Damascius seems compelled to redefine the Platonic meaning of eros, hitherto always defined as a drive for truth or being.[54] For Damascius, this quest itself must be seen as a quest for appearances:

[Objection:] But it is Being that intellect desires. [Answer:] It may desire Being, but it attains Being as an object of knowledge. Perhaps we should say that its desire is also of Being insofar as it is known since desires naturally correspond to the capacity to attain the objects of desire, and it follows that, for the knower, to attain Being is to attain it insofar as it is known.

In stark contrast to the Neoplatonic identity thesis, for Damascius, knowing and being known consist in alterity:

[Question:] what does it mean to say, "capable of being known," and how does this differ from Being? [Answer:] Something is an object of knowledge insofar as it exists in relation to another, whereas it is Being by virtue of what it is in itself.

Damascius' point is not that all is illusion or that reality subsides into mere appearances. Nor would he recommend the abandonment of metaphysics and the acceptance of a life based on phenomenal presentations. Rather, his point is that Being in itself should not be grasped as being, or a being, or an object, as something distinct and outside of a knower substantially different from Being. In truly unified knowledge, Being is not something attained, and hence no desire for Being can be satisfied. We have already looked at this passage from Damascius' discussion of the Unified, one of the three aspects of the noetic triad:

There is something intelligible, which you should know in the flower of the intellect.

If you turn your own intellect toward it and know it as an object, then you will not know it . . .

I ask you to know this without strain; turn back the sacred eye of your soul and bring the empty mind into that intelligible, until you comprehend it since it is outside the intellect. (C-W I.105.3–5; 9–13 = Or. Ch. fr. 1)

---

[53] Plato *Symposium* 206a; *Meno* 77e.
[54] Cf. *Enneads* III.6.9.

As Damascius comments, in unitive knowledge, the mind does not attempt to assimilate the object to itself. Rather, the mind completely abandons itself (ἀφιεῖσα ἑαυτήν), and itself becomes the object; the object no longer exists (ὡς οὐκ ὄντα μηδὲ ἐπιζητοῦσα), and hence the mind no longer desires to discover it. Here, one can no longer speak of intellect knowing being. Because intellect offers its separate identity to the aspect of the One it contemplates as unity, it is not possible to posit intellect as an absolutely separate and distinct hypostasis. In quoting the phrase "outside the intellect" from the Chaldean Oracles, Damascius suggests that intellect is not separate from the One. This non-dual approach brings the One into all the hypostases without thereby collapsing them. Again using metaphorical language, Damascius describes the experience in which intellect disappears:

When first we try to see the sun we see it from afar. But as we get closer to it, we actually see it less: finally we don't see it or anything else, since we have ourselves become the light. There is no more eye of enlightenment. (C-W I.84)

Everything short of the absolute is a manifestation of that principle; when Damascius limits intellect's knowledge to the appearance of being, he suggests that Being still falls short of the goal that eros implies but that intellect can never discover.

Conclusion

In the *Peri Archon*, Damascius criticizes the foundational premises of Procline metaphysics in his attempt to renew the contemplative form of his tradition and to guide his school by means of a radically nondual philosophy. Perhaps it will be helpful to summarize the substance of his criticisms by glancing at those propositions in the *Elements of Theology* directly abrogated in the *Doubts and Solutions Concerning First Principles*. Damascius criticizes Propositions 7, "Every productive cause is superior to that which it produces"; 11, "All that exists proceeds from a single first cause"; 35, "Every effect remains in its cause, proceeds from it, and reverts upon it"; 75, "Every cause properly transcends its resultant," and possibly several of the propositions concerning the doctrine of Henads.

The self-refuting nature of metaphysical discourse goes some way toward explaining the apparent heterodoxy of many of Damascius' statements, which can accordingly be seen more as metalinguistic than as metaphysical. When he insists upon the separation of the knower and the known or assimilates the One to the notion of totality, he knowingly breaches fundamental Neoplatonic principles: for Plotinus the One is by definition transcendent, and so forth. Why should Damascius be able to get away with such arguments, when no Neoplatonist in his right mind would agree to them in the first place?

Here I think we see a certain forgetfulness on the part of the tradition. Perhaps what happens in the case of Damascius is that the critique of discursivity that lies at the heart of the tradition must be reperformed and reenacted by means of textual practices. Damascius' method of teaching consists in taking away intellectual supports. He often refers to the effect at which he aims as a 'radical purification' of our conceptions.[55] If his criticisms of intellection or of causality appear to be unorthodox, we should nevertheless refrain from accusing him of reducing intellect to the level of discursive thinking or holding the One to be commensurate with ordinary objects.

Perhaps the most surprising passage in the *Doubts and Solutions Concerning First Principles* occurs near the end of the treatise, where Damascius appears to eschew traditional metaphysics in favor of revealed wisdom:

> We use human language to speak about principles that are divine in the highest possible degree. We cannot conceive or name them without being compelled to use our own ideas about realities that far exceed every mind life, and being. Even when the Gods instruct some of us concerning these or other matters, they [do not teach] such [thoughts] as the Gods themselve have. Instead, they use an appropriate language when instructing Egyptians Syrians, or Greeks . . . and so transmit matters of great import to human beings by using a human dialect. (C-W III.140.11–25)

Damascius concludes his first aporia on the nature of the Ineffable by reaffirming that it is neither a cause nor not a cause, neither a source nor not a source, that it is neither one nor many. By reper forming this critique of discursivity, Damascius achieves his aim in the quiescence of discursive thinking. The only remaining approach to the One is, he says, "by keeping quiet, by remaining in the secre

---

[55] *diakatharis, apokatharein.*

recess of the soul and not leaving it" (I.15.14). No doubt he did not write *Doubts and Solutions Concerning First Principles* for neophytes or beginners in philosophy. It is a highly technical and intellectually demanding work that assumes familiarity not only with Plato but also with the history of Neoplatonism and with various forms of esoteric theology. It is written for those who belong to the tradition but whose intellectual activity impedes their progress. Finally, it is meant for those whose doubts are almost insurmountable, who remain dissatisfied with dogmatism and unconvinced by elaborate metaphysical constructions. For such people, the only way to remove doubt is to remove thought altogether. This radical solution may remind us of the earlier Skeptical *epoche* of the Hellenistic Academy. And yet, this strong medicine is prescribed for those who, eschewing every panacea, will only be satisfied with an absolute cure for what ails them. Finally, the sole remedy for ignorance is, in Damascius' words, perseverance in unknowing.

Appendix: Damascius on Intellectual Reversion
(C-W II, pp. 148–152.8)

Context: Damascius has been discussing The Unified, the last henad of the noetic triad that comprises Damascius' second hypostasis. The Unified is the aspect of this hypostasis that communicates with other levels of being; it is the source of further emanation because multiplicity proceeds from The Unified. In this section, Damascius is ultimately considering whether or not The Unified can be known by the intellect. The portions translated constitute a digression on the nature of knowledge.

In the first part of this passage, Damascius defines knowledge as a reversion or return to a higher station of being. But if reversion occurs only at the level of intellect, then there is still a fundamental distance between that which reverts (the knower) and that to which the knower reverts. In the second part of this passage Damascius elaborates on the limits of knowledge: knowledge seeks its object and conforms to it. Yet this quest can only come about because of a separation between the knower and the known.

But gnosis is, as the name makes clear, a thought that is in the process of coming to be, and that means intellection. As for intellection (νόησις), because it inclines or reverts to [the fact of something's] Being and to the [affirmation, "it] is," it could justly be called "a state of return" (νεόεσις). But as it is, using a more elevated diction and achieving euphony by contracting [the vowels] into *eta*, we call it νόησις. And so too intellect (nous) is named from the fact that it returns to Being. Now nous returns both by means of substantial and vital reversion but in the third rank and as it were distantly, by means of gnostic intellection, and because nous is gnostic, and so it returns by means of actuality or in actuality, but neither substantially nor by means of the vital power. And that is why this kind of intellection is something that is involved more with becoming, and this is also more apparent to us, because it is especially distinct. And that is why the majority of philosophers define intellect in terms of [intellectual reversion]. But also before this there is the distinct and delimited hypostasis that exists before reversion and it was necessary to call this *noesis* before the gnostic reversion because it is first in reaching Being from the state of procession, and from this return nous gets its name, and before gnosis it both returns and reverts already.

And perhaps gnosis is the coming to be of Being and of substance. The knower certainly becomes substantial by means of the return to Being in the act of gnosis, but not in a primary way, but rather in a kind of substantiation that is nevertheless characterized by becoming. And that is why nous is the realities, as Aristotle too says.

Names should fit closely with realities, however ingenious one's terminology. That nous subsists and that gnosis is projected as the return to Being, and that every return is of something that once proceeded and is now already separate and therefore in need of return, and that return does not eliminate separation, but rather it actually leads back that which is separate, insofar as it is separate, into that from which it has divided itself and proceeded, all of this is evident even from the name, gnosis.

But what is [the essence] of knowledge? Is it a halo, taking as it were the first place in the procession of light that comes about in the knower from the object known? Certainly sense perception accords with the perceptual object, and the representation subsists according to impression, and so with opinion and discursive thought; the latter accords with the object of thought, the former with the object of opinion. In general then knowledge subsists according to the object of knowledge (γνῶσμα), if this expression is allowed, and the object of knowledge is that which can be known, but [as it] already subsists in the knower. [Another way to put it is to say that] knowledge accords with this object of knowledge but it is not the object of knowledge. **Question:** What then is the experience of the knower when it does not yet know? **Answer:** It seeks out the object of knowledge. Therefore knowledge is the attainment of the object of knowledge *qua* object of knowledge. For if in fact it attains Being, this is [only] insofar as Being is an object of knowledge. **Question:** What then is the nature of the object of knowledge and how does it differ from Being? **Answer:** [The difference is this:] the object of knowledge is related to another, whereas that which is what it is in itself is Being.

Perhaps this [way of putting it] indicates what belongs to either of them, but what their nature is has not yet been shown. Being is the hypostasis, but the object of knowledge is as it were the manifestation of the hypostasis. And one might say that the hypostasis is one thing in the case of the material form, but quite another in the case of the sensible [particular]. The sensible aspect falls outside of it and makes it known, making it known until the point of sense-perception, and so comes about in way that corresponds to sense-perception. That is also the way that manifestation [is related to] Being, as if it were a light that precedes Being [until it reaches] the knower, running out to meet the knower as the latter ascends. The light is coordinate with Being and it becomes one with it and it accomplishes and satisfies its desire for Being because of the completion of its intrinsic illumination. **Question:** So then intellect does not know Being, but [only] the manifestation of Being? **Answer:** [It knows] Being insofar as it is manifest, and it is manifest in accordance with the object of knowledge. And even if intellect could know Being, in exactly the way that it knows that which is capable of being known, nevertheless all that is capable of being known would be entirely [present] as an object of knowledge. The result is that intellect does know Being, but necessarily, as we say, according to the manifestation [of Being]. **Question:** But it is Being [that Intellect] desires. **Answer:** It may desire Being, but it obtains it as an object of knowledge. And perhaps it would be better to say that its desire is also for Being according to the object of knowledge. After all, desires and the attainments [of desire] have identical objects, and correspondingly for the knower, the attainment of Being is according to that which is known. **Question:** What do we mean by the expression, "manifestation?" **Answer:** The manifestation borders on the secondary principles and it furnishes itself in proportion to the measure of those wishing to enjoy it and to enfold the illumination that precedes it. **Question:** Is it therefore the case that the whole [of Being] is not knowable, but rather only the illumination, just as the color alone is visible, but not the underlying substrate? **Answer:** Yes, emphatically. But this should cause no surprise, but rather be a necessary consequence, that Being is something that belongs to the first principles but remains always out of the reach of the second principles and hence, ineffable. For in this way too that which is entirely out of bounds and ineffable is uniformly related to everything else, and each of the other things is toward its secondaries by itself ineffable and also becomes ineffable toward something. And this is especially unremarkable, as I said, but one might perhaps wonder whether intellect knows [just] the preceding illumination of Being, and not Being itself, that is, according to its manifestation. The **Answer** is that the manifestation of Being is the name for this prior illumination, [which is] not, however, a kind of emanation from it, as the light that surrounds the earth is from the sun. Rather, it is as if someone were to see the sun itself by means of its natural brilliance. **Question:** Then [intellect] knows only the surface [of Being], since it knows the manifestation of Being in the way [that one sees] a color? **Answer:** Being is intelligible through and through; there is no part of it that does not shine out and hasten to be revealed, just as you would say of a crystal or of some other transparent object that it is visible as a whole, because the nature of what is visible permeates it throughout.

Nevertheless, the body is one thing and that which is manifest throughout something else, just as in the intelligible order the manifestation would be other than Being. And the same thing will result, first, that [knowledge] is not of Being, but of the manifestation which is other than Being (for in the case of that which is completely transparent, it is not the body that is visible, but only the color). Next, in the case of something that is completely indeterminate, will we be able to distinguish manifestation as one thing, and Being as another, which then is like the substance for its manifestation, or differs from it however it in fact does?

To this we reply as follows: The Being that is what it is, insofar as it is just Being, is without distinction.

10

Conclusion: Reading Neoplatonism

Throughout this book, I have been talking about the "Neoplatonic tradition" as if this phrase referred to a well-defined phenomenon such as a group of philosophers who, in company with each other, formulated a self-consistent set of doctrines.[1] Yet it is not just the complexity of Neoplatonic scholasticism, particularly its subtle integration of Aristotelianism, Stoicism, and Platonism,[2] nor the major shifts in its philosophical vocabulary, such as the influence of Iamblichean theurgy precipitated, that makes it so difficult to locate the factors promoting the continuity of the school. Although the broad outlines of what we today might call a philosophical system can be seen in many of the philosophers who today fall under this sobriquet, the fact remains that the Neoplatonists themselves traced their philosophical genealogy in strikingly different ways. A time span of three centuries makes an unbroken succession of teachers and students an unlikely way to account for the cohesiveness of the tradition.

I have ended this book with the work of Damascius, the last Platonic Successor. Despite his official ties to the ancient Platonic school, his own membership in the tradition is anything but straight-

---

[1] As Eric Havelock writes,
> This word, with the concept it expresses, is taken for granted by all scholars and specialists. It describes an accepted presence in history. "Tradition" can be used to cover almost anything. The more ready its use, the more excuse it seems to provide for not going any further. Few, if any, ask the question, What sort of thing is a "tradition"? What is it made of? How does it work? (Havelock, *The Muses Learn to Write*, p. 67.

[2] On this scholastic dialectic, see Theiler and Dorrie.

forward. In the midst of the upheaval, persecution, and ideological pressures exerted on him, with a millenium separating him from classical Athens, Damascius seemingly had to rediscover or renew the tradition whose last proponent he became. One very clear example of Damascius' renewal of tradition can be found in the concluding pages of his *Doubts and Solutions Concerning First Principles*. There Damascius adds a theological appendix, which consists in short summaries that describe:

> The traditions that belong to other theologians concerning the intelligible diacosm; perhaps from these traditions we can experience a still greater reverence, indeed the greatest possible, for that transcendental union.[3]

Damascius proceeds to report three versions of the Orphic theology, alludes to Eudemus' theological interpretations of Homer, Hesiod, and Pherecydes of Syros, and ends with Eudemus' summaries of Babylonian,[4] Sidonian, and Persian theologies.[5] These concluding chapters reveal that Damascius did not think that his philosophy was or could be restricted to a specific culture; as we saw for Proclus' *Platonic Theology*, Damascius also presumed that his own work belonged to a perennial philosophy whose universality he discovered in the writings of traditions he realized were still more ancient than Platonism.

Yet his *Life of Isidore* allows us to gauge the difficulties that beset Damascius, not only because of his affiliations with a minority tradition but because of the collusion and intellectual influence pedaling that he feared had insinuated themselves among his colleagues In it, one can read Damascius' terse and caustic account of Horapollo, a colleague who lacked a philosophical disposition and deserted the Platonic camp for the Christians, out of "sheer greed.' (ἀπλήστου τινὸς ἐπιθυμίας).[6] Again, Damascius complains about the philosopher Ammonius, who, "being very fond of money and always

---

[3] Damascius *Peri Archon* C-W III.159, 10–15.
[4] Damascius' summaries of an ancient Babylonian theogony are by and large in agreement with second millenium B.C.E records such as the *Enuma Elish*. See C-W III, pp. 234–235 and Burkert, *The Orientalizing Revolution*.
[5] Damascius *Peri Archon* III.159 and following, C-W.
[6] Damascius *Vitae Isidori*, fragment 317 (Suda III 615, 17, s.v. "Horapollon"). Zintzen p. 253, 5–6.

calculating with a view to business, came to an agreement with an official who oversaw such matters and belonged to the prevailing opinion [sc. Christianity]."[7] These passages give the impression of isolation, as if this last official representative of Platonism had become the school's only defender while its integrity collapsed from within.

These brief examples make it clear that Neoplatonism is engimatic: what forces allowed this tradition to renew itself and incorporate conceptual structures and religions both indigenous and borrowed? It is easy for us to read through the fragments of Damascius' *Life of Isidore*, replete as it is with the story of the pagan philosopher, Hypatia (later martyred at the hands of an angry Alexandrian mob), or through Proclus' *Against Philoponus on the Eternity of the World*[8] (or indeed through any number of earlier works exhibiting a particular axe to grind, such as Porphyry's *Letter to Anebo*), and see that their formulations have been hammered out on the forge of intractable ideological differences. We know, for example, that pagan and Christian cosmologists argued about whether or not the natural motion of any sublunar body could be properly circular, a question posed as an inquiry into natural science but answered from the perspective of religious dogmatism. Since in the epoch we are considering, ideological consciousness pervades philosophical discourse to such a degree, it is all too easy for the modern reader to approach these texts with suspicion, even to dismiss them as the product of a highly interested, ideologically fraught, community of thinkers. How then are we to understand the claim of this same group of thinkers when they insist on the pristine nature of their philosophical tradition because, as they maintain, that tradition rests on an innate faculty capable of discovering and revealing universal truth?[9]

I think it is important to consider the issue of our relationship to

---

[7] Damascius *Vitae Isidori*, fragment 316 (Epitoma Photiana 292). Zintzen 1967, p. 251, 11–13.

[8] For a history of the dispute between John Philoponus and Proclus on the eternity of the world, see Sorabji 1987.

[9] In just one example that comes immediately to mind, a historiographer like Hayden White, who claims that political authority structures all discourse, would no doubt be interested in the political factors that might lead the Neoplatonists to posit this faculty.

a textual tradition from which we necessarily stand apart. As Gadamer writes in his reflections on the problem of historical distance in interpretation:

> We started by saying that a hermeneutical situation is determined by the prejudices that we bring with us. They constitute, then, the horizon of a particular present, for they represent that beyond which it is impossible to see. But now it is important to avoid the error of thinking that the horizon of the present consists of a fixed set of opinions and valuations, and that the otherness of the past can be foregrounded from it as from a fixed ground.
>
> In fact the horizon of the present is continually in the process of being formed because we are continually having to test all our prejudices . . . Hence the horizon of the present cannot be formed without the past.[10]

I take it that what Gadamer means is something like the following. The realization that one does *not* belong to a tradition, that it stands outside the framework of one's particular historical world, offers the opportunity for a genuine dialogue with that tradition. Encountering this other perspective can uncover the prejudices that limit one's own understanding. It now becomes possible to see the present as no longer so circumscribed from within, but rather as informed by other traditions.

The purpose of this book is to help the reader take on, insofar as possible, a view that is situated within or that provisionally accepts some of the fundamental principles of Neoplatonic philosophy. In the preface to this book, I suggested that the identity theory of truth, the doctrine that intellect is identical with its objects, is perhaps the foundation of the philosophical enterprise we know as Neoplatonism. Without at least a notional confrontation with this theory, the texts that belong to this tradition are at risk of being completely opaque or uninteresting to the modern reader, for whom it is possibly almost axiomatic that truth is structured like or by language, that truth at any rate must always already be framed by the discourse that defines a certain epoch, and so forth. In the preceding chapters, I have tried to show that this doctrine of intellectual, or unitive, knowing entails precisely that truth is not structured like language and is not a product of any discourse. Hence, intellectual knowing does not posit an intentional object that is directed toward some state of affairs in the world, nor does it admit of the subject-object dichotomy

---

[10] Gadamer 1989, p. 306

that lies at the heart of, for example, Western grammar. More than this, intellectual truth is not available for transmission in any discursive form. It is this last point that must now be expanded.

Already we have seen that the textual tradition forming our only record of Neoplatonism is incomplete in crucial ways. This incompleteness is not only owing to the frequent reticence evinced by Neoplatonists to transmit their teachings in a written form. If Porphyry's anecdote is credible, Plotinus himself continued to teach and committed nothing to writing until he was almost the age of fifty; instead, he concerned himself with the difficulties presented by individual students during the course of personal instruction.[11] According to Longinus, the most esteemed members of the Platonic school engaged primarily in oral teaching, devoting themselves to refining their students' understanding;[12] Plotinus' own teacher, Ammonius, wrote nothing and possibly enjoined his followers to maintain a similar practice.[13] Emphasis on face-to-face teaching and personal transmission from master to student is altogether in keeping with the Neoplatonic contemplative praxis that purported to cultivate a wisdom existing outside the parameters of language, as I hope to show.

The anecdotal material clearly documents the intimacy of the student-teacher relationship, an intimacy developed often throughout several decades of association.[14] Although it would be difficult for the modern reader to estimate what this meticulousness concerning a given student's comprehension of the doctrines entailed, one conclusion certainty presents itself: the written record of such philosophical associations necessarily left a great deal unrecorded. This gap in the written representation of Neoplatonic teaching and doctrine is more or less empirical; it can be alluded to without invoking or entering into postmodern discussions concerning the priority of

---

[11] *Life of Plotinus* 4.10–12 (Armstrong's translation): "In the tenth year of the reign of Gallienus [,] Plotinus was about fifty-nine years old. I, Porphyry, when I first joined him was thirty. From the first year of Gallienus[,] Plotinus had begun to write on the subjects that came up in the meetings of the school."

[12] *Life of Plotinus* 20.

[13] *Life of Plotinus* 3.30.

[14] *Life of Plotinus* 3–4. Plotinus studied with Ammonius for eleven years; Amelius had been with Plotinus for eighteen years when Porphyry joined them at the age of thirty.

texts for the historical recoverability of an extra-textual world.[15] I am not here concerned with the frequently raised problem of comparing writing to orality or written language to spoken language, important as this issue is, given that Plato himself is often placed at the fulcrum of the transformation of ancient oral culture. Nor again am I interested in rehearsing the "oral-teachings" problem in terms of how it bears on the esoteric Plato and on the Neoplatonic-Pythagorean tradition that purportedly preserved these teachings. For my purposes, it is enough to notice that personal instruction was an important element in Neoplatonic teaching methods, as it was in the earlier Hellenistic schools. What then did such instruction accomplish, and how does it bear on the problem of Neoplatonic textuality? I turn now to consider some difficulties that must be faced as we encounter what has in fact been expressed in the textual tradition. These difficulties exist by virtue of the insight that the tradition as a whole seeks to communicate and to embody, with which language itself is in a certain respect out of alignment.

Damascius' student, Simplicius, wrote a *Commentary on Aristotle's Categories*, at the beginning of which he discusses the *skopos*, or province of Aristotle's treatise: are the ten categories (γένη) that Aristotle enumerates words, realities, or conceptual entities? By sharply delineating these approaches, Simplicius underscores a semantic theory, according to which "propositions . . . are complex expressions, and these are not realities."[16] Even if the categories are deployed semantically (καθὸ μέντοι σημαντική ἐστιν ἡ λέξις)[17] to refer to actual things, it is best to think of them as conceptual entities (νοήματα) that symbolize, or are images of, genuine substances (σύμβολον οὖσα τῆς ἐν τοῖς οὖσιν οὐσίας).[18] Concepts are not realities, although the soul's fall into embodiment and consequent forgetfulness of reality necessitate sight, hearing, and speech (φωνή), while speech itself constitutes the soul's outermost activity.[19]

Turning now to the signifying expressions themselves, according to Aristotle, substance is "what is primarily signified in language,"

---

[15] Cf. White, *The Content of the Form.*
[16] Simplicius, *CAG* VII. Cf. Hoffman 1987a and 1987b.
[17] Proemium *Simplicii in Aristotelis Categorias Commentarium* 11, 1.
[18] Proemium *Simplicii in Aristotelis Categorias Commentarium* 11, 19.
[19] Proemium *Simplicii in Aristotelis Categorias Commentarium.* 13, 5.

while "other things are predicated of substance."[20] Hence the structure of language as conceived throughout this tradition involves grammatical subject and object, a conceptual apparatus by means of which a speaker approximates the genuine references of these signifying expressions, and the (at least notional or operative) distinction between the speaker and that to which the speaker makes reference.

But this structure, based as it is on a system of distinctions ideally mirrored in the categories deployed by the philosopher of language,[21] is entirely unsuitable for expressing certain kinds of truth, as when that truth does not even vaguely resemble the grammatical structures that imply the distinction between substance and accident, between the speaker and what the speaker says.[22]

To make this asymmetry clear, let us consider Plotinus' attempts to describe the moment at which the soul attains to self-knowledge, the moment when the apprehension that soul is not other than the intellect becomes central to the act of soul's own awareness. In this relationship to intellect, the soul comes to apprehend truth, in the Neoplatonic sense according to which intellect is the ground of truth, since it is only in intellect that real being is known. As Plotinus puts it, "that is the locus of truth."[23] He goes on to describe this kind of awareness as:

Truly intelligible, both knower and known, self-apprehended and not dependent on another in order to see, completely self-reliant in the act of seeing, since what it sees, that it is, and yet it is known by us [sc. the soul] by means of that itself, so that for us [the soul], awareness of it comes about through itself. Or how else would we be able to speak about it? That is its nature: it can be grasped more clearly by itself, and we can only grasp it through it. And so, it is through conceptions of this kind that our own soul is led up to it, that is when our soul establishes itself toward it as an image of it. (*Enneads* V.3.8.40–49)

Plotinus touches on this kind of experience more briefly in *Enneads* VI, where he is actually discussing the soul's apprehension of the One in unitive knowing:[24]

[20] Proemium *Simplicii in Aristotelis Categorias Commentarium* 9, 25–27, quoting Aristotle.
[21] Proemium *Simplicii in Aristotelis Categorias Commentarium* 9.
[22] Here I am deeply indebted to Sells's excellent discussion, chapter 1.
[23] *Enneads* V.3.8.36: ἐκεῖ γὰρ τὰ ἀληθῆ.
[24] For an extremely subtle and penetrating discussion of this passage, see Bussanich 1988, pp. 146–7. Bussanich's analysis of Plotinus' mystical language here is unparalled by other Commentators.

But when the soul wishes to see [the One] by itself, it is just by being with it that it sees, and by being one with that it is one, and it is not capable of thinking that it possesses what it seeks, because it is not other than that which is being known. (VI.9.3.10–13)

In this conclusion, I cannot do justice to the incredible richness of these descriptions, both of which point to moments in which soul, as the seat of discursive thinking, comes to a realization that leads it outside the strictures of discursive thought. The first passage begins from the perspective of intellect as the ground of truth, but ends with the soul's experience of self-knowledge, which consists in a displacement of self-identity. Whatever else may be said about this passage, it should be apparent that the kind of awareness under discussion seemingly defies the grammatical and semantic structures just touched on. For it is just at the moment when truth is apprehended that it ceases to be something that could be articulated in language: the thinker is thinking about something whose realization displaces the very fact of the thinker's being who he thought he was. Moreover, this kind of thinking, though it is an image of the reality under discussion, consists in the thinker actually becoming that which is being thought. Hence the meaning of the pronoun *auto* shifts its referent in the very act of the soul's coming to describe its experience. Here subject and predicate, noun and verb, shift places with what before was an extra-linguistic element, and the conceptual structure of self-knowledge consists in the displacement of that very structure, as when Plotinus says that "it is through conceptions of this kind that [the] soul is led up to it."

Perhaps this last paragraph has been difficult to follow. It was intended to be. Plotinus suggests that in this kind of thought, genuine self-knowledge, language arises afterward as an awkward translation of a truth whose essence is to break free of discursive structures. It is for this reason that the texts that seek to convey or even to inculcate self-knowledge at once fail to accomplish their purpose. By understanding this failure of the text, we can also conversely allay some of our anxieties about the text. Here, it is not that the text presents itself as containing an abstract, disembodied world that intrudes upon the embodied, concrete identity of the reader, threatening to elide the latter in a truth that it fails, ultimately, to deliver. Quite the reverse occurs: the text points out that the reader is in possession of a lexicon that is much too subtle to appear on the page. The text submits to the authority of the reader, who, it has just admitted, is "completely self-reliant in the act of seeing." Objections to this kind of reading are no doubt prolific. In the preceding text, we encounter through language a self-reflexive moment that disrupts the structure of reflexivity inasmuch as the initial locus of awareness referred to in the text (the soul) is displaced by another kind of consciousness: "it is known by us [sc. the soul] by means of that itself, so that for us [the soul], awareness of it comes about through itself." Therefore this text purports to describe something that could only be called pristine awareness, immediacy of apprehension, or even self-authorizing consciousness. No reasons are adduced to persuade the reader that this reflexivity, so difficult to capture in language, is any more available outside the text. Moreover, the obvious difficulty presents itself that such an experience would seem to depend for its communication on its realization in language, on the markers that delineate the subject of discourse.

It is worth pausing to consider this objection. As we have seen, the reader of Neoplatonic texts faces several challenges. On the one side, the texts expound a number of doctrines that in all likelihood were also explicated within a course of personal instruction. Of course, this instruction is not fully represented in the texts themselves, which more often than not seem highly exegetical and concerned with other canonical texts. On the other side, the philosophical core of this tradition purports to rely on nous, the faculty of unitive knowing. This unitive knowledge is, as we have already seen, seemingly at odds with language itself. If it does not strike the reader as futile to suggest that so much is left out of these texts despite their constituting our sole means of access to the Neoplatonic tradition, it nevertheless will be helpful to recall what is actually presented in the texts.

Throughout the history of Neoplatonic textuality, it has been of primary importance to press language into the service of the Ineffable. At times this effort has meant the manifest invention of fictions of language, as when the Chaldean Oracles are written in an Imperial imitation of Homeric Greek and yet are purported to contain the secrets of Babylonian wisdom, or when Orpheus is represented as the preceptor of Pythagoras. At other times, this fictional aspect of the tradition seems to encroach on historical configurations, as, for example, the events reported in hagiographic narratives. An effective Neoplatonic hermeneutics would seek to understand Neoplatonic writings in terms of an ongoing invention of tradition in the very specific sense that the texts rely on the participation and willingness of the reader to enter into the practice of interpretation. Not only to take up the puzzles and enigmas offered by such fundamental principles as the three primary hypostases, the One, the Intellect, and the Soul, with the advice of Plotinus in mind to "make oneself the vision" or to "exchange the image for the reality" but also to ask oneself why these texts still speak to us, despite their difficulty and demands, is to enter into this practice. Thus whatever fictions are perpetrated within the confines of the text for the purpose of contriving a tradition, this invention is more accurately realized in the perpetuation of the tradition through an earnest confrontation with the very puzzles offered by these texts.

In this book I have been talking about specific kinds of language – traditional narratives, mathematical symbolism, visionary exercises, divine names, and aporetic discourses – all of which are deployed to entice the reader, like the Dionysus of the fable whom the Titans captivated with their mirror, into the drama, or action, of the text. But this central drama implied by many Neoplatonic texts throughout the tradition is the *anagoge*, the soul's ascent and assimilation to reality, whether that effort is conceived as theurgy, contemplation, or gnosis. Hence philosophy can be articulated in the imperative mode: "First become godlike" (*Enneads* I.6.9.33); "Retreat to yourself and see" (*Enneads* I.6.9.8); "One must put aside everything else and abide in this alone and this alone become..." (*Enneads* VI.9.9.50). At the other end of the linguistic spectrum, this *anagoge* can be described in the form of a visionary geography that is also an exegetical device, as when Proclus reads the *Phaedrus* myth as a description of mystic ascent: "Therefore the same method of *anagoge* is also [used by us], and on account of this the method employed by theurgy becomes more credible."[25]

In the preceding sentence quoted from Proclus, *anagoge* is a concept explicated by an allusion to a myth recounted in one of Plato's dialogues. This reading backwards into the history of Platonism is again part of the invention of tradition that is so crucial to Neoplatonist hermeneutics. But what is even more critical for this herme-

---

[25] Proclus *Platonic Theology* IV, p. 29.3–6 (S-W).

neutics is the ability to read not into the past but into the present. This is where the Neoplatonic conception of symbolism becomes integral to the act of reading. In following Plotinus' exercises involving the visualization of the luminous sphere or Proclus' geometric imaginations, readers turn aside from the text to notice their own minds, now illuminated or highlighted under the influence of the text. Both of these authors use a dialect sanctioned by tradition, whether Pythagorean, Orphic, or Platonic, to present a new meaning to the reader. This meaning to which the symbol points is recovered through an extra-textual effort on the part of the reader or student, although the directions offered by means of the symbol can facilitate this procedure.

In his treatise "On Well-Being," *Enneads* I.4, Plotinus touches briefly on what happens when the mind becomes aware of nous, the faculty of unitive knowledge. The mind comes to be aware of an activity that is "before awareness,"[26] and it does this by "turning thought back on itself,"[27] an event that comes about quite naturally when the mind's productions come to a halt, leaving it finally "in peace."[28] As Plotinus says, the discursive mind is usually active in thought production, but when this kind of activity is brought to a rest, the result is that the mind functions like a mirror.[29] The discursive mind in setting aside its discursive activity becomes transparent. This transparent self-awareness consists in "perceiving directly, while preserving that prior awareness, that intellect and thought are active."[30] Thus there is a direct awareness of awareness that coincides with a freedom from attachment to particular thoughts. This is the objectless knowing that characterizes intellect. In treatise I.4, this kind of practice is said to be accompanied by the cultivation of detachment from emotional states, the "fearlessness in all matters," that allows such mental stability to develop. The Neoplatonists often use symbols as expedient devices through which to communicate the nature of such practices as concentration, absorption in the object

---

[26] *Enneads* I.4.10.6: τὸ πρὸ ἀντιλήψεως ἐνέργημα.

[27] *Enneads* I.4.10.8: ἀνακάμπτοντος τοῦ νοήματος.

[28] *Enneads* I.4.10.13–14: περὶ ψυχὴν ἡσυχίαν μὲν ἄγοντος τοῦ ἐν ἡμῖν τοιούτου. ᾧ ἐμφαίνεται τὰ τῆς διανοίας.

[29] *Enneads* I.4.10.10: ὥσπερ ἐν κατόπτρῳ περὶ τὸ λεῖον καὶ λαμπρὸν ἡσυχάζον.

[30] *Enneads* I.4.10.16–17: καὶ οἶον αἰσθητῶς γινώσκεται μετὰ τῆς προτέρας γνώσεως, ὅτι ὁ νοῦς καὶ ἡ διάνοια ἐνεργεῖ.

of contemplation, and self-directed attention. More than this, the symbolon is often used as the contemplative object; it is offered as a focal point for sustained, concentrated attention and as a mirror in which the mind can reflect back to itself its own "quiet, radiant, motionlessness."

Therefore it is necessary to admit that the texts cannot stand by themselves for the tradition, and that the tradition comprises more than could be contained in a text. The text reminds the reader that philosophical understanding is not conceptual but, in a certain sense, practical. Today it has become somewhat fashionable to suggest that allusions to practice or *askesis* can be assimilated to the text.[31] On this approach, such things are no more than the fictions of a textual enterprise that simply invents its own hermeneutical context. At any rate, if this were so, if contemplative *askesis* were a philosophical or linguistic trope, it is legitimate to ask what difference this would make to the text or how one could tell the difference. For the Neoplatonists, all the difference in the world. But if a reader does not take any steps beyond the text, the difference will no longer be visible.

One could go further in this discussion of the fictionality of tradition and suggest that the highest form of Neoplatonic hermeneutics might posit philosophy as, in the last result, mere fiction. After all, is this not fundamentally the position of Damascius, for whom the foundational premises of first philosophy, including causal explanation and the existence of a first principle, are shown to be the creations of ignorance? As Damascius succinctly puts the matter:

But now it is time to place a seal on our talk about the One, and say that it is not that which we say is nor what we know as simultaneously one and all things, but rather, what we labor to bring forth from these things (I am speaking here of gnostic labor), it is That . . . And it is this that the philosopher Proclus in his *Monobiblos* calls the Ineffable Axiom (or Principle of Signlessness).[32]

[31] On the problems of language and experience in the textual representation of *askesis*, see Katz, *Mysticism and Language*.

[32] Damascius, *Peri Archon*, I, p. 86.10, C-W.
Νῦν δὲ ἐκεῖνο περὶ τὸ τοιούτου ἑνὸς ἐπισφραγιζόμενοι λέγομεν, ὅτι ὃ μὲν λέγομεν οὔτε ἔστιν οὐδὲ γιγνώσκομεν ὡς ἓν καὶ ὡς πάντα ὁμοῦ, ὃ δὲ ἀπὸ τούτων ὠδίνομεν (ὠδῖνα φημι γνωστικήν) τοῦτό ἐστι . . . Καὶ τοῦτό ἐστιν ὅπερ ὁ φιλόσοφος Πρόκλος ἐν τῷ μονοβίβλῳ ἀπόρρητον ἀξίωμα κέκληκεν, τὸ κατὰ τὴν ὠδίνουσαν ἐκεῖνο γνῶσιν.

Conclusion: Reading Neoplatonism

Damascius too practices philosophy in the imperative mode; indicative statements that convey philosophical truths are set aside as a part of this imperative. This imperative is nothing other than the realization that discursive thinking, far from being able to transmit or convey philosophical truth, can actually present the greatest hindrance to the apprehension of that truth:

Now knowing takes places by means of intuitive seeing, or by means of syllogism, or it is just a diluted and obscure sort of vision that sees things from a distance, as it were, but which nevertheless relies on logical necessity, or else, [knowledge is] simply a specious form of reasoning that doesn't even have access from afar, but simply conceives of certain ideas on the basis of other ideas. By means of such thinking, we habitually recognize the material order or privation or in general that which has no reality.[33]

The truth that has been in question throughout this book begins in self-knowledge, since as Damascius is at pains to remind us, the mind's ordinary habit "conceives of certain ideas on the basis of other ideas." But this habit separates the mind from reality, from its own being and from genuinely encountering the reality of other beings. Hence, in the juxtaposition of traditions that occurs when someone today reads the texts of Neoplatonism, it is not enough to concede that a meaningful hermeneutics comes about if readers succeed in translating the language of Neoplatonism into a language that belongs to them. To read Neoplatonism is not just to interpret the texts of Neoplatonism, to make them speak again through meanings now realized in or appropriated by a textual interpretation. I quote once more from Gadamer, this time as a caveat:

interpretation is not a means through which understanding is achieved; rather, it enters into the content of what is understood . . . The interpretation places the object, as it were, on the scales of words.[34]

This quotation suggests that exegesis is the goal of interpretation and understanding, or that one can equate understanding with exegesis. Throughout this book, we have seen that Neoplatonic exegesis itself is only a trope for a kind of understanding that never fully surfaces in language. What I have been arguing in this book is that reading Neoplatonism involves precisely the opposite approach: we must take the object, the text, off the scales of words.

[33] Damascius *Peri Archon* I.67, C-W.
[34] Gadamer 1989, p. 398.

243

References

Primary Sources: Ancient Authors

ALCINOUS

[Alcinous] 1993. *Handbook of Platonism*. Translated with Commentary by J. Dillon. Oxford.

Whittaker, J. 1990. *Alcinoos, Enseignement des doctrines de Platon*. Les Belles Lettres. Paris.

ARISTOTLE

Barnes, J. 1975. *Aristotle's Posterior Analytics*. Oxford.

Charlton, W. 1970. *Aristotle's Physics, I, II*. Translated with Introduction and Notes. Oxford.

Hicks, R. 1980. *Aristotle De Anima*. With Translation, Introduction, and Notes. Cambridge.

Ross, W. D. 1924. *Aristotle's Metaphysics*. A Revised Text with Introduction and Commentary. Oxford.

Ross, W. D. 1955. *Aristotles' Physics*. A Revised Text with Introduction and Commentary. Oxford.

Ross, W. D. 1949. *Aristotle's Prior and Posterior Analytics*. Oxford.

Commentaria in Aristotelem Graeca (CAG). 1882–1909. 23 vols. Berlin.

DAMASCIUS

Chaignet, A. 1989. *Damascius le diadoque. Problemes et solutions touchant les premiers principes*. 3 vols. Traduits par A.-Ed. Chaignet. Paris. Reprinted, Brussels, 1964.

Damascius Successoris. 1899. *Dubitationes et solutiones de primis principiis*. 2 vols. In *Platonis Parmenidem*. Edited by C. E. Ruelle. Paris.

Damascius. 1995. *Commentaire du Parménide*. Edited by L. G. Westerink and J. Combès. Paris.

References

Damascius. 1986–91. *Traité des premiers principes.* 3 vols. Trans. by J. Combès. Text by L. G. Westerink. Paris.

Damascius. 1977. *Commentary on the Phaedo. The Greek Commentaries on Plato's Phaedo.* Vol. II, *Damascius.* Edited by L. G. Westerink. Amsterdam.

Damascius. 1967. *Damascii vitae Isidori reliquiae.* Edited by C. Zintzen. Hildesheim.

Galpérine, M. 1987. *Des premiers principes. Apories et résolutions.* Lagrasse. (Translation)

HELLENISTIC PHILOSOPHERS

Long, A. A., and D. Sedley. 1987. *The Hellenistic Philosophers.* 2 vols. Vol. 2, *Original Texts.* Cambridge.

Von Arnim, I., ed. 1903–24. *Stoicorum veterum fragmenta.* 4 vols. Leipzig.

HERMETICA

Hermetica. 1968. *Hermetica: The Ancient Greek and Latin Writings which Contain Religious or Philosophic Teachings Ascribed to Hermes Trismegistus.* Edited and translated by Walter Scott. Vol I, *Texts and Translation.* Reprint, London. New English translation in B. Copenhaver, *Hermetica.* Cambridge. 1992.

Hermetica. 1991. *Corpus Hermeticum.* Tome 1. Traités II–XII. Edited by A. D. Nock. French translation by A.-J. Festugière. 1946. Reprint, Paris.

IAMBLICHUS

Iamblichus. 1966. *Les Mystères d'Egypte.* Texte établi et traduit par E. des Places. Paris.

Iamblichi. 1975. *De communi mathematica scientia liber.* Stuttgart.

Iamblichus. 1953. *De Anima.* Translation and Commentary by A. J. Festugière. In *La Révélation d'Hermes Trismégiste,* appendix 1, 3: 177–248. Paris.

[Iamblichus] 1922. *Theologoumena arithmeticae.* Edited by V. de Falco. Second edition by U. Klein. Stuttgart, 1975.

Dillon, John M. 1973. *Iamblichi Chalcidensis: In Platonis dialogos commentariorum fragmenta.* Edited with Translation and Commentary by John M. Dillon. Leiden.

Iamblichus. 1989. *Protrepticus. Protreptique.* Jamblique; texte établi et traduit par E. des Places. Paris

JULIANUS

Julianus. 1989. *The Chaldean Oracles.* Edited and translated by R Majercik. Leiden.

Julianus. 1971. *Oracles Chaldaiques.* Texte établi et traduit par E. des Places. Paris.

References

OLYMPIODORUS

Olympiodorus. 1990. *Prolégomènes à la Philosophie de Platon.* Edited by Westerink and J. Trouillard. Paris.

ORPHIC FRAGMENTS

Kern, O. 1922. *Orphicorum Fragmenta.* Berlin.

PLATO

Plato. 1980. *Platonis opera recognovit brevique adnotatione critica instruxit Ioannes
Burnet.* 5 vol. Oxford.
Plato. 1961. *The Collected Dialogues of Plato, Including the Letters.* Edited by Edith
Hamilton and Huntington Cairns. With introduction and prefatory
notes. Translator ed. by Lane Cooper and others. New York.

PLOTINUS

Plotinus. Atkinson, M. 1983. *Plotinus, Ennead V.I.: On the Three Principal Hypostases.* A Commentary with translation. New York.
Bertier, J., L. Brisson, A. Charles, and J. Pepin. 1980. *Enneades.* VI, 6.
French and Greek. *Traité sur les nombres: Enneade VI, 6 [34].* Introduction,
texte grec, traduction, commentaire et index grec. Paris.
Beutler, R., and W. Theiler. 1960–71. *Plotins Schriften.* Griechischer Text,
deutsche Übersetzung, Anmerkungen. Bände II, III, IV, V a-b, VI. Ham-
burg.
Bussanich, J. 1988. *The One and Its Relation to Intellect in Plotinus: A Commen-
tary on Selected Texts.* Leiden.
Fleet, B. 1995. *Ennead III.6: On the Impassivity of the Bodiless.* Oxford, New
York.
Hadot, P. 1988 *Traité 38: VI, 7 Plotin.* Introduction, traduction, commentaire et notes. Paris.
1964, 1976, 1982. *Plotini Opera.* Edited by P. Henry and H.-R. Schwyzer.
Editio minor. 3 vols. Oxford.

PORPHYRY

Porphyry. 1975. *Sententiae ad intelligibilia ducentes.* Edited by E. Lamberz. Leipzig.
1982. *La vie de Plotin.* Paris.

PROCLUS

Proclus. 1970. *A Commentary on the First Book of Euclid's Elements.* Translated by
G. Morrow. Princeton. Second edition by I. Mueller. 1992.

References

1954. *Commentary on the First Alcibiades of Plato.* Edited by L. G. Westerink. Amsterdam. English translation by W. O'Neill, The Hague. 1971.

1963. *Proclus. The Elements of Theology.* 2nd ed. Edited by E. R. Dodds. Oxford.

1968–87. *Platonic Theology. Theologie Platonicienne.* Edited by H. D. Saffrey and L. G. Westerink. 5 vol. Paris. *Procli in Platonis Theologiam.* Portus ed. Hamburg. 1618. Reprint, Frankfurt. 1960. English translation by Thomas Taylor, *The Platonic Theology,* London. 1816. Reprint, New York. 1986.

1908. *Proclus' Commentary on Plato's Cratylus.* Edited by G. Pasquali. Teubner.

1903–6. *Proclus' Commentary on Plato's Republic. Procli in Rem publicam commentarii.* 2 vols. Edited by G. Kroll. Leipzig. Reprint, 1965.

1903–6. *Proclus' Commentary on the Timaeus. Procli in Platonis Timaeum.* 3 vols. Edited by E. Diehl. Leipzig. Translated by A.-J. Festugière. 5 vols. Reprint, Paris, 1966–8.

1961. *Proclus' Commentary on Plato's Parmenides. Procli Commentarium in Platonis Parmenidem.* In *Procli opera inedita.* 2nd ed. Edited by V. Cousin. Paris. 1864. Reprint, Hildesheim.

1987. *Proclus' Commentary on Plato's Parmenides.* Translated by J. Dillon and G. Morrow. Princeton.

1891. *Eclogae de Philosophia Chaldaica.* Edited by H. Jahn. Halis Saxonum.

1873. *Procli diadochi in Primum Euclidis Elementorum Librum commentarii ex recognitione Godofredi Friedlein.* Leipzig.

SENECA

Seneca. 1977. L. Annaei Senecae. *Dialogorum Libri Duodecim.* Edited by L. D. Reynolds. Oxford.

1965. L. Annaei Senecae. *Ad Lucilium Epistulae Morales.* Tomus II. Edited by Reynolds. Oxford.

SIMPLICIUS

Simplicius. 1907. *In Aristotelis Categorias Commentarium.* Edited by A. Kalbfleisch. *CAG,* vol. VIII.

1989. *Commentaire sur les categories.* Traduction, commentée sous la direction d'Illsetraut Hadot. Leiden.

1995. *On Aristotle's On the Soul 1.1–2.4.* Translated and annotated by J. Urmson, and P. Lautner. Ithaca.

THEO SMYRNAEUS

Theo Smyrnaeus. 1878. *Theonis Smyranei: Expositio rerum mathematicarum a legendum Platonem utilum.* Edited by Hiller. Teubner.

References

Secondary Sources

Alfino, M. 1990. Plotinus on the possibility of non-propositional thought. *Ancient Philosophy* 8:273–84.

Annas, J. 1992. Socrates the Sceptic. In *Oxford Studies in Ancient Philosophy*. Supplementary volume. Oxford; New York.

Annas, J., and J. Barnes. 1994. *Sextus Empiricus: Outlines of Scepticism*. Cambridge; New York.

1985. *The Modes of Scepticism*. Cambridge; New York.

Athanassiadi, P. 1993. Persecution and response in late paganism: The evidence of Damascius. *Journal of Hellenic Studies* 113:119–29.

Balme, D. 1987. Teleology and necessity. In A. Gotthelf and J. G. Lennox, eds., *Philosophical Issues in Aristotle's Biology*. 275–85. Cambridge; New York.

1990a. *The Toils of Scepticism*. Cambridge; New York.

Barnes, J. 1983a. Pyrrhonism, belief, and causation. In M. Burnyeat, ed., *The Skeptical Tradition*. Berkeley. Reprinted in Aufstieg und Niedergang der Römischen Welt II 36.4 (1989).

1983b. Immaterial causes. In *Oxford Studies in Ancient Philosophy*. Vol. 1.

Beierwaltes, W. 1991. *Selbsterkentnis und Erfahrung der Einheit*. Frankfurt.

1990. *Begriff und Metapher*. Heidelberg.

1987. Proclus ein "systematischer" Philosoph? In *Proclus: Lecteur et interprète des Anciens*. Paris.

1965. *Proklos: Grundzüge seiner Metaphysik*. Leiden.

1961. Plotins Metaphysik des Lichtes. *Zeitschrift für Philosophische Forschung* 15:334–62.

Bernard, W. 1987. Philoponus on self-awareness. In R. Sorabji, ed., *Philoponus and the Rejection of Aristotelian Science*, 154–63. Ithaca.

Bett, R. 1997. *Sextus Empiricus: Against the Ethicists*. Oxford.

1989. Carneades' *Pithanon*: A reappraisal of its role and status. *Oxford Studies in Ancient Philosophy* 7.

Black, M. 1978. Afterthoughts on metaphor. In S. Sacks, ed., *On Metaphor*. Chicago.

1977. More about metaphor. *Dialectica* 31:431–57.

Blume, H. D., and F. Mann. 1983. *Platonismus und Christentum: Festschrift für Heinrich Dörrie. Jahrbuch für Antike und Christentum*. Ergänzungsband 10. Aschendorff.

Blumenthal, H. J. 1996. *Aristotle and Neoplatonism in Late Antiquity*. Ithaca.

1987a. Plotinus, 1951–1971. In H. Temporini and W. Haaser, eds., *Aufstieg und Niedergang der Römischen Welt*. Band 36.1.

1987b. Neoplatonic elements in the De Anima Commentaries. In R. Sorabji, ed., *Aristotle Transformed*. Ithaca, NY.

1978. 529 and its sequel: What happened to the Academy? *Byzantion* 48: 376–81.

1971. *Plotinus' Psychology: His Doctrines of the Embodied Soul*. The Hague.

Blumenthal, H. J., and E. G. Clark, eds., 1993. *The Divine Iamblichus*. London.

249

References

Boss, G., and C. Steel. 1985. *Proclus et son influence*. Actes du Colloque de Neuchâtel.

Brisson, L. 1995a. Premises, consequences, and legacy of an esotericist interpretation of Plato. *Ancient Philosophy* 15:117–34.

1995b. *Orphée et l'Orphisme dans l'Antiquité gréco-romaine*. Aldershot; Brookfield.

1991. Damascius et l'Orphisme. In *Orphisme et Orphée, en l'honneur de Jean Rudhardt. Recherches et Rencontres* 3:157–209. Genève.

1990. Orphée et l'Orphisme à l'epoque impériale. In *Aufstieg und Niedergang der Römischen Welt* II 36.4. 2867–2931.

1987. Proclus et l'Orphisme. In *Proclus, lecteur et interprète des Anciens*. CNRS. 43–103.

1985. Les Théogonies Orphiques et le papyrus de Derveni: Notes critiques. *Revue de l'Histoire des Religions* 202:389–420.

Burge, T. 1993. Vision and intentional content. In E. Lepore and R. Van Gulick, ed., *John Searle and His Critics*, 195–214. London.

1986. Cartesian error and the objectivity of perception. In P. Pettit and J. McDowell, *Subject, Thought, and Content*. Oxford.

Burkert, W. 1992. *The Orientalizing Revolution*. Cambridge, MA.

1982. Craft versus sect: The problem of Orphics and Pythagoreans. In B. Meyer, and E. Sanders, eds., *Jewish and Christian Self-Definition*, 1–22. Philadelphia.

1972. *Lore and Science in Ancient Pythagoreanism*. Translated by Edwin L Minar, Jr. Cambridge.

Burnyeat, M., 1982 Idealism in Greek philosophy: What Descartes saw and Berkeley Missed. *Philosophical Review* 111:3–40.

1976. Protagoras and self-refutation in later Greek philosophy. *Philosophical Review* 85:44–69.

Bussanich, J. 1997. Mystical elements in the thought of Plotinus. In *ANRW* 36.7. 5300–5330.

1992. The invulnerability of Goodness. In J. Cleary, ed., *Proceedings of the Boston Area Colloquium in Ancient Philosophy*, vol. 1. pp. 151–94. Boston.

1988. *The One and Its Relation to Intellect in Plotinus*. Philosophia Antiqua Leiden.

Cadava, E., ed. 1991. *Who Comes After the Subject?* New York.

Calame, C. 1991. Eros initiatique et la cosmogonie orphique. *Recherches e Rencontres*, no. 3:27–247.

Cameron, A. 1969. The last days of the Academy of Athens. In *Proceedings o the Cambridge Philosophical Society*, 195.

Casadio, G. 1986. Adversaris orphica et orientalia. *Studi e Materiali di Stori della Religione*. 52.291–322.

Charles, A. 1971. L'Imagination, miroir de l'ame chez Proclus. In *Le Néopla tonisme*, 241–9. Paris.

Charles-Saget, A. 1982. *L'Architecture du divin: Mathématique et philosophie che Proclus*. Paris.

References

Cilento, V. 1971. *Paideia antignostica: Riconstruzione d'un unico scritto da Enneadi III.8, V.8, V.5, II.9.* Florence.

1967. *Stile e linguaggio nell filosofia di Plotino. Vichiana* 4.

Code, A. 1985. Aristotle: Essence and accident. In R. Grandy and R. Warner, eds., *Philosophical Grounds of Rationality.* Oxford.

Combès, J. 1990 Damascius entre Porphyre et Jamblique. *Philosophie* 26:41–58.

1978. L'un humain selon Damascius. *Revue des Sciences Philosophiques et Théologiques* 62:161–6.

1977. Damascius et les hypothèses négatives du Parménides. *Revue des Sciences Philosophiques et Théologiques* 61:185–220.

1976. Négativité et procession des principes chez Damascius. *Revue des Études Augustiniennes* 22:114–33.

1975. Damascius, lecteur du Parménides. *Archives de Philosophie* 38:33–60.

Cooper, J. 1987. Hypothetical necessity and natural teleology. In A. Gotthelf and J. Lennox, eds., *Philosophical Issues in Aristotle's Biology.* Cambridge.

Corbin, H. [1960.] *Avicenna and the Visionary Recital.* New York.

Corrigan, K. 1981. The internal dimensions of the sensible object in the thought of Plotinus and Aristotle. *Dionysius* 5:98–126.

Coulter, J. 1983. *The Literary Microcosm.* Leiden.

Davidson, D. 1980. *Essays on Actions and Events.* Oxford; New York.

1978. What metaphors mean. In S. Sacks, ed., *On Metaphor,* 29–46. Chicago.

Derrida, J. 1982. *Margins of Philosophy.* Translated by Alan Bass. Chicago.

1981. *Dissemination.* Translated by Barbara Johnston. Chicago.

Descartes, R. 1990. *Meditations on First Philosophy.* Bilingual ed. Edited by G. Heffernan. Notre Dame.

Deutsch, N. 1995. *The Gnostic Imagination.* Leiden.

Dillon, J. 1987. Iamblichus of Chalcis. In *ANRW,* Part II, 36.2. 863–78.

1977. *The Middle Platonists.* Ithaca.

Dodds, E. R. 1960. Numenius and Ammonius. In *Entretiens Hardt* V:3–61.

1951. *The Greeks and the Irrational.* Berkeley and Los Angeles.

1928. The *Parmenides* of Plato and the origin of the Neoplatonic One. *Classical Quarterly* 22:129–42.

Doerrie, H. 1976. *Platonic Minora.* Munich.

Edelstein, L., and I. G. Kidd. 1989–90. *Posidonius.* Fragments. 2nd ed. Cambridge; New York.

Eliade, M. 1964. *Shamanism: Archaic Techniques of Ecstasy.* New York.

Emilsson, E. 1996. Cognition and its object. In L. Gerson, ed., *Cambridge Companion to Plotinus.* Cambridge.

1993. Plotinus on the objects of thought. *Archiv für Geschichte der Philosophie* 77 Bd., pp. 21–41.

1991. Plotinus and soul-body dualism. In S. Everson, ed., *Psychology,* 148–65. Cambridge.

1988. *Plotinus on Sense-Perception.* Cambridge.

References

Everson, S. 1997. *Perception in Aristotle.* Cambridge

1991. The objective appearance of Pyrrhonism. In S. Everson, ed., *Psychology.* Cambridge.

Farrell, F. 1994. *Subjectivity, Realism, and Postmodernism.* Cambridge.

Ferrari, G. R. F. 1987. *Listening to the Cicadas.* Cambridge.

Ferwerda, R. 1965. *La Signification des images et des metaphores dans la pensée de Plotin.* Groningen

Festugière, A.-J. 1968. Contemplation philosphique et art theurgique chez Proclus. In A.-J. Festugière, ed., *Études de Philosophique Greque,* pp. 585–96. Paris.

1951–4. *La Révélation d' Hermes Trismégiste.* 4 vols. Paris.

Filoramo, G. 1990. *A History of Gnosticism.* Cambridge.

Finamore, J. 1985. *Iamblichus and the Theory of the Vehicle of the Soul.* Chico.

Findlay, J. N. 1974. *Plato. The Written and Unwritten Doctrines.* London

Fishbane. M. 1981. *The Garments of Torah.* Albany.

Fossum. J. 1985. *The Name of God and Angel of the Lord.* Tübingen.

Fowden. G. 1989. *The Egyptian Hermes: A Historical Approach to the Late Pagan.* 2nd ed. Princeton.

1982. The pagan holy man in late antique society. *Journal of Hellenic Studies,* n.s., 29:33–59.

1977. The Platonist philosopher and his circle in Late Antiquity. *Philosophia* 7:359–83.

Frede, D. 1991. The cognitive role of *phantasia* in Aristotle. In M. Nussbaum and A. Rorty, eds., *Essays on Aristotle's De Anima.* Oxford.

Frede, M. 1987a. Stoics and Skeptics on clear and distinct impressions. In M. Frede, *Essays in Ancient Philosophy.* Minneapolis.

1987b. *Essays in Ancient Philosophy.* Minneapolis.

1987c. The original notion of cause. In M. Frede, *Essays in Ancient Philosophy.* Minnesota.

Gadamer, H-G. 1989. *Truth and Method.* Translated and revised by Joel Weinsheimer and Donald Marshall. Originally published as *Warheit und Method.* Tübingen, 1960.

Gaiser, K. 1980. Plato's enigmatic lecture "On the Good." *Phronesis* 25:5–37

Galpérine, M. 1971. Damascius et la théologie négative. In *Le Néoplatonisme.* Paris.

Garin, E. 1983. *Astrology in the Renaissance: The Zodiac of Life.* London; Boston.

1961. *La cultura filosofica del Rinascimento italiano.* Firenze.

1960. Le 'Elezioni' e il problema dell' astrologia. In E. Castelli, ed., *Umanesimo e esoterismo,* 21. Padua.

Gasché, R. 1986. *The Tain of the Mirror.* Cambridge, MA.

Gersh, S. 1978. *From Iamblichus to Eriugena.* Leiden.

1973. *Kinetos Akinetos.* Leiden.

Gerson, L. 1997. Epistrophe Pros Eauton. *Documenti e Studi Sulla Tradizione Filosofica Medievale* 8:1–30.

References

1994. *Plotinus.* Arguments of the Philosophers Series. New York.
Ed. 1996. *Cambridge Companion to Plotinus.* Cambridge.
Gill, C. 1991. Is there a concept of person in Greek philosophy? In S. Everson, *Psychology.* Cambridge.
1990. *The Person and the Human Mind.* Oxford.
Gillespie, M. A. 1995. *Nihilism before Nietzsche.* Chicago.
Glucker, J. 1978. *Antiochus and the Late Academy.* Göttingen.
Gotthelf, A. 1987. Aristotle's conception of final causality. In A. Gotthelf and J. Lennox, eds., *Philosophical Issues in Aristotle's Biology.* Cambridge.
Graeser, A. 1972. *Plotinus and the Stoics.* Leiden.
Griswold, C., ed. 1988. *Platonic Writings/Platonic Readings.* New York.
Gurtler, G. 1989. *Plotinus, the Experience of Unity.* New York.
Guthrie, W. K. C. *Orpheus and Greek Religion.* Princeton.
Hadas, M. 1958. *The Stoic Philosophy of Seneca.* New York.
Hadot, I. 1978. *Le Problème du Neoplatonisme Alexandrin: Hierocles et Simplicius.* Paris.
Hadot, P. 1995. *Philosophy as a Way of Life.* Translated by Michael Chase. London.
1987a. Théologie, exégese, revélation, écriture, dans la philosophie greque. In M. Tardieu, ed., *Les Regles de l'interpretation.* Paris.
1987b. *Exercises spirituels et philosophie antique.* 2nd ed. Paris.
1987c. Structure et themes du Traité 38 (VI. 7) de Plotin. In H. Temporini and W. Haase, eds., *Aufstieg und Niedergang der Römischen Welt.* Band 36.II.
1985. *Plotin, Traité 38 (VI 7).* Paris.
Halperin, D. 1990. Why is Diotima a woman? In J. Winkler and F. Zeitlin, *Before Sexuality.* Princeton.
Hancock, C. L. 1985. *Energeia.* Ph.D. diss., University of Loyola.
Hankinson, J. 1995. *The Sceptics.* New York.
1992. Actions and passions: Affection, emotion, and moral self-management in Galen's philosophical psychology. In J. Brunschwig and M. Nussbaum, eds., *Passions and Perceptions,* 184–222. Cambridge.
Hatfield, G. 1986. The senses and the fleshless eye: The meditations as cognitive exercises. In A. Rorty, ed., *Essays on Descartes' Meditations.* Berkeley.
Havelock, E. 1986. *The Muse Learns to Write: Reflections on Orality and Literacy from Antiquity to the Present.* New Haven.
Helleman-Elgersma, W. 1980. *Soul Sisters.* Hildesheim.
Hierocles. 1974. *Hierocles in Aureum Pythagoreorum Carmen Commentarius.* F. G. Koehler, Stuttgart.
Himmelfarb, M. 1993. *Ascent to Heaven in Jewish and Christian Apocalypses.* Oxford.
Hoffman, P. 1987a. Categories et langage selon Simplicius–La question du "skopos" du traite Aristotelicien des "Categories." In *Simplicius, sa vie, son oeuvre, sa survie.* Actes du Colloque International de Paris (28 sept.– 1er oct. 1985). Berlin; New York.

References

1987b. Sur quelques aspects de la polemique de Simplicius contre Jean Philopon: De l'invective à la reaffirmation de la transcendance du ciel In *Simplicius, sa vie, son oeuvre, sa survie.* Berlin; New York.

Huntington, C. W. 1989. *The Emptiness of Emptiness.* Honolulu.

Irwin, T. 1989. *Classical Thought.* Oxford.

1988. *Aristotle's First Principles.* Oxford.

Janowitz, N. *Icons of power: The pragmatics of ritual in Late Antiquity.* Unpublished manuscript.

1989. *The Poetics of Ascent.* Albany.

Judovitz, D. 1988. *Subjectivity and Representation in Descartes.* Cambridge.

Kahn, C. 1991. Aristotle on thinking. In M. Nussbaum and A. Rorty, eds. *Essays on Aristotle's De Anima,* 359–81. Oxford.

Katz, S. T. 1992. *Mysticism and Language.* New York.

Kenny, A. 1992. *The Metaphysics of Mind.* Oxford.

Kingsley, P. 1995. *Ancient Philosophy, Mystery, and Magic.* Oxford.

Kosman, A. 1986. The naive narrator: Meditation in Descartes' meditations In A. Rorty, ed., *Essays on Descartes' Meditations.* Berkeley; Los Angeles.

1975. Perceiving that we perceive: "On the Soul, III.2." *Philosophical Review* 84:499–519.

Krämer, H. J. 1990. *Plato and the Foundations of Metaphysics: A Work on the Theory of the Principles and Unwritten Doctrines of Plato with a Collection of the Fundamental Documents.* Translated by J. R. Catan. Albany.

1959. *Arete bei Platon und Aristoteles: Zum Wesen und zur Geschichte der Platonischen Ontologie.* Heidelberg.

1964. *Der Ursprung der Geistmetaphysik.* Untersuchungen zur Geschichte des Platonismus zwischen Platon und Plotin. Amsterdam.

Lacan, J. 1978. *The Four Fundamental Concepts of Psycho-Analysis.* Translated by A. Sheridan. London.

Lakoff, G., and M. Turner. 1989. *More than Cool Reason.* Chicago.

Laks, A. 1992. Substitution et connaissance: Une interprétation unitaire (ou presque) de la théorie aristotélicienne de la métaphore. In Rorty, ed *Essays on Aristotle's Rhetoric.* Berkeley; Los Angeles.

Laks, A., and G. Most 1997. *Studies on the Derveni Papyrus.* Oxford.

Lamberton, R. 1985. *Homer the Theologian.* Berkeley; Los Angeles.

Larsen, B. D. 1972. *Jamblique de Chalcis: Exegete et philosophe.* Aarhus.

Lautner, P. 1994. Rival theories of self-awareness in Late Neoplatonism. *Bulletin of Institute of Classical Studies* 107–16.

Lee, J. S. 1978. The omnipresence of being: A study in Plotinan metaphysics Ph.D. diss., University of Connecticut. Storrs.

Leroux, G. 1990. *Plotin traité sur la liberte et la volunté de l'Un.* Paris

Levinson, S. 1983. *Pragmatics.* Cambridge; New York.

Lim, R. 1995. *Public Disputation, Power, and Social Order in Late Antiquity.* Berkeley.

Linforth, I. 1941. *The Arts of Orpheus.* Berkeley; Los Angeles.

Linguiti, A. 1990. *Principi primi e conoscenze nel tardo neoplatonismo greco.* Accademia toscana di scienze e lettere. Serie Studi 112. Firenze.

References

Lloyd, A. C. 1990. *The Anatomy of Neoplatonism*. Oxford.

——— 1986. Non-propositional thought in Plotinus. *Phronesis* 31:258–65.

——— 1982. Procession and division in Proclus. In A. C. Lloyd and H. J. Blumenthal, eds., *Soul and the Structure of Being in Late Neoplatonism: Syrianus, Proclus, and Simplicius*. Liverpool.

——— 1969–70. Non-discursive thought–an enigma of Greek philosophy. *Proceedings of the Aristotelian Society* 70:261–74.

——— 1964. *Nosce Teipsum* and *Conscientia*. *Archiv für Geschichte der philosophie* 46: 188–200.

——— 1955–6. Neoplatonic logic and Aristotelian logic. *Phronesis*1:58–72, 146–60.

Long, A. A. 1991. Representation and the self in Stoicism. In S. Everson *Psychology*. Cambridge. Reprinted in A. A. Long, *Stoic Studies*, 1996.

Mackie, J. L. 1974. *The Cement of the Universe: A Study of Causation*. Oxford.

Marion, Jean-Luc. 1993. Generosity and phenomenology: Remarks on Michel Henry's interpretation of the Cartesian *cogito*. In S. Voss, ed., *Essays on the Philosophy and Science of Rene Descartes*. Oxford.

Mates, B. 1996. *The Skeptic Way*. Oxford.

McDowell, J. 1993. Intentionality *De Re*. In E. Lepore and R. Van Gulick, eds., *John Searle and His Critics*, 215–25. London.

——— 1986. Singular thought and the extent of inner space. In P. Pettit and J. McDowell, eds., *Subject, Thought, and Content*. Oxford

Menn, S. 1998. *Descartes and Augustine*. Cambridge.

Merlan, P. 1973. *Monopsychism, Mysticism, and Metaconsciousness: Problems of the Soul in the Neoaristotelian Tradition*. The Hague.

——— 1953. *From Platonism to Neoplatonism*. 2nd ed. 1960. The Hague.

Modrak, D. 1987. *Aristotle: The Power of Perception*. Chicago.

Moutsopoulos, E. 1985. *Les Structures de l'imaginaire dans la philosophie de Proclus*. Paris.

Nagel, T. 1986. *The View from Nowhere*. Oxford.

——— 1974. What is it like to be a bat? *Philosophical Review* 83:435–50.

Newman, R. 1989. *Cotidie meditare*. Theory and practice of the meditatio in Imperial Stoicism. In *ANRW* II 36.3. 1473–1517.

Nussbaum, M., and A. Rorty, eds. 1991. *Essays on Aristotle's De Anima*. Oxford.

Obbink D. 1993. Cosmology as initiation vs. the critique of the Orphic mysteries P. Derveni Col. 16. Paper presented at Princeton University Conference on the Derveni Papyrus. Princeton.

O'Meara, D. 1993. Plotinus. *An Introduction to the Enneads*. Oxford.

——— 1989. *Pythagoras Revived: Mathematics and Philosophy in Late Antiquity*. Oxford.

Oosthout, H. 1991. *Modes of Knowledge and the Transcendental*. Amsterdam and Philadelphia.

Pearson, B. 1992. Theurgic tendencies in Gnosticism and Iamblichus's conception of theurgy. In T. Wallis, ed., *Neoplatonism and Gnosticism*, 253–76. Albany.

Pépin, J. 1986. Cosmic piety. In A. H. Armstrong, ed., *World Spitituality: An*

References

Encyclopedic History of the Religious Quest. Vol. 15, pp. 408–35. Crossroad, NY.

1970. Plotin et le mirroir de Dionysius. In *Revue Internationale de Philosophie* P. Pettit and J. McDowell, eds. 1986. *Subject, Thought, and Content.* Oxford.

Peuch, H. 1957. Plotin et les Gnostiques. In *Entretiens Hardt* V: 181–92. Geneva.

Priest, S. 1991. *Theories of the Mind.* Boston.

Putnam, H. 1983. *Realism and Reason.* Cambridge.

E. Ragland-Sullivan and M. Bracher, eds. 1991. *Lacan and the Subject of Language.* New York.

Rappe, S. L. 1998a. Skepticism in the sixth century? Damascius' *Doubts and Solutions Concerning First Principles. Journal of the History of Philosophy.* 36.3 337–60.

1998b. Damasius' Skeptical affiliations. *The Ancient World* 29, no. 2.

Reale, G. 1997. *Toward a New Interpretation of Plato.* Translated from the tenth edition and edited by J. R. Catan and R. Davies. Washington, DC.

Redding, P. 1996. *Hegel's Hermeneutics.* Ithaca.

Reinhardt, K. 1924. *Kosmos und Sympathie.* Munich.

Rich, A. N. M. 1960. Plotinus and the theory of artistic imitation. *Mnemosyne* ser. 4.13:233–9.

Ricoeur, P. 1977. *The Rule of Metaphor.* Translated by R. Czerny, K. McLaughlin, and J. Costello. Toronto.

1974. *The Conflict of Interpretations.* Evanston.

Rist, J. 1967. *Plotinus: The Road to Reality.* Cambridge.

Roloff, D. 1970. Plotin. *Die Großschrift* III, 8-V, 8-V, 5-II, 9. Berlin.

Rorty, A., ed. 1976. *The Identities of Persons.* Berkeley; Los Angeles.

Rorty, R. 1979. *Philosophy and the Mirror of Nature.* Princeton.

Rosan. L. 1949. *The Philosophy of Proclus.* New York.

Rusten, J. 1985. Interim notes on the Papyrus of Derveni. *HSCP* 89:121–40

Saffrey, H. D. 1992. Accorder entre elles les traditions théoloquies: Une charactéristique du Néoplatonisme Athénien. In E. Bos, ed., *On Proclus and His Influence in Medieval Philosophy,* 35–50. Leiden.

1990. *Recherches sur le Néoplatonisme après Plotin.* Paris.

1987. Analyse du Commentaire de Damascius sur la deuxième Hypothèse du Parménide. Introduction, chapitre II, *Proclus, théologie platonicienne* Livre V. H. D. Saffrey and L. Westerink 1968. Paris.

1971. Abammon, pseudonyme de Jamblique. In R. Palmer and R. Hamerton-Kelly, eds., *Philomathes: Studies and Essays in the Humanities in Memory of Philip Merlan,* 227–39. The Hague.

1965. Introduction to *Proclus, théologie platonicienne.* Livre I. Paris.

Schibli, H. 1990. *Pherekydes of Syros.* Oxford.

Schleiermacher, F. D. E. 1836. *Schleiermacher's Introductions to the Dialogues of Plato.* Translated by William Dobson. Cambridge. Reprint, Bristol. 1992

Schlette, H.-R. 1974. *Das Eine und das Andere. Studien zur Problematic Problemati des Negativen in der Metaphysik Plotins.* Munich.

Scholem, G. 1978. *Kabbalah.* New York.

References

Schroeder, F. 1994. Review of Beierwaltes 1991 in *Ancient Philosophy* 14, no. 2.

1992. *Form and Transformation*. Montreal; Buffalo.

1989. Presence and dependence in the Plotinian philosophy of consciousness: συνουσία, συναίσθεσις, and σύνεσις. In H. Temporini and W. Haase, eds., *Aufstieg und Nedergang der Römischen Welt*. Band 36.2.

1980. Representation and reflection in Plotinus. *Dionysius* 4:37–59.

1978. The Platonic Parmenides and imitation in Plotinus. *Dionysius* 2:51–73.

Schubert, V. 1968. *Pronoia und Logos*. Die Rechtfertigung der Weltordnung bei Plotin. *Epimeleia* 11. Salzburg.

Schwyzer, H.-R. 1960. "Bewusst und Unbewusst bei Plotin." In *Entretiens Hardt* V:343–90. Geneva.

Seaford, R. 1986. Immortality, salvation, and the elements. *HCSP* 90:5–9.

Searle, J. 1995. *The Construction of Social Reality*. New York.

1993. Reference and intentionality. In E. Lepore and R. Van Gulick, eds., *John Searle and His Critics*. London.

1983. *Intentionality*. Cambridge.

1979. Metaphor. In A. Ortony, ed., *Metaphor and Thought*. New York. Reprinted in Martinich A. 1990. *The Philosophy of Language*.

Sellers, P. 1997. *Delimitations: Pheneomenology and the Demise of Metaphysics*. Bloomington.

Sells, M. 1994. *Mystical Languages of Unsaying*. Chicago.

Shaw, G. 1995. *Theurgy and the Soul: The Neoplatonism of Iamblichus*. College Park, PA.

1993. The geometry of grace: A Pythagorean approach to theurgy. In H. J. Blumenthal and E. G. Clark, eds. *The Divine Iamblichus*, 116–37. London.

Sheppard, A. 1982. Proclus' attitude to theurgy. *Classical Quarterly* 32:212–24.

1981. *Essays on the Fifth and Sixth Books of Proclus' Commentary on Plato's Republic*. Gottingen.

Silverman, H. J. 1994. *Textualities: Between Hermeneutics and Deconstruction*. New York.

Skulsky, H. 1986. Metaphorese. *Nous* 20:351–69.

Smith, A. 1978. Unconsciousness and quasi-consciousness in Plotinus. *Phronesis* 23.

1974. *Porphyry's Place in the Neoplatonic Tradition*. The Hague.

Sorabji, R. 1990. *Aristotle Transformed*. Ithaca, NY.

1983. Myths about non-propositional thought. In *Time, Creation, and the Continuum*. Ithaca.

Ed. 1987. *Philoponus and the Rejection of Aristotelian Science*. Ithaca; London.

Soskice, J. M. 1991. *Metaphor and Religious Language*. Oxford.

Steel, C. 1978. *The Changing Self: A Study on the Soul in Later Neoplatonism*. Translated by E. Haasl. Brussels.

Stock, B. 1996. *Augustine the Reader: Meditation, Self-knowledge, and the Ethics of Interpretation*. Cambridge, MA.

References

Strange, S. 1992. Plotinus' account of participation. *Journal of the History of Philosophy* 30:4.

1987. Plotinus, Porphyry, and the "Categories." In H. Temporini and W. Haase, eds., *Aufstieg und Niedergang der Römischen Welt*. Band 36.2.

1981. Plotinus' treatise on the genera of being: An historical and philosophical study. Ph.D. diss., University of Texas. Austin.

Strömberg, R. 1946. Damascius: His personality and significance. *Eranos* 44: 175–92.

Tambiah, S. J. 1979. *A Performative Approach to Ritual*. London.

Tardieu, M. 1990. *Les Paysages reliques*. Routes et haltes syriennes d'Isidore à Simplicius. Bibliotheque Ecole Hautes Études. Science et Religion 94. Paris.

Ed. 1987. *Les Regles de l'interpretation*. Paris.

Tarrant, H. 1998. Introduction to *Olympiodorus, Commentary on Plato's Gorias*. Translated with full notes by K. R. Jackson, K. Lykos, and H. Tarrant. Leiden.

1997. Olympiodorus and the surrender of paganism. In L. Garland, ed., *Conformity and Non-conformity in Byzantium, Byzantinische Forschungen* 24: 179–90.

1984. *Scepticism or Platonism*. Cambridge.

Taylor, C. 1989. *Sources of the Self*. Cambridge, MA.

Taylor, C. C. W. 1990. Aristotle's epistemology. In S. Everson, ed., *Companions to Ancient Thought*. Vol. I, *Epistemology*. Cambridge.

Theiler, W. 1966. *Forschungen zum Neoplatonismus*. Berlin.

1964. Einheit und unbegrenzte Zeiheit von Plato bis Plotin. In J. Mau and E. Schmidt, eds., *Isonomia*. Studien zur Gleichheitsvorstellung im griechischen Denken, 89–109. Berlin.

1960. Plotin zwischen Platon und Stoa. In *Les Sources de Plotin*, 65–103. Geneva.

Trouillard, J. 1982. *La Mystagogie de Proclos*. Paris.

1974. L'Activité onomastique selon Proclus. In *Entretiens Hardt*. Vol. 21, *De Iamblique à proclus*. Geneva.

1972a. La Notion de Dunamis chez Damascios. *Revue des Études Greques* 85: 353–63.

1972b. *L'Un et l'âme selon Proclus*. Paris.

Wagner, M. R. 1982a. Plotinus' world. *Dionysius* 6:13–42.

1982b. Vertical causation in Plotinus. In R. Baine Harris, ed., *The Structure of Being*. 51–72. Albany.

Wallis, R. T. 1987. Scepticism and Neoplatonism. In H. Temporini and W. Haase, eds., *Aufstieg und Niedergang der Römischen Welt*. Band 36.I.

1972. *Neoplatonism*. London. Second edition, with foreward and bibliography by L. P. Gerson. Bristol. 1995.

Warren, E. 1964. Consciousness in Plotinus. *Phronesis* 9:83–97.

Wedin, M. 1992. Aristotle on the mechanics of thought. In A. Preus, ed., *Aristotle's Ontology. Essays in Ancient Greek Philosophy*. Vol. V. Albany.

West, M. L. 1983. *The Orphic Poems*. Oxford.

References

White, H. 1987. *The Content of the Form. Narrative Discourse and Historical Representation*. Baltimore.

Wilkes, K. 1991. Psuche versus the mind. In M. Nussbaum and A. Rorty, eds., *Essays on Aristotle's De Anima*. Oxford.

1988. *Real People*. Oxford

Wilson, D., and D. Sperber. 1988. *Relevance*. Cambridge, MA.

Wilson, P. 1995. Speaking in hieroglyphs. *Alexandria* 3. Phanes.

Witt, R. E. 1975. Iamblichus as a Forerunner of Julian. In *De Jamblique à Proclus*. Geneva.

1930. Plotinus and Poseidonius. *Classical Quarterly* 24:198–203.

Wurm, K. 1973. *Substanz und Qualität*. Berlin and New York.

Yates, F. 1966. *The Art of Memory*. Chicago.

1964. *Giordano Bruno and the Hermetic Tradition*. Chicago.

Zizek, S. 1993. *Tarrying with the Negative: Kant, Hegel, and the Critique of Ideology*. Durham.

Zuntz, G. 1971. *Persephone: Three essays on Religion and Thought in Magna Graecia*. Oxford

Index

General Index

Academy, closing of, 197; last scholarch, 197
akatalepsia, 7, 213, 222
akousmata, 13, 14n
Alcibiades, 150; as failed initiation candidate, 153; as initiation candidate, 152
Alcinous, 6, 9
Ammonius (5th century), 8, 9, 10, 11
apatheia, 59, 61, 63
Aphrodite, 163
Aristophanes: *Birds*, 146, 148, 149, 150; *Clouds*, 153, 256; in *Symposium*, 144n
Aristotle: on first philosophy, 26; *see also* individual works in Index Locorum
ascent literature, 109, 111, 170, 191
askesis, xvi, 20, 112, 242

Barnes, J., 36n
Beierwaltes, W., 91, 97, 103n, 131, 133–5, 222n
Being: in *Doubts and Solutions Concerning First Principles*, 203, 214, 221
Black, M., 77n
Blumenthal, H., 19n, 32n, 53n, 94, 97
Brisson, L., 147, 162
Burge, T., 82
Burkert, W., 117n, 137
Burnyeat, M., 67, 91
Bussanich, J., 42n, 43n, 44n, 58n, 125n

Camillo, G., 129–30
causal explanation, 33–8; Aristotelian, 38–9; Plotinus' criticisms of, 35–42
causation, 33, 36; Damascius' criticisms of, 202, 206, 207; Hume's account of, 38; interdependent, 38, 42; Plotinus' theory of, 38
center, 105, 124, 125, 135
Chaldean Oracles, 1, 3, 118, 140–1, 159; "Do not deepen the plane," 138;

fragment, 3, 112; in Proclus' *Platonic Theology*, 169, 177, 186
Chronus, 146, 160, 162; *see also* gods, Orphic
circle, 124, 125, 133–5
Combès, J., 201n
concentration, 18, 80, 106
Corpus Hermeticum, 108–10, 112, 128–30
cosmic egg, 146, 149, 150

Damascius: cites three versions of Orphic theology, 147; Orphic lore in, 147–8, *see also* Index Locorum
Davidson, D., 37n, 98
Demiurge: Gnostic interpretation of, 31; in *Platonic Theology*, 180–1, 187
Derrida, J., x, xiv n, 112, 113, 122
Derveni papyrus, 79, 145, 148, 149, 162, 163
Descartes, 47, 68, 73, 78; and Augustine, 49; Cartesian dualism, 48, 68; Cartesian subject, 47, 68, 51; meditation and, 51, 78; *Meditation secunda* paragraph, 9, 69; self-transparency, 48, 51; thought experiments, 67, 82
detachment, 85–8, 105, 135; *see also* apatheia
Dillon, J., 31, 203, 208
Dionysus, 143, 144, 145, 149n, 156, 162, 164–6; *see also* gods
Diotima, 150, 152, 153, 156
discursive thinking, 2, 42, 58, 63, 73, 74, 99, 101; critique of, xiii, 94, 104–5, 225–6
divine names, 179–82
doubt, 78; *see also epoche*
dream state, 45, 62–3
dreamer, 62–3
dyad, 125

eidos, 113
Eliade, M., 154n

261

Emilsson, E., xiii n, xiv n, 19, 60n, 62n, 64n, 65n, 67, 102n
endeixis, 209–11
ephectic, ephectics, 6–10
epistemology, 27, 30, 45, 52, 71
epistrophe, 127, 133, 135; *see also* self-reflection
epoche, 58, 62, 203, 227
esoteric doctrines of Plato, xv, 122
essence, 29, 34, 39, 43–4
essentialism, 33, 39–40
Eudemian theogony, 146
exegesis: in the Commentators, 8–11; in Iamblichus, 13–14; Middle Platonic, 6–7; of Plato, 4–11; in Proclus' *Platonic Theology*, 169 ff.
exegetical tradition, ix; in *Doubts and Solutions Concerning First Principles*, 201; in *Platonic Theology*, 167 ff., 193
explanation, 33

Farell, F., 25n, 45, 46n
Ferwerda, R., 92, 94
Ficino, M., 130
flower of the soul, 177, 224
Forms, 101
Frede, M., 68, 210

Gadamer, H., 234, 243
Gasché R., x n, 56
geometric figures, 121–2, 124, 125, 131, 134–5, 138
Gerson, L., xiv n, 2n, 30, 46n, 47n, 55n, 56n, 65n
gods: Chaldean, 188–9; Hermetic, 108; Orphic, 160; in *Platonic Theology*, 188; replicated in Proclus, 162

Hadot, P., 49, 50
Havelock, E., x n, 231n
Hellanikus, 149, 150, 161
Henads, 214–15, 223
hermeneutics: Neoplatonic, 122, 240–3
Hermetic literature, 108, 109, 111–12, 128; in Renaissance, 129–30
Hieronymus, 149, 150, 161; *see also* Orphic Theogony
Hymn to Zeus, Orphic, 158–60

Iamblichus, 118, 158, 159; author of *Protrepticus*, 13; dispute with Porphyry concerning the One, 204; *On the Common Mathematical Science*, 138; on theurgy, 173
identity theory of truth: *see* identity thesis
identity thesis, xiii, 27, 29, 70, 73, 74, 102, 217; Damascius' rejection of 220–1
imagery in *Enneads*, 91, 104, 108, 109
imagination, 128, 130; as passive intelligence, 131; Proclus' theory of, 132, 173
imperative philosophy, 240
incorrigibility, 68–72
Ineffable, 204, 208–9, 216
initiation, 20, 143, 148, 151; and Eros, 151, 153; in *Platonic Theology*, 189–90
intellect, xiii, 27, 30, 36, 63, 65, 74–6, 85–6, 102; analogous to perception, 218; does not belong to the human psyche, xiv n, 19n; in *Doubts and Solutions Concerning First Principles*, 217; not properly speaking a faculty, 19n
intentionality, 57, 58, 73, 106; definition of 73n; and discursive thinking, 99
interpretation: of *De anima*, 52–6; of Platonic texts in Proclus, 171, 185
introspection, 20, 52, 66, 67, 68, 82–3, 89

Kingsley, P., 117n, 145, 146n, 156
Krämer, H., xv n, 4n, 122, 124n

Lamberton, R., 175n
language: in the *Enneads*, 107; incapable of transmitting wisdom xiii, 93, 94, 238–9; metaphoric, 92; and Neoplatonism, 117; ritual features of, 108; in Simplicius' commentary on the *Categories*, 236–7; theurgic, 174, 184
Lewy, H., 138
Lloyd, A. C., 67n, 71n, 75n, 92, 223n

Marcus Aurelius, 49
mathematical symbolism 120–2, 124, 127–8
meditatio, 49–50
meditation: Cartesian, 78–9; in the *Enneads*, 79, 103; on the sphere, 79–81; Stoic, 49–50
Meditations on First Philosophy, 49, 68; *Meditation Secunda* paragraph nine cited, 69
metaphor: comparison, 95; in the *Enneads*, 92, 94–5, 98, 108, 113; and metaphysics, xiv, 112; pragmatic, 96, 97; theories of creative, 98, 108
metaphysical discourse, 112–13
method, geometric, 124; mathematical versus geometric, 136; non-discursive 2–3, 18–21, 87; in Proclus, 132, 133
Middle Platonism, 5–6, 31n
monad, 124, 136
Moutsopoulos, P., 131
myth: Orphic, Plato and, 149–56; Proclus and, 158, 175, 185–6

Nagel, T., 3, 28, 29
Neoplatonic tradition, 118–20; continu

ity of, 1; defining features of, xi, 2;
exegetical, 119–20
Nichomachus of Gerasa, 131
non-discursive thinking, xvi n; 20–1, 93,
100, 101, 106, 123, 128, 134
nous, xiv, 1, 20, 30, 108, 109, 239, 241

offering according to capacity, 139
Olympiodorus, 6–10; Commentary on
the *Phaedo*, 144, 165
O'Meara, D., 118, 133n, 136n, 142n
One: Damascius' philosophy of, 200–1,
204–6, 225; as divine name, 182, 183
Orpheus, 143, 145, 148, 150, 158
Orphic cosmology, 143, 149, 164
Orphic fragments, 157
Orphic Theogony, 146, 157, 160; three
versions of, 146, 158

parakolouthesis, 56, 57
Parmenides: Damascius' Commentary on,
199; in *Doubts and Solutions Concerning
First Principles*, 199, 200; in *Platonic
Theology*, 159–60, 167–8, 191
pathos, 59, 60, 66, 219
perception, 99–100; of perception in
Aristotle's *De anima*, 52–6
Peri Archon, see Dubitationes et Solutiones
Peri philosophias, 120–1
peritrope, 209
Phaedo, 146
Phaedrus, 102, 187, 191
Phanes, 145, 149, 150, 152, 164; *see also*
Orphic Theogony
phenomenalism, 83, 194
philosophia perennis in Proclus' *Platonic
Theology*, 169; Damascius' views on,
232
Plato, 102, 113; lecture "On the
Good," 120; and Orphic myth, 143;
unwritten doctrines of, 120; writings
cited by Proclus, 159, 167–8
Platonic Theology, chapter 8 passim; as esoteric interpretation of Plato, 159,
179
Platonic tradition, x; versus Pythagorean
tradition, 118–19, 159
poetry, Proclus' theory of, 175–6, 180
point, 124, 126, 136
Porphyry, 86; conflict between P. and
Iamblichus over theurgy, 14–5; Neoplatonic ethics of, 17
pragmatics, 97
prayer, 89
proem, Orphic, 152
prosektikon, 53
prosoche, 50, 53
Protagoras, 8
providence, 40–1n; *see also* teleology
Pseudo-Simplicius, 54
Putnam, H., 25n, 37

Pythagoras, 118, 137–42
Pythagorean symbolism, 117, 121, 123,
125, 137; in Proclus, 133, 136, 169
realism, 25–6
representational gap, 28, 70, 73, 88
res cogitans, 47, 49n, 51, 55, 69, 70
Rhapsodic Theogony, 146, 157, 161
Rhetoric metaphor in, 95, 97
Ricoeur, P., ix n, 12, 16, 19, 95
ritual language, 113, 170, 171, 175,
179, 192–3
ritual narrative, 21, 164, 194
ritualism, 137, 139
Rorty, R., 47n, 48n, 68

Sacred Discourse, *see* Rhapsodic Theogony
Searle, J., 25n, 64, 95n, 96n
self, 86, 87–8; socially constructed, 155
self knowledge, 71–3, 76, 127; and incorrigibility, 68, 71, 74–77; *see also* self-
transparency
self-perception, 64
self-reflection, 19–21, 54–6, 58, 67, 127–
9
self transparency, 48, 63–4, 69, 72, 77
Seneca, 49, 50
Sextus Empiricus, 7, 68, 72, 219
Shaw, G., 15n, 136n, 137n, 138, 142n,
170n, 177
Simplicius, 197, 210, 236
Skeptical reading of Plato, 7–10
Skepticism, 46, 212
Skeptics, 68, 71, 72, 76, 219, 222
Socrates: as Orpheus, 150; as shaman,
154, 155; in *Symposium*, 150
Sorabji, R., 92, 233n
speech offering, 170
sphere, 79—80, 89, 104, 127
statues, *see* theurgy
stephanos, 153
subject, 72, 86; Cartesian, 51, 58, 66,
105
subjectivism, 28, 58, 69
subjectivity, 81, 85, 87
sunthema, 176–7
symbol, 117; definition of, 12; Pythagorean, 126; as ritual object, 3, 11, 21,
140; in theurgic rites, 139
symbolon, 171, 174; ascent and descent
by means of, 177; and interpretation
12
Symposium, 144, 148, 149–56
Syrianus, 148, 157, 159, 164; author of
On the Concordance of Orpheus, Pythagoras, and Plato Regarding the Oracles, 157

teleology, 33–4; Aristotelian, 34, 37–8;
Platonic, 33, 34

tetrakys, 137
text: ambiguous status of, 126; nature of, x; Neoplatonic, xii; theurgy and 172, 192, 195
textual strategies, ix, xiii, xv; and ritual, 196
textuality ix; practices within varieties of Neoplatonic, xiii, xv, 192; as self-presence, xv n
Theaetetus, 8
theory of Forms, 26
theurgic ritual, 173
theurgy, 138–9; dispute between theurgy and philosophy, 11, 172, 177n; and Neoplatonism, 15, 172; in the *Platonic Theology*, 170, 179
thought experiments: Cartesian, 67; in the *Enneads*, 79–81, 83–5, 117
Timaeus, 30–5, 112
Titans, 143, 149, 165
tradition, 16, 117, 231; as context for exegesis, 17, 194; and ideology, 233;

Neoplatonism as minoirity tradition, 232; and text, 242
Trouillard, J., 136n, 174n, 180, 181, 183
truth: non-discursive, xv–vii; non-representational, 93, 101

unwritten doctrines, xv, 4, 120–2

visionary text, 129–30, 133, 144, 170, 184
visual experience 106–7
visualizations, 103–5, 111

West, M., 147, 149, 156, 162
Williams, B., 29, 30
"worst difficulty" argument, 86

Yates, F., x, 129, 130

Zeus, 163–4

Index Locorum

Agathias
 2.30–4: 197
Anonymous
 Corpus Hermeticum
 treatise:
 IV.4: 112
 X.103: 112
 XI: 110–11 (quoted in full);
 171
 XI.8: 128
 XII.10b: 111
 XIII.11b: 111n
Derveni papyrus
 column XXI: 163
Orphic Fragments
 21a: 149
 25: 164
 68:187
Aristotle
 Analytica Posteriora
 71a16: 33n
 1641b25: 32
 De anima
 404b16–27: 121
 425b12 ff: 53
 429a3: 100, 218
 429b4: 101n
 430a18: 75
 431a1: 73, 100
 431b4: 101n
 431b5: 74n
 De memoria
 450a 1–7: 101n
 De partibus animalium
 1640a 33–b4: 38–9
 Physica
 184a10: 26

Aristoxenus
 Elements of Harmony
 II,30–1: 121
Damascius
 Dubitationes et Solutiones
 I 1.1: 204
 1.1–5: 206
 1.1–14: 204
 2.9–12: 206
 6.5–10: 211
 6.10: 242
 22.15–20: 208
 24.7–10: 205
 24.11: 202, 216
 42: 209
 62.3: 213
 62.4–7: 213
 80.19–81.2: 215
 82.19–82.6: 215
 84.9–12: 225
 II 13.1–5: 205
 14.1–6: 205
 105.3–5: 141
 105,18–21: 141
 148–52.8: 227–30
 149.4–11: 221
 149.23–5: 221
 150.20–4: 221
 III 140.11–25: 226
 Vitae Isidori
 110: 9
 316: 233
 317: 232
Elias
 In Categorias
 Proemium
 109.24–110.8: 8–9

Index

Iamblichus
De Communi Mathematica Scientia
  22.66: 138
  22.67: 138
De Mysteriis
  177 n
  7.42: 15
  96.13: 15, 172
  233: 139
  272.8–12: 178
Protrepticus
  29, p. 132: 13
  34, p. 247: 13
  p. 137: 14
  pp. 137–8: 14
Vita Pythagorae
  147: 138
Marinus
Life of Proclus: 157
Olympiodorus
Prolegomena Philosophiae Platonicae
In Phaedonem
  I.3: 165
  I.5: 165
  VII.1: 7
  X.27: 7
  XI25: 10
Philoponus
In De anima
  76: 121n
  465: 55
Plato
Laws
  716a: 149
Parmenides
  132b4: 46
  132b11–c11: 46
  132b7–c5: 86
Phaedo
Phaedrus
  274c–275a: x
Republic
  510–11: 134n
  560e: 151
Symposium
  189 ff.: 149–56
Timaeus
  29c1: 31n
  30b1: 31n
  34a9: 31n
  45b3: 30n
Plotinus
Enneads
  I 1.9.17–21: 74
     4.10.6: 241
     4.10.8: 66, 241
     4.10.10: 241
     4.10.13–14: 66, 241
     4.10.16–17: 66, 241
  II 1.9: 74n
      9.8.22: 34n
  III 2.1.15: 41n
       6.5.1: 62

     6.5.10: 60
     7.5: 75
     8.6.24: 73
     8.8.41: 87
  IV 3.17.12: 124
      4.43.16: 104
      4.5.20: 70
  V 1.12.1: 3n
     1.12.15: 3n
     1.2.14–20: 111n
     1.3.16–20: 65
     1.4.19–21: 104n
     1.5.6: 125
     1.7.13.15: 102
     1.8.11–15: 5
     2.2.2–5: 72
     2.3.17: 58; 64, 99
     3.1.1–15: 64
     3.1.22: 74n
     3.3: 57
     3.5.1–15: 99n
     3.5.25: 28n
     3.6.8–10: 76
     3.6.24: xiv n
     3.6.36: 61
     3.7.19: 57
     3.8.40–9: 237
     3.9.28: 77, 114
     3.10.23.26: 102
     3.10.35: 28n
     3.11.1–4: 125
     3.13.15: 102
     3.17.23: 104
     3.17.35: 64
     3.23–7: xiv n
     5.1.38–40: 73
     5.1.62: 100
     5.2.18–20: xiv n
     5.5.11: 64
     8.3.12: 77
     8.4.26: 35, 93n, 99
     8.4.48–53: 5
     8.4.54: 102
     8.6: 107
     8.7: 32
     8.7.41: 40
     8.9.1–3: 103
     8.9.3: 79, 104
     8.9.9–14: 105
     8.9.11–89
     8.11.24: 56 n.
     9.3.27: 72 n
     9.5.5: 75
     9.6.8.: 64
     9.7.14–17: 47
     9.8.3–4: 47
  VI 1.21.10–1: 61n
      1.22.12–3: 61n
      4.7.22–6: 105
      5.5.1: 124
      5.8.6: 113
      5.9.1–5: 81
      7.1.1–11: 41

Plotinus, *Enneads,* VI *(cont.)*
  7.1.37: 38
  7.2.35: 35
  7.2.44: 40
  7.3: 38
  7.6.2: 35
  7.7.31: 35
  7.8.41: 40
  7.9: 38
  7.10.40: 36
  7.12: 42, 64, 111
  9.3.10–13: 238
  9.8.20–1: 124, 127
Porphyry
 Sententiae
  32, p. 23: 18n
  32, p. 25: 18n
  32, p. 29: 18
  32, p. 37: 18
 Vita Plotini
  3–4: 235
  3.30: 235
  4.10–12: 235
  18.10: 85
  20: 235
Proclus
 Eclogae de Philosophia Chaldaica
  1 16–19: 180
  5 8–11: 176
 In Primum Euclidis Elementorum Librum
  12.11–6: 132
  16: 173
  141: 140
  141.22: 133
  142.2–5: 133
  147.15: 138
 In Cratylum
  6.13: 179
  51.20.18–22: 181
  133.77: 167
 In Parmenidem
  808: 167
  809: 167
  896: 173, 174
  1076: 174
 In Alcibiadem
  177n
 In Rempublicam
  I 3.161: 176
    40.1–4: 173
    78.25: 175
    85.1: 159

  II 46.18–22: 135
 In Timaeum
  I 85.17–9: 135
    273: 180; 181
  II 246: 118
    255: 180
  II 148: 134
  III 168: 158
 Institutio Theologia
  proposition:
  7: 207; 225
  11: 203,225
  15: 69
  35: 225
  75: 225
  80: 36 n
 Theologia Platonica
  I 1.3.21: 174
    1.4.20.1–25: 170
    2.3.1–5: 179
  II 6.40.1–5: 182
    6.40.5–10: 182
    6.41.1–5: 182
    6.92: 183
  IV 9.192.24–193.5: 191
    9.192.5: 190
    9.193.15–6: 190
    34.233: 137
  V 5.22.3–10: 187
Pseudo-Simplicius/Priscianus
 In De anima
  165.29: 62
  290.6–8: 54
Seneca
 De Brevitate Vitae
  3.17–30: 50
 Epistles
  99.10: 50
Sextus Empiricus
 Adversus Mathematicos
  I.310–311: 72
 Pyrrhoneae Hypotyposes
  II.70–2: 219
  II.104–13: 210
Simplicus
 In Aristotelis Categorias Commentarium
  Proemium:
  9, 25–7: 237
  11, 1: 236
  11, 19: 236
  13, 5: 236
 In De anima, see Pseudo-Simplicus

Made in the USA
Coppell, TX
18 April 2022

76738308R00173